Successful
Business Networking
Online

Endorsements

This will be a great resource for all kinds of business-people adapting to the new world of online networking. The range of contributors and topics addressed guarantees that anyone will find some valuable nuggets of wisdom they can employ in their daily business.

In my academic role, it will be a fantastic resource to help equip the next generation of entrepreneurs and business leaders with essential digital networking skills. Successful Business Networking Online challenges us to think about how we can create new online networking spaces for our students and how to build their confidence to participate in a wide range of new opportunities that digital networks create.

This should be an essential resource for all Business School libraries.

Professor Gary Bosworth, Newcastle Business School,
Northumbria University

I highly recommend this wonderful book written by Ladey Adey! She lives and breathes the true art and practice of Networking, believes in it and the power it has. I would say, *"It's a crucial part of her DNA— Dedicated Networking Always"*. Through this exciting book, learn how you and your business can succeed using the online networking phenomenon. It is jam packed with great tips, tactics and advice to put into use immediately. This book is a MUST read for today's post-pandemic networker!

Andrea R Nierenberg: Networking Strategist and Award winning
Author of 7 networking books including;
Savvy Networking, and Networking that Really Works.

Business Networking has transformed itself. Built on good foundations it has entered the digital age. This important book supports business people to network naturally in this sphere and celebrates the new dawning of online networking. A modern approach, which shows you the way to be a successful networker using today's technology. I heartily recommend Successful Business Networking Online to all BNI members and business people across the world.

Dr. Ivan Misner, Founder of BNI and NY Times Bestselling Author.

Successful Business Networking Online

Build your
Business using
Powerful *Online*
Connections

Publications

Ladey Adey

Dedication

To everyone who attends Business Networking events online and offline. For the amazing people who organise these events so I and others can enjoy the meeting and gain clients

We've created a new world approach to business networks.

I give praise to **God** and lean into the promise for His blessing for this book and trust it also blesses its readers and their businesses.

Special Dedication

To my husband and best friend - **Denis Peter** – my rock - who supports all my ideas. He knew that if I was to meet the challenge of writing this book he would become my butler and chief bottle washer! It's the behind the scenes stuff which enable authors to write!

To **Abbirose**, my daughter and Creative Director of our Children Books. She edited the book whilst doing the illustration work for our next children's book in the *Little Unicorn* series.

She made time when the typed pages landing next to her computer accompanied with the words, *"Please edit"* and requests to create pictures too.

To **Candice,** my daughter and my grand-daughter **Sofia Rose**, who keep my sanity. Candice sends lots of pictures and videos of their days - enhancing my purpose in life.

Love You All - to the Moon and Back

Contents

A Changing Networking World

Karen Wilbourn

OH, how the networking world has changed,
Networking in particular, often viewed as a game.
Broken promises of referrals and introductions,
Sat round a table of countless solicitors!

SILLY meeting times of 6 am, punished for non-attendance,
Then endeavouring to make amends.
Reciting your name, company and kiss-off line,
Hoping to be remembered time after time.

BUT not anymore, the networking world has changed,
We now have the luxury of not playing the old game.
Login to online networking, be quiet, be loud or just sit and observe,
No sense of feeling lost; fat, thin, young, old, no one cares any more.

YOU have their attention, in the comfort of your home,
Times have changed there's a new 'normal' to roam.
Your work schedule now fits into flexible times,
Putting first your life and your kids plus your fitness climbs.

MEET new people, join new groups, no more wasting time,
Searching Google maps to find the shortest or fastest route.
Saving on petrol and traveling times,
Parking fees and costly fines!

AT the click of a button, faces amazingly appear,
No pre-requisite of being just down the road.
Meeting in different towns or even countries, work we now complete,
Communicating to suit our own personal beat.

BUSINESSES will re-open and life will resume,
But never forget the new 'normal' working to a different tune.
It will make us calmer, it will make us nicer,
Let's ensure we learn to listen, take note and all be kinder.

The History of Business Networking

Networking is the No. 1 unwritten rule of success in business.
Sallie Drawcheck

I compiled this timeline using, in my opinion, significant points in history as the formation of business networking, as we know it today. For the most part, women were excluded or actively discouraged from joining networking and trading activities, even from the coffee houses in Georgian Times. However, I'm sure there were some notable exceptions of brave, forward-thinking and enterprising women. It wasn't until the Victorian era that women were able to form and attend official networking meetings. Come with me on a fascinating journey through time!

Cavemen: Upon the realisation that their social links would benefit by collaboration, cavemen ceased fighting one another. This discovery brought mutual satisfaction and continued support - perhaps there were even guttural gestures round a fire between different tribes - this was the birth of networking.

It might have been survival networking: trading between groups or tribes. Of course, networking went beyond the 1-2-1; when one tribe introduced a tribe to another, networking expanded and the beginning of referral networking was born.

I can imagine a fruit collection specialist and a hunting expert discovering a natural trade-off. They realise they can all eat better by working together and sharing their spoils! Perhaps, creating the original Masterchef! I can visualise a group of women with expert skills in tanning animal skins and making coverings (clothes). They offer to swap their excess skins to a group with skills in making shelters and providing firewood. You get my drift and if you want to read more about these times, then you might enjoy the fictional saga, *Clan of the Cave Bear* by Jean M Auel.

A Historical Timeline

2000 BC The earliest form of **banking** began in Assyria, India and Sumeria, formed by merchants who issued grain loans to farmers and traders. This moved into Ancient Greece and the Roman Empire with evidence of money lending.

33 BC Roman Baths became more than a place to wash. Original baths used an extensive aqueduct system to provide the water. Large bathhouses were communal meeting places where high-ranking military officers, politicians, philosophers and businessmen could gather and network!

Baths offered a complex of libraries, reading rooms, perfumery booths, restaurants, games rooms, snack bars and stages for theatrical and musical performances. In the early days, there were 170 small baths in Rome; by 300 AD that number had climbed to over 900 baths.

50–51 AD A visit by **Apostle Paul** on a missionary visit to Corinth and the network of Christians began to spread today's estimate of 2.3 billion people.

117–476 During the Roman Empire groups of businessmen specialising in a craft would meet together as a Corpus or Collegia which are recognised today as **Guilds**.

1000 The first **Guild** was recorded and mentioned in Town Charters. In all industries, Guilds were formed. Artisans and merchants came together, as a brotherhood in a single trade, for mutual aid, to ensure the continuity of their work and skills to benefit their business. The raison d'être of the Guilds have roots similar to our trade unions, syndicates and guess what? Yes, business networks.

Guilds, full of business people, became central to the economic growth of city and town life and had political and social standing. If you look around your local town, you'll probably find a lovely Guildhall building. These were contracted and financed by Guild members of old, as a meeting place and we still use these buildings today. There are over 100 Guilds still in existence with wonderful names such as Worshipful Company of Worsted Weavers, Company of Fellmongers and The Incorporated Trades of Irvine, each with Facebook pages and the like!

1407 The first modern bank **Banco di San Giorgio** was founded in Italy. Banking could only spread through business networking, as its survival is via those driving the economy, aka business people!

1472 The oldest bank still in operation is **Banca Monte dei Paschi di Siena,** and was founded in Siena, Italy.

1599 The term **Chamber of Commerce** appeared for the first time in Marseille, France.

1652 London's first **coffee house** established was by **Pasqua Rosée.** Rosée was a servant of the Levant Company who imported coffee from Turkey.
A plaque commemorating this can be seen on a pillar of the Jamaica Wine
House. It's known as the '**Jampot' Coffee House**, and located in London's Financial District. **Samuel Pepys** diaries records visiting the 'Jampot' in 1660. By **1663** there were 82 known coffee houses within London City walls.

The purpose of the coffee house was to maximise interaction between customers within a welcoming and creative environment. A penny would be charged for entrance and politics were discussed freely – much to the frustration of **Charles II** who tried to ban them in **1675.**

1662 Rembrandt painted **The Syndics of the Drapers' Guild** in which he depicted a professional association – a guild, of merchants and artisans associated with the textile industry.

1695 The Bank of England was established as the first recognised 'modern' bank.

1695 The first record of a **Secret Society** meeting, though they were no doubt around before this date, but *shsssh* don't tell anyone! To name a few; **International Order of St Hubertus (1695), Freemasons (1745), Odd Fellows (1812), Knights of Pythias (1864)** they all had one purpose: to help one another in business.

1712 Button's Coffee House was in operation and was one of thousands of coffee houses in London (today it's a **Starbuck's** site). Coffee houses continued to be a centre for networking, attracting a particular clientele and Buttons drew playwrights, authors, poets, journalists and members of the public. It was acceptable to sit next to a stranger and ask their view on a book or for their opinion of the latest news.

1744 Gentlemen Golfer's Competition was played – some serious networking and relationship building happened here, culminating with the winner **John Rattray** being saved from hanging for his involvement in the **Jacobite Risings of 1745** by the intervention of **Duncan Forbes of Culloden.**

1851 The Great Exhibition of the Works of Industry of All Nations took place – the brainchild of **Prince Albert**. It was an amazing networking event. *'Oh, to go back in time.'*

1895 Margaret Murray Washington created the **Tuskegee Woman's Club** during her tenure as **Lady Principal of Tuskegee, Alabama.**

1903 The Institute of Directors was founded with 23 leading businessmen, headed up by **Lord Avebury** (best known for introducing the Bank Holidays Act of 1871). **Lady Margaret Mackworth** became the first female president in **1926**.

1905 The Rotary Club was formed in America between three business acquaintances and within seven years had become an International movement.

1921 The Soroptomist International (Womens' sisterhood) began in Oakland, California. The first group to be established in UK, London was in 1924.

1927 The Round Table (a Gentleman's Club) was founded in Norwich, Norfolk, UK.

1934 California Vitamin Company came up with the concept of Multi-Level Marketing. This paved the way for companies such as **Avon (1939), Tupperware (1948), Amway (1959), Mary Kay (1963), Forever Living (1978)** amongst many others.

1951–1970 During this time, **network groups** of marginalised business people were set up, such as women and African-American groups. Pertinent subjects could be addressed in a *'safe and supportive'* meeting, for instance, ways to combat the *'glass ceiling'*, addressing barriers to professional success.

1969 The Internet was launched. October 29th is regarded as its birthday when ARPANET used telephone lines to interface multiple computers, one in LA & the other near San Francisco.

1971 The first email was sent by **Ray Tomlinson.**

1974 The Federation of Small Businesses was started by Norman Small.

1985 BNI (Business Network International) was founded by **Dr Ivan Misner.** It has over 270,000 members and over 9,700 groups worldwide. Groups made a pivot to meet online during Covid-19.

1975–2000 Smaller **networking clubs** were set up to bring together business people within a town or city.

1990 The World Wide Web was invented. Sir Tim Berners-Lee also launched the first Web Page on 13th November 1990.

1993 First Web Browser called **Mosaic** was launched.

1996 First web-based email system, Hotmail arrived on the scene.

1998 Google was launched by **Larry Page** and **Sergey Brin**.

2000–2020s Technology improves and apps arrive putting **networking online** on the map and breaking down geographical barriers.

2003 LinkedIn was launched – to put business and professional people in touch with one another and encourage online recruitment.

2003 Skype was founded and was one of the first to provide video calls.

2005 Facebook groups were first launched to colleges.

2005 YouTube is created by **Chad Hurley**, **Steve Chen** and **Jawed Karim**.

2011 LinkedIn groups were made available.

2011–2020 The apps for video conferencing and virtual meetings are used more regularly, **Google Hangouts, Adobe Connect, WebEx, Microsoft Teams** but it would be **Zoom** which becomes the popular choice..

2020 Zoom quadruples its daily users as networking ONLINE explodes. New online groups are set up on a daily basis as an effect of lockdown. Consequently, networking ONLINE became the new business networking reality. Online business networking offered every day of the week including Sundays. Revolutionary groups are beginning to emerge such as **Community Conversation Groups.**

2020 World Online Networking Day is established on October 29th by **Ladey Adey**

Foreword

Nigel Botterill

Your network is your net worth.
Porter Gale

In the good old days of 2019, BC (Before Covid-19), it was a lot of effort to go to a networking event. You had to contend with public transport or, if you own a car, allow travel time for traffic, find a parking space, design business cards, get them printed, arrive home late/leave home early, and about another 100 steps that I've missed out!

Now, in the new world that has been thrust upon all of us, to be a positive contribution on a Zoom call, all you have to do is brush your hair and click. The difference is that in the old world we had expensive, complicated and difficult processes that we were already used to. So they didn't count as effort.

The '*new normal*' requires all of us to engage in new effort – things that we're not used to – which is what this book is all about. We didn't ask for this shift and the old ways disappearing might not feel like much of a benefit. But it is.

Online networking is part of the new normal.

It's here to stay.

It ain't going away.

When I was a kid I loved board games: Monopoly, Connect 4 and Othello, that sort of thing. Every time, the people that introduced me to the game taught me how to play the game. The instructions in the box were about how to play the game.

But I was much more interested in how to win the game – and that's what this book is all about. Most people don't think about the different rules for winning, as opposed to just playing.

But Ladey does, in this book.

Her deep understanding and love of networking oozes from every page but the contributions from people who know their *'networking onions'* so to speak – the winners, whose collective experience in face-to-face networking spans over 650 years, is what makes this book special.

It sets you up to win in the 'new normal' game of online networking. The impact of that on your business, and your life, could be profound. Enjoy – but pay attention!!

Nigel Botterill, Founder and CEO: Entrepreneurs Circle.
Best Selling Author: Botty's Rules and Build Your Business in 90 days

Introduction

A New Era of Business Networking

Only the minority have mastered the
true art of business Networking.
Unknown

Networking has a long history – since the beginning of human interaction between tribes as previously suggested in the Historical Timeline. At what part in our evolution did humans begin to realize that they had something to sell, something to offer, which somebody else needed and they could barter for mutual benefit? I suggest that networking is a natural part of the human condition but business people have evolved this skill and organised it. Business people know that networking done well brings a steady supply of new and returning customers.

Let's speed up to today, the 2020s, into the Internet era and the online scene. Networking evolves as technology becomes widely used and familiar. It seems to me, we've come to a transformation point in business networking history and a book is an obvious way to capture and record the phenomenon in which we are actively living. It's acknowledged that **Networking Online is now the new 'normal'**. Networking online has hit the tipping point into commonplace business activity. Its underlining principles and basic functions remain the same as face-to-face networking, yet there are subtle differences, nuances and refinements. I would suggest to be successful in business networking it's important to know how online networking works, its etiquettes and differences to in-person networking. Armed with this knowledge your business can gain and prosper from this essential activity.

The Online Networking Explosion

Turning to the Internet for business networking has been a direct response by business people continuing to trade through times of pandemic, specifically Covid-19, and lockdown. Our businesses need to survive and thrive or 'bounce back' (to coin the government phrase) and continue. A networking marketing strategy is the way to do this.

Business people and entrepreneurs are solution-focussed people, uppermost in their minds is the desire to keep existing customers happy, find new clients and make money. They have contributed to the online communication explosion. It has exploded for one reason and one reason only, the Covid-19 pandemic, 2020. Most world governments were of one mind in their approach to beat and eradicate the pandemic. We had to change our behaviour, we had to isolate ourselves and go into lockdown. It has affected every life, lifestyle and culture, all 7.8 billion of us.

We had to accept the closing of borders, lockdown of cities and towns; free travel, internationally and locally, was banned. We had to change the way we lived, how we educated our children, how we worshipped and how we interacted with one another physically. Meeting, mingling and mixing, the foundation of business networking with chats over coffee were no longer allowed, we had to 'isolate' from each other, and were no longer allowed to meet in groups.

We were not allowed to physically interact with one another, as had been our habit and cultural pattern throughout the centuries. The way we lived our life changed enormously from the moment the government announced: *"You will not leave your house unless you are a key worker, work on the frontline or have a frontline business"*. All was closed; airports, restaurants, retail, cinemas - all entertainment and non-essential business shutdown. The government categorised the definitions of which business were essential, furlough began (though not for the first time in history) and meetings and group gatherings were disallowed

Supermarkets had to change the ways they dealt with people with only one person from a household allowed to shop, maintaining 'social distancing' (staying two metres apart from one another). Physical barriers went up, plastic screens between the cashier and the customer, children taught they couldn't play with one another and new ways of separating us from each other were implemented.

This 'halt of trading' didn't even happen in the war years, then trade and entertainment continued. The year 2020 brought pandemic fears to the world in an unprecedented way.

My Personal History

My love affair with business networking began with my first meeting in 2007, at an Athena Network® meeting. I enjoyed this women's network so much I bought a franchise for Lincolnshire. I spent many hours organising networking meetings and establishing other networking groups including golf and charity networks. Pre-lockdown, I would attend around 10-13 in-person events per month, whereas during lockdown, I averaged 37 events per month. This unexpected increment has boosted my business, brand profile and connections!

Using Technology as a Networking Tool

As the world's Covid-19 storm continued with little sign of abating, networking organisers had to reconsider their operations. Business had to find a new way of relating with one another and selling their services, (selling business to business, or business to customer). The way we did it, thankfully, was to use the technology at our fingertips. Online became the new means of communication with Google Hangouts, Skype, and Zoom, and Microsoft Teams becoming some of the new tools. Even the older generation had to learn the technology to keep in touch with family, carers and to shop.

This is why and how online networking mushroomed and exploded in its usage. 'Normal' is engaging through the computer replacing physical face-to-face meetings. It would have been seen as Science Fiction at any other time in history, but now it is our reality.

This new reality is fascinating; how it's being used, and what effect it will have on business and business people. Is it a case of just taking the usual way of networking, the usual set up and just doing it online? Well, I don't think so, it's more sophisticated than that. Comparing face-to-face networking with online networking shows advantages and openness alongside disadvantages and limitations, which may be surprising. Online is an exciting new way to network with huge financial savings, although the loss we would feel were it to replace face-to-face interaction completely would be too great. However, online networking may have a new place in our future for the betterment of our businesses.

It raises the question, how do we effectively network to grow our email lists; to grow our customer base; and to provide services and make money? That is why we're in business - to do something we want to do and to make money; for all the essential stuff like pay bills and have extra for personal interests; and to invest back into the business.

The Timing of this Book

As business people, we are creating history as we live through this incredibly challenging time of pandemic, I wanted to record how networkers have responded to make the best of a bad situation and by doing so, change the face of business networking forever. As I explore, research and invite contributors to add their viewpoints about online networking I shall give you tips and hacks on how to successfully engage in online networking groups. Alongside this, I've asked prominent business people I've met via networking, to write guest features about business networking from their own unique perspectives. These articles are written especially for you and create a 'secret sauce' to successful business networking online.

This book is for ambitious business people using networking online (possibly for the first time) who want to know: the best online networks to attend, how to make online networking an essential part of strategic business marketing planning, know the correct etiquettes and make more sales via business networking.

You will find this book is jam-packed with pertinent information. It has morphed into a networking book in its own right with links to over 100 people who have contributed and refined this book with their input. Do go and look on their websites and if you contact them mention this book. If you feel you'd like to add something contact me *(ladey@ ladeyadey.com)* and let me know, I'd love to hear from you and you could be accredited in Version 2 of this book!

Enjoy and happy online networking.

Ladey

Anthony Thomson - Co-Founder of 86 400 and Metro Bank

Ladey Adey (LA): When I first contacted you through LinkedIn, I mentioned that my friend, Nathan Eaves, informed me that you'd set up the Metro Bank, by networking, and using networking systems. I didn't know whether that was true or whether that was an urban myth? You replied it was half true. So can you unpack that for me a little please?

Anthony Thomson (AT): I can, in fact, Metro Bank, in a sense came out of networking. At the time, I was the Co-founder and Chief Executive of the *Financial Services Forum*, which is a membership organization for senior executives in the Financial Services Industry. Its aim was to improve marketing on the basis that good marketing would be good for the consumer. We wrote a series of articles for our own physical and online magazine. I'd heard of a very interesting bank in America, so, in 2007, I went across there to meet the Founder and through this introduction came the idea for Metro Bank, so networking was part of the genius of the founding of Metro Bank.

I began work on it in 2008 and we launched in 2010 with one branch in Holborn, London. As you know, all the big banks had thousands of locations, and everybody said, *"Well, how are you going to compete with just one store?"* The answer was, *"We will build it street by street, literally postcode by postcode".* So, we had our team of people meet with businesses in the 300-400 metres surrounding us, then the half mile, then one mile surrounding us. We introduced ourselves, told them what we were doing, and invited them to come along to our launch event, at which they could open an account.

This is how Metro Bank started scaling its customers - literally going out and talking to people in the community. Then, the *'Flywheel Effect'* came into being, marking our growth, which was; they told their friends, who told their friends, who told their friends and within four years, we had one million customers.

LA: It's that telling about and referring on, which is what networking is about. Is Metro Bank continuing to open more branches today?

AT: Yes, I believe it is but as you might recall, I stepped down as Chairman back at the end of 2012. Since then, I founded and chaired the UK's first digital bank, which is Atom Bank, which was delivered on people's mobile devices and in 2019, my wife and I moved to Sydney, Australia.

When I decided to come to Australia, I didn't really know anybody. I just knew one or two people who had been out here. They introduced me to people, who introduced me to people who introduced me to more people. Initially, I spent a year coming over for one week each month and, on one of those visits I met a really interesting guy who was the Managing Director of *Cuscal*, a successful payments company. They had great technology, lots of resources, and wanted to launch a bank but had never done it and, literally over lunch, we agreed that we shared a similar view of the world, a similar strategy for building a bank, and we agreed to work together.

LA: Excellent. Will you be using more online networking within the marketing strategy to bring in businesses and customers in the future?

AT: Well, 86 400 Digital Bank is delivered through a mobile device, so the entire bank is online. We have acquired customers through digital marketing, but increasingly, our customers come through our existing customers, referring us to friends. We provide all sorts of digital support and incentives to enable them to do that. So, I think if we look at the way business worked 10-15 years ago, pre-digital, it was physical networking and mobile devices have allowed us now to make that 'digital' networking. Clearly, the biggest network in all this is Facebook and that couldn't have existed pre the Smartphone. One could argue that the PC introduced digital networking but the smartphone has really elevated it to, probably, the premier medium of networking today.

LA: How do you think this current situation of the pandemic, Covid-19 and the lockdown that everyone is experiencing is affecting either networks or the way we're communicating online?

AT: I think there are several answers to that. From a personal perspective, I communicate with all of my family via tools like Zoom, Houseparty, LinkedIn, Facebook and WhatsApp - we've all been forced to do that and in a way that opportunity didn't exist not so long ago. These are relatively new networking techniques.

From a business perspective; whilst our business is domestic (Atom Bank and Metro Bank before that were domestic) our investors and our business partners were international. I think for the very first meeting, it was important to meet face-to-face, but subsequent meetings invariably took place via digital channels. As bandwidth has improved (and networks too) it has become easier and easier to do that. I suppose the question is, will that strategy or traditional way of meeting in person for the first introduction and then communicating by phone or video thereafter continue, or will first meetings now take place through online channels like this?

LA: We are in very interesting times. It's only a matter of weeks since I first contacted you through LinkedIn and here we are having our first meeting, online through Zoom. It's going to be very interesting, how things change once we're given our freedom back.

AT: I think that's the key question: will it change behaviours?

LA: In your book 'No Small Change' you say, "Marketing is the art and science of persuasive communication". Can you explain this a little bit more?

AT: At the risk of putting it in the vernacular, you can only sell people crap once. So ultimately, you have to have a good product. It was Ralph Waldo Emerson, the 19th century American philosopher who said, "If you build a better mousetrap, the world will beat a path to your door." Well, the reality is, they won't because the world is full of better mousetraps or better products and services for consumers. Unless they become aware of them, they're not going to buy them. We're in an incredibly media rich environment, exposed to hundreds of thousands, thousands upon thousands, messages a day. Marketing is the process by which you bring your new products to the attention of prospective consumers. Expose people to the features and the benefits and hopefully persuade them to buy. As I say, marketing is very powerful but it has to have a good product underpinning it.

LA: I noticed, you detail the 'Marketing Seven P's' and how they related to digital world. In this book, we're exploring aspects of online networking, I'd like to ask you from your marketing expertise how do you see the online marketing developing?

AT: Well, as you say, it has already developed this is not an uncommon occurrence. If you take the area in which I've spent most of my experience, which is financial services, your contact centres have been around for the better part of 30 years. The idea of connecting people remotely is not a new one. It is opportunities presented by broader bandwidth and video, which enables the opportunity to introduce you to more people. I don't think what's happening today is new it's just an evolution of a process. It's been done for a long time.

LA: There is always a tipping point though when a product or services becomes so popular that it is as though it's always been part of our lives. I remember when the video recorder first came out; only certain people could afford to buy them, now everyone has a recording device in their home. It's that movement when it changes from use by a small number of businesses to everyone taking advantage of it isn't it?

AT: There's a great image which looks at the uptake of technologies and how long it took for each to reach 50 million users. For instance it took 22 years for the Television, 12 years for the cell phone and less than 4 years for iPods. So, it's the proliferation of new technology which enables this into the broaden network community. You couldn't have it if only two people had a smartphone.

LA: That is true and it's the pace, isn't it? As you said, it's got quicker and quicker. Do you have any concerns at all about online or digital being too quick or too hasty?

AT: No, no, not at all, I think it is for some people. It changes per generation, as people of my generation, and a generation younger than me, like you, are not digital natives. We are new to this land whereas our kids and grandkids are growing up absolutely immersed in the use of this technology. My good friend, *Chris Skinner*, says, *"It's only a matter of time and evolution until they start having opposable thumbs."*

LA: Do you see yourself as a marketer or a banker?

AT: Absolutely as a marketer, first and foremost, a marketer - this is where my area of interest lies. It happens to have been very specifically applied to banking for the last 11-12 years. I don't know how long I can keep saying I'm not a banker. I'll try it for as long as I can and say that I'm a marketer.

LA: So how did banking become the sphere that you've done so much work in?

AT: Almost by accident. One of my very early jobs was marketing for financial services and marketing insurance. I went from there to start an agency, which specialized in the marketing of financial services. Back in the 80s, it became the biggest of its kind in Europe. I sold it to publicists, who were second largest advertising agency group in the world at that time. I then co-founded the Financial Services Forum, which I mentioned previously, which is about improving marketing effectiveness in financial services. This, in turn, led to looking at marketing in banking, which led to the launch of Metro bank; digitization and the introduction of the iPhone led to the launch of Atom bank. My wife led to us moving to Australia, which led to 86 400. It's a series of serendipitous forks in the road, I guess.

I think the likelihood is, I will always have been in some form of marketing. Banking is just the path that presented itself to me over the last decade. Who knows what the next 10 years will bring?

LA: Do you still use networking and how does networking look to you in today's light?

AT: Yes, in the sense that I think one always needs to be inquisitive; there are lots of interesting people out there doing interesting things. I'm always pleased to connect to them, to find out what other people are doing, and where I can, to help people with the developments of what they're doing. You know, there's a balance to be had, you can't do that all day every day. I find things like LinkedIn incredibly interesting. I get approached by all sorts of people with all sorts of thing, interesting ideas, some of which I can help with, some which I can't, some of which I think are completely stark raving mad. I think to where we started with this conversation, a lot has now moved into the online arena but nonetheless, I still enjoy meeting people face-to-face.

Principles of Business Networking

My golden rule of networking is simple: Don't keep score.
Harvey MacKay

Principles are fundamental truths, with business networking principles standing the test of time, therefore remaining unchanged throughout the centuries. It's fascinating to think we're applying these same attributes today as we attend face-to-face or online meetings.

I often wonder what is the real genealogy of business networking. As I've suggested, networking may have evolved from traders and individual business men wanting to expand their sponsors and influencers as necessary within the business culture of their particular time. We are still witnessing this today with changes due to the 2020 pandemic, a milestone in business enterprise.

P T Barnum

Group structures and settings may have changed throughout the centuries, but etiquette and technique remain the same from one century to another and are influenced by people such as P T Barnum (1830s) to Dale Carnegie (1930s).

Dale Carnegie

We never imagined the virtual network meeting would take on as much importance as it has today in the 21st Century.

People buy from People

I'm a huge advocate for networking and love to think of myself as a 'Connector' of people. I have been networking for over 4 years now and can honestly say the majority of my business has come as a result of networking.

The power of networking is not to be underestimated and is a fabulous way of meeting local business people; make great connections and new friends. Online networking extends the reach from meeting other business people locally, into the national and international sphere.

Networking has to be part of your marketing strategy. Building good relationships is vital in business and getting yourself 'out there' in front of people is more valuable than paying for digital advertising which may or may not hit the right audience.

Deborah Firmstone, Founder: Queen Bee & Co

No Limp Lettuce Handshakes

I've always loved networking; face-to-face, social and online. Whilst I love hugs and air kisses, I must admit that I'm a huge advocate of online networking. Think of all the positives... no limp lettuce handshakes, no awkward pauses and no travelling!

There are huge positives: saving huge amounts of time, not having the awful dilemma of what to wear or even having to style the back of your hair!

Sandra Garlick MBE, Founder: Woman Who Achieves Academy

Principle One:

Networking is a Long Term Business Endeavour

Who you hang around with matters - a lot (including online!)
Nigel Botterill

Is the purpose of business to make money? Yes! It matches this definition: *A business can earn a profit for the products and services it offers.* There may be other underlining values for going into business, such as providing a service or a much-needed product to benefit other people's lives, but ultimately if a business doesn't make money then it's a hobby masquerading as a business!

To make money, you need a steady and regular stream of customers, agreed? Professional business networking is a way of finding customers or people who may put you in contact with new customers. So why wouldn't business and professional people invest time to involve themselves in business networks?

In 1904, at an inaugural dinner for the Institute of Directors, Lord Avery, summarised the purpose of business networking. He referred to the objectives of the Institute, but it's applicable to all networks. Lord Avery said, "*...it should be the centre from which they might obtain information upon various points of interests; that it should be the meeting ground on which they might consult together.*"

Finding the Best Network for You

Every business network is different, so use your skills, business savvy and intuition to make each work for your business. Which are the best business networks for you and your business?

Create a wish list of what you want from a business network - it may be to achieve your wish list you need to attend more than one network. Some points you may wish to include:

- A network of business people and entrepreneurs who stretch, stimulate and inspire their members.
- A network which generates new business.
- A network who are friendly, welcoming and have a social aspect.

It's Not Easy!

by Meryl Shirley,
Founder: _The Good Business Network_

Good networking involves much more than just turning up at a meeting. It requires being active, not passive, intentionally building a rapport with a fellow human being, as well as having a good product to 'sell'. It goes beyond the popular 'model' of people buying from those they like, know and trust into something more. You have an end product that people want for a particular reason - a lifestyle, an attitude to life, a product with perceived value and impact. Being genuine when networking is essential but it involves; preparing yourself to hold your head up high, valuing yourself and what you do, and to manage your _'imposter syndrome'_ allowing you to show your true self in the best light.

It can be off putting when people see networking as a place to sell their stuff. I don't think people want to network with people who only care about paying their mortgage every month. Yes, we all need to pay our bills, however making this your goal in networking is a very old-fashioned approach to business - getting what you can and selling to people without any thought of who they are.

Sales generated through networking are based on a different kind of relationship. There is a realisation that networking is about being visible or making an impact, but the challenge is to ask HOW are you presenting yourself? Are you visible and making an impact for the right reason?

In order for people to want to buy from you - the ultimate goal of networking, people need to know you are trustworthy, that you deliver on what you say you will, and you are a person with good values; integrity for want of a better word. Someone who networks well genuinely cares about others.

F *continued* As far as I'm concerned, good networking is not about cultivating thousands of contacts, or looking at people for what you can get from them; it's about doing something for, or with, someone because you have built a rapport and a genuine relationship. I'm not sure that it can be taught; people can often sense if another is genuine. This style of networking is learnt through being immersed in a healthy business culture, forming genuine relationships and it comes from the heart.

⌐ A network which shares pertinent business information. A network where the participants look for collaborators and are active referrers.

There's often a negative perception towards networking groups - people worry that it might be too "sale-sy" or that it may be about trading favours with strangers. Actually, it shouldn't be either. To reiterate, the purpose of attending meetings is to expand your business contact base in order to reach and contact more customers.

Principle Two:

Mastering the Art of Business Networking

I was told many years ago that nobody has
a monopoly on wisdom – and most of the answers
we need can be found within our network of contacts.
Mike Stokes

There's a common purpose at an event or meeting. Every person is there to meet a new contact for the betterment of his or her business. It doesn't matter who they are: the founders, directors, workers, professionals working for others, or representatives of a charity- they all need leads and want to be introduced to people who can become their customer or supporter. What business wouldn't want more of this?

Your Commitment

Your commitment in attending any network is:

⌐ Time - they say, *"Time is money,"* so it's a valuable investment.

- Money - including the cost of membership and meeting fee. Are you getting return on your money?

- Energy - to connect to others, raise your profile and add to your business network - where possible, help others to connect with one another.

It all goes back to the old adage, *'What you put in (to a network) is what you get out!'*

Meeting Format

An individual will set up a networking event or organisation in a region or online and invite local businesses and professionals to attend. They're often located in hotels or places with large rooms. The meeting will have a pattern or agenda, which can include all or some of the following:

- General networking - people mingle and exchange pleasantries, meet new faces and greet the people they already know.

- Formalised networking - organised so people can exchange business cards and arrange further meetings.

- An elevator pitch as a means to find out who is in the room. Participants are expected to give their name, company name, and a short outline of what they do (it's surprising what you can say in one minute!) It's an art form in itself and often fills people with dread, at least initially. I've devoted Chapter 3 to the subject!

- A speaker - there's little guarantee about the quality of the speaker! I've heard so many over the years of varying presentation styles and content, but I try to find at least one nugget of information from every guest speaker.

- Notices – information of interest to business people, local or national events, council information etc.

- Calls to Action (often during the one-minute pitch).

- Asks for help, referrals or introductions you need.

- Follow-ups (in your own time outside the meeting).

The most important job after a meeting is the 'follow-up'. Your choice is to either contact people who you've had a conversation with and collected business cards from or moan that it's been a waste of time and money. Nonetheless, you'll have booked into the next meeting to do it all over again!

How Often?

Face-to-face meetings can take place weekly, fortnightly, or monthly. Some organisations even boast of providing a group which you could attend every day! You're only restricted by geography and inclination!

Meetings are often at the following times: pre-breakfast, breakfast, lunch, early evening and night-time and may or may not include food. Online Meetings can take place anytime, any day and anywhere and only include virtual food and drink (i.e. you bring your own!). Beware though, watching people eat on screen is horrid and will damage your brand, so when taking any food breaks initiate your 'Stop video'!

Duration

Typically up to two hours, any longer than this and it's more of a workshop. Cost: Meeting fees range from free to £30 a meeting. Along the way, networking may expand your social circle and develop into a friendship, that's the 'icing on the cake'!

Passionate Networking

**by Margot Grantham,
Co-founder: WDG Research**

Let's think about passion for a moment ...

... and I don't mean that sort of passion! The 'passion' I'm referring to is having a passion for your business. Are you passionate about what you do? Does passion drive your business? Are you so passionate about your business that you want to share your passion with others? Is that why you attend networking groups? My background is in Marketing and we were always banging on about the 4 P's: Product, Packaging, Promotion and Place. What about the 5th P – PASSION? Without this P we risk inertia or achieving no more than the status quo. Passion is the change agent in business.

F continued

Passion makes you feel highly energised in a positive manner. It is an energy force – it helps people achieve against all odds: climb mountains, excel at sport, build empires.

On the subject of building empires: Howard Schultz, former chairman and CEO of *Starbucks*, took a small coffee business and expanded it to over 30,000 stores worldwide. Over thirty years ago on a visit to a piazza in Milan, he noticed how passionate the Italians were about their coffee. He found their passion infectious and enthused about it to his wife. Back home he set about transforming his Seattle coffee-bean store. Before long, his zeal convinced his investors to buy into his concept of bringing Italian-style cafés to America - and the iced frappaccino was born!

Passionate people are visionaries. They are inspiring, captivating, motivating and fun. They excel in their careers as they do in their lives, working hard to make things happen. Some are even a little bit crazy! But, they are great people to work with, just as they are fantastically productive employees to have. Passionate employees create passionate, loyal customers, as any management guru will tell you.

Yes, passion is contagious and like a virus it spreads rapidly. It is most virulent when conveyed face-to-face, online and by word of mouth making networking a highly effective carrier.

As you build relationships in your networking groups, your passion and enthusiasm will spread and encourage others to achieve what they otherwise may not have considered. This is the virtuous spiral that develops when you share your passions and your values widely. In this virtuous spiral, your relationships will continue to feed your passion as business is exchanged and people feel confident in how they feel about you and what they know about your business.

By the way, you will never find a passionate entrepreneur hanging around a lacklustre business. Like oil and water, they don't mix well... they flow at different speeds!

I said that passion is a virus, which might seem inappropriate in a world reeling from Covid-19, but see it as a good virus infecting your contacts with your enthusiasm.

Principle Three:

It's Who You Know

*Your success will be determined 90% by you
and 10% by the outside world.
It's what you think and do that will make the difference.*
Nigel Botterill

They say that business networks are about who you know. This is true and is dependent on the level of the definition of 'know!' You can know 'of' someone, know someone by sight, know someone by name, know someone because you meet up regularly at an event, know someone because you have met with them on a 1-2-1 basis, and know someone because they are part of your circle of influence and social group. How well people know what you do in your business varies too. Networking is about deepening those relationships, so when you say you know someone, it's more than seeing their name on a badge or screen. It takes time, interest and commitment.

Business networking is a way to strengthen the bond with other business people who could help you. It opens doors that otherwise would remain closed – but it takes persistence and mutual interest for this to work, and for personal and business relationships to flourish.

The adage, *'People do business with people they know, like and trust'* is the mantra for a majority of networking groups. This quote has been attributed to *Mark Twain*. It's unlikely that he was the originator of this phrase, but that's good marketing!

This is one reason why networking groups like long-term members, as they get to know, like and trust each other well. The downside is the group appears 'cliquey' and unappealing to new arrivals. They feel like outsiders, making the true winners the networking organisation itself who are making money! Hey, business networks are a business too!

Types of Networking

- 💻 Regular online and offline meetings hosted by the same person, same place, same day, same time and duration.
- 💻 Events, including trade shows.
- 💻 Golf, sport and community groups.

A Change for the Better!

ViewPoint

The Covid-19 pandemic has forced different thinking on businesses across the world, challenging mindsets, beliefs and, *"That's how we've always done it!"* attitudes at every turn. Networking has not escaped its effects. I have done a lot of networking in person over the years; suddenly all of it is *'in pixel'* instead.

The biggest difference is just how much of the darned stuff (video calls) it is possible to pack in. Wednesday mornings are particularly busy for me, it seems; frequently with three or four back-to-back meetings on Zoom *(oh, how we all went from terrified novice to accomplished veteran almost overnight!).* All without a penny spent on travel, parking, coffee and the rest.

Yet while the medium may have changed, the underlying principles have not. It remains that, networking is all about the relationship, and how we can develop them for (hopefully) mutual benefit. It still pays to approach any networking event with a non-salesy, *"How can I help and add value?"* attitude. The events themselves are simply a starting point from which longer conversations can grow.

The online environment is, I believe, a great leveller, neutralising the environment and making it ideal for a novice networker to dip their toe in the process. The very nature of the networking beast should ensure that more accomplished folk will demonstrate by their actions the effective methods of picking up the conversation and moving the process forward. In due course, the transition to in-person meetings will be less scary than jumping straight in at the deep end.

As the future charges at us, I believe the best networking opportunities will offer a mix of in-person and in-pixel meetings, and consequently evolve into a new, more inclusive 'normal', which in itself will broaden the opportunity to do business.

Rob Purle, Founder: *A Change for the Better*

Principle Four:

Networking is not Direct Selling

Networking is like lifting weights at the gym:
If you use the 'proper form' - you do it consistently over
a long period - it can be very effective.

Brian DeChesare

There's a huge difference between networking and selling, and if the two get mixed up, there can be dire consequences! This is one of the worries which stop people from attending networking events – *"Am I going to be sold to?"* Perversely, we like to sell our stuff, but we don't necessarily like to be sold to! Or, perhaps it's HOW we're being sold to that's the real problem. Do you think of the salesman as the old encyclopaedia salesman at the door, or the double-glazing person on the phone? Both have reputations for not going away until you buy.

You may have had that experience at a face-to-face networking meeting too, when somebody approaches you, stuffs a business card in your face and says, "I am such and such, and my product will..." before you know it they carry on, with zero interested in you. They just yak, yak... *"I do this, I do that, and I do the other, and you need to buy now."*

This is a big turnoff - they have confused networking as a platform for direct selling. Networking is more subtle. It isn't the other extreme of *"no selling allowed,"* but it's about a platform to promote products and services through relationship-building.

The purpose of networking is to let people know what you do, and they have the choice whether they go any further with you; either for themselves, their business or for their clients. The fun of networking is finding synergy between you and other like-minded business people and then working with one another.

A good analogy for networking is that it's a bit like dating. When you go on your first date, you see the woman or the man of your dreams and you don't jump in with, *"Hey, I want to marry you and have babies with you. Let's start now and forget all the dating rubbish"*.

You don't go there! Perhaps eight months or a year down the line you might say, *"You know, when I first met you, I knew that you were the one for me and that we would end up spending the rest of our lives together."*

21

However, not on that very first date, or you would find your companion, quite rightly, running for the hills! You have to play the game, you have to develop the relationship to see what fits, how you match - and it is the same with networking.

Networking (and particularly online networking) can fast track the opportunities for finding business by the introduction to other business people and by increasing the number of groups you belong to, or events you attend. During lockdown, networking online has become the obvious way to continue with business interaction.

Online networking has advantages over in-person meetings, but even so, the principles of networking and promoting your business remain the same. You have to tell people your story and it needs to be part of your marketing strategy. This includes deciding on the number of networking meetings to engage with.

Attending more meetings is easier online. You don't have to fight with traffic and worry about the travel arrangements. There are still other points to manage, though. You have to turn up on time (some hosts don't allow you in after 5 minutes!) and you have to show you're interested when on screen. It's against online networking etiquette to be obviously working on your emails while someone else is talking. A good networker looks at the camera regularly, shows interest and actively listens to what other business people are saying.

All seasoned networkers know business is ultimately about listening. You listen, you discern and ask yourself, is this person:

- 💻 Someone I want to do business with?
- 💻 Someone whose products and services I actually need that will help my own business or improve my personal life?
- 💻 Someone who understands my business and what I stand for?
- 💻 Someone who is trustworthy?
- 💻 Someone I want to go further with, know more about them, their business, their products, their family, their interests and their life?

This is networking. What qualities do you see? Do you like this person? If the answer is yes, you may not need their services, but you like them enough to recommend them to others in your network. We all have personal networks made up of family, friends, colleagues, ex-colleagues and business contacts (it is like an extensive Christmas card list).

Promotion at a Networking Meeting

If direct selling is frowned upon at networking events, how can you promote yourself and your services? There are lots of techniques and acceptable ways. Organisers will help this by providing a product or 'bumf' table, or by setting aside a time when you can showcase your product online or run a slideshow of your services. Overall, you are repeating in innovative ways, who you are, why you're offering your product or service and how to contact you or what you'd like people to do. The latter is known as a Call to Action (CTA).

As humans, we never lose our love for stories, and stories make you stand out during networking time. When given the opportunity (one minute or more) to speak to the others in the room, say, "I've been thinking about my business, and last week I met... and they said..." Then give a short testimonial story or a story around a feature of your product or service. Even online with individual screen time, you have to engage with others and you don't want them reaching for the mouse to check their emails!

The Seven Second Rule

Make yourself memorable, because it only takes seven seconds for people to make a judgement of whether they like you or not! Researchers have concluded it takes an average of seven seconds for us to sum one another up and record a *'first impression'*. Only seven seconds to decide if you like a person, or want to get to know them more!

You may have listened to the song *7 Seconds* by Youssou N'Dour featuring Neneh Cherry, which poignantly captures the time it takes for our judgemental behaviour to kick in!

If seven seconds is the time given for face-to-face interaction, what is it for online interaction? We know online interaction is faster, so are we deciding in less than seven seconds whether or not we want to do business with an individual? What a frightening thought and it puts the one-minute pitch into perspective! They do say, *"You don't get a second chance to create a first impression!"*

They have applied the seven-second rule to websites - how long it takes someone to decide if they want to read on and stay on the page or click to another site. Research from website testing tools like *Clickdensity*, shows that two seconds is a good rule of thumb for people staying on a page!

I think there's more to this initial assessment than meets the eye. In the in-person networking scenario, we have the benefit of using all our senses, including smell and touch, which are impossible in online interactions. Yet, our brains are wired to make instant decisions, and this seems contradictory to the networking mantra of building relationships, which can take years. Perhaps it takes longer if the initial seven seconds has resulted in a negative first impression.

Missing the Buzz

The Franchise sector does a lot of face-to-face meetings so it's almost as if we've been forced into the online world. For my business, I've welcomed this.

I am a member of Encouraging Women into Franchising (EWIF) and because of lockdown we've met via Zoom. Although meeting online is really good, I don't think it will entirely replace face-to-face networking because you don't get quite the same buzz around the room.

Online working is changing the way we think about conducting our business. For instance, I think initial meetings will take place online with a face-to-face meeting coming later. We take part in exhibitions and some of these have transformed into virtual exhibitions.

The technology allows us to have a chat room, book 1-2-1 appointments with people and even have a virtual person to 'man' the stand. Display materials are in PDF formats so they can easily be downloaded or sent to people via email. The in-person exhibitions can be a killer for your feet and your back so sitting on a chair and attending a virtual one is a great idea.

All in all, we are going forward into a 'new normal'.

Julie Taylor, Founder: Franchise Resales

Principle Five:

Seek Strategic Win-Wins

One person gives freely, yet gains even more;
another withholds unduly, but comes to poverty.
Proverbs 11:24

Choose your network wisely. It has to be a key element in your marketing strategy and business plan. You need to know your customer (potential and otherwise) will be in the room. As a publisher with a clientele of business people who want a book to work like a business card which open doors to speaking engagements, the networks which suit my business are ones where ambitious business people gather. The key here is 'ambitious,' with driven business leaders.

Who's your ideal customer and which networks do they attend? Link up with great networkers who love to refer business to others; they are the connectors in life. Discover businesses with complementary skills and assets to your own, so that alliances can be made. Make networking an adventure where you want to create win-win-win situations for you, other businesses and the client. Some actions to take:

- ⌨ Align your networking activities to your Business Plan.
- ⌨ Draw up a networking schedule and plan for the week and month.
- ⌨ Look at the previous year's business performance and notice any trends. Are there any peak periods and why?

Freedom of Online Networking

The new networking online frees up my time, allowing me to concentrate more on my business. It saves me time and money, no longer wasting hours travelling to meetings (as someone with disabilities this has always been a trial for me). I can connect with people from all over the world. It gives me access to a larger potential client base.

Nicola Gaughan,
Founder: *Iconic Creative Consultants*

Adapt, Survive and Thrive

A popular Western business theme is change management, emphasising people's inability and even reluctance to change. This has produced a lucrative industry for change management consultants. Well, why not? We pay people for advice to steer us through difficulties, relationships problems, organisational and technical issues...there's quite a long list.

However, we humans are incredibly adaptive to changing circumstances; our survival and progress over millennia proves this. While I am impressed by the capability of artificial intelligence to learn (a little worrying for us – will "they" take over?) I am convinced that human adaptability surpasses this. The Covid-19 outbreak shows this, as lockdown has compelled us to find alternative ways of communicating, working and maintaining our psychological well-being.

Due to the interconnectedness of business, the sudden global shutdown created a sense of confusion, dislocation from normality and bereavement. In my case, the end users of my leadership and management development services couldn't receive these, since there could be no gatherings for seminars and we couldn't travel. So, I adapted by providing: regular, but not too frequent, personal contact using email and other media; short written pieces of encouragement and advice; Vlogs to inspire and motivate; less frequent, longer articles and one-to-one conversations using various media.

It is clear that we have no prior experience to call upon that mirrors the traumatic circumstances of 2020's Covid-19 crisis. However, if we can be intentionally positive it provides our innate adaptability with a powerful springboard for action.

It also summons our uniquely human capacity for resilience, inspiring confidence that we can adapt, survive and thrive in a changing world.

Dr Chan Abraham,

Founder: Leadership International, Golden Acorns, Daybreak Ministries & Revival NOW!

Principle Six:

Measure and Move On

There is no point in just putting something out in the ether and not listening to the echoes.

John Harrington

It doesn't matter how nice the group is that you attend (the majority of business people are very nice people), but you have to measure the return on investment you are getting from a networking group.

- Are you meeting people that will further your business and bring in new customers?

- What is the 'rate of return' on the time and money you're giving to networking or could some other activity give you a better outcome?

- It must be more than counting the number of networking events you attend (you can fill each and every day with those), it has to be more than the number of business cards you collect or LinkedIn connections you make.

- What's your measure of whether this particular network is good for you and your business?

- Are you with a group who you can rely on for help and advice, and who you want to help and mentor in return? If not, go and find another network, which helps your business grow and be profitable.

- Ask yourself regularly if attending a particular business network is for you.

There are billions of business people regularly attending networking meetings every week, and there seems to be little evidence that this has subsided since the conversion to online networking meetings. Obviously, there are some industries that gravitate more comfortably to this type of sales generation, primarily those in the service professions (accountants, solicitors, coaches and trainers) and less from the face-to-face industries such as builders, hairdressers and beauticians – but there's no hard and fast rule.

I'm always intrigued when I see headlines on blogs or in newspapers such as *'Why networking events are a waste of time'*, *'Why I stopped going to business events'* or, *'Is it time to stop going to networking events?'*

Just because it doesn't work for one individual who's to say it won't work for another? I strongly suspect the writers are really complaining about the 'organisational or strictly formatted' meetings and still network, albeit in an individualist and informal way!

If you're feeling despondent about a network, leave before you infect it with negativity. Find other ways to keep in contact with the business people you've connected with and then research other networking groups who reflect your aims and ethos, and whose style and modus operandi make you excited to attend.

Extra Principle:

The Ethical Networker

An ethical networker is someone who the organisers want at their party (event). It's someone who has an approach to networking which brings out the best in themselves and others, who are viewed as successful business networkers and embody these five networking principles:

- Respectful of the network, other people and themselves.
- Avoid being part of a 'networking clique or huddle'.
- Don't 'pounce' on newcomers as if they are fresh 'business meat'!
- Follow-up with people they have spoken to.
- Ready with a referral and a positive word for other business people.

In fact, you can add to the list by considering the qualities you admire in fellow networkers and how you'd like to emanate these qualities and be an ethnical networker.

Are you there yet, or do you have some learning to do?

In **C**onversation **W**ith

Alisoun Mackenzie - TEDx Keynote Speaker and Life Coach

Ladey Adey (LA): Alisoun, how long have you been running networking groups?

Alisoun Mackenzie (AMcK): Ever since I started in business almost 20 years now, that's scary! I found that I couldn't find the right networking groups that I wanted to join. There were some good ones, but they didn't do it completely for me, so I created my own.

LA: What makes your network different from other business networking groups?

AMcK: They are very heart-centred and value-based networks. My events are about connecting with people from a place of love, kindness and with compassion in their hearts, getting to know each other, sharing information, providing inspiration, and enabling people to shine in a collaborative way. They are also holistic, often starting with breathing exercises or meditation. I come from a perspective we're better when we create opportunities for people to share wisdom and expertise, rather than one person holding all the wisdom.

LA: Have the groups always been for women?

AMcK: No, not until recently. I used to serve a mixed audience. My first network was called the Feel Good Hub, which was for therapists, coaches, trainers, everybody in the world of personal development and healing, who wanted to connect and support each other to help them grow their business. Since 2005, I've also run more intimate mastermind groups (4-6 people) rather than 30-50 people at networking events.

I like the intimate connections, support and opportunities that occur when a small group of 4-5 business owners meet up regularly.

LA: How does networking work within a mastermind group?

AMcK: Well, you're not 'working the room' in the same way as the large face-to-face meetings, so it's easier and quicker to develop much deeper relationships. I've found that members in a mastermind group engage fully with one another and want to do business together.

LA: How has the pandemic and lockdown affected your business?

AMcK: Initially, having just launched the Impact Retreat side of my business, it felt as though my business had fallen off a cliff. Now, after some strategising, I looked at what people needed and started offering free online classes, which, of course, is just another way of networking. The first one was on *Emotional Resilience* and I also launched the *Woman of Impact Book Club* and started running regular community calls to support women in my network.

LA: Do you think people will want to carry on networking online, or do they prefer the face-to-face meetings?

AMcK: I don't think I, or any of the people I've spoken to, particularly want to go back to the way it was completely. I mean, there's no doubt most of us want to have more personal interaction, but we're beginning to realise how much more can be achieved online. I think it's going to affect how we view office space and working from home.

This time last year, I facilitated a big conference for over 100 people, but I didn't have live streaming. Nowadays, I think all large events need to plan to add live streaming and online networking to people as a contingency and to open up their events to a wider audience.

LA: Tell me about how your charity work operates and how that embraces networking.

AMcK: About ten years ago, I started volunteering with a charity to do humanitarian work with young genocide survivors in Rwanda. Initially, I needed to raise money for the project and for my trips, and the only way I could think of doing that while running a full-time business was to incorporate my fundraising into my business.

So, I started making bracelets and taking them along to sell at networking events. People bought and wore the bracelets, which, in turn, raised funds and raised my visibility. I found fundraising for my humanitarian trips created more opportunities to speak, which, in turn, led to more paid work. I was surprised at how my fundraising and humanitarian work really helped me grow my business network. It made me more memorable and increased paid business on the back of it.

When I think about the connections and new partners I've made by my charitable work, I would never in a million years have thought I could have such personal conversations. When you connect from your heart and you do something that you feel is meaningful, other people who have the same values and share the same thoughts will connect with you. It doesn't matter 'who' they are.

Fundraising has become a core component of my business. Last year, I led a team who raised money to build a school in Cambodia. Now, my business gives women the opportunity to participate in projects where they raise the funds to build a school in Asia, then visit the school and enjoy a pampering retreat.

My network has grown on the back of my fundraising because I focussed on engaging other business owners to be part of this as well. Many people in business have loved supporting and donating to these projects. I make it easy for my contacts, my clients and my business network to be part of something good, even if they don't want to go off and visit Rwanda themselves.

LA: How do you view networking and how does it work for you?

AMcK: I think of networking not as *"I have to go to a business network event"*, but in the wider context of networking, such as volunteering: if you volunteer and help out in other ways, you start to meet different people, who become part of your personal network or community.

For most of us, the best way to get clients is by referrals. First, you build the connections and friendships, and then people refer you and vice versa, based on what they've seen and experienced. Networking isn't about going out to get business; it's about giving to others first before making any request. People need to understand what you offer in order to refer to you. If people ask you what you're doing or what you're up to, then share it with them.

LA: So you need to share your 'passion'?

AMcK: Yes, passion is inspiring and intoxicating, but it must be authentic. It's not about going into volunteering or fundraising in order to get business. Absolutely not that. It's thinking about groups other than business networks as a way of networking. Consider your hobbies; if you're a member of a local book club, a ski club, a sailing club, a tennis club, or even on a parent/school committee, these are all forms of networking groups. They're just not called that. So it's actually thinking of networking in a broader context. It's about building connections with people.

LA: You have established an online book club for women. Will this form a networking trend?

AMcK: I've been thinking about a book club for a while and so put it 'out there' by sending one email and one post across social media platforms. Initially, 30 women signed up, which blew me away! They're obviously all interested in reading books, but there's more. I feel heart-centred business women are looking for something more, to have meaningful conversations about inspiring books written by women.

Women like to talk and I think we're at a very exciting stage for the evolution of women. As the old male paradigms of society and success start to crumble around the world, we're moving into a time where a softer side, a more feminine viewpoint needs to be seen and heard. Not in a way that puts men down, but where there's more equilibrium, respect and harmony between male and female energy and respective needs.

When I say softer, I don't mean in a passive way but one where women are claiming their voice and rights. A lot of women in the world are now in positions where they can choose what they want to do, create opportunities for themselves, choose their working hours, choose the type of relationships they want to be in. As a result, there are more women exploring their voice; women can be a powerful force of change in the world.

This is why I decided to just *'lean in'* to see what would happen if I launched an online book club for women who want to make an impact. Let's see where it goes, see where the conversations take us. I'd love to see what sparks start to unfold as people connect with one another, go off and do things on the back of the book club. It's early days and I've got no attachment to any outcome. What I do know is, there's a growing tribe of women who are really keen to have deep and meaningful conversations, which they're not able to get anywhere else.

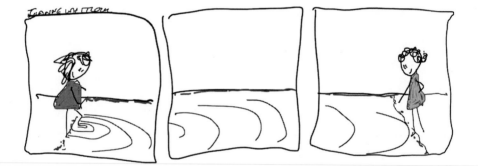

The Online Networking Strategist

The richest people in the world look for and build Networks,
everyone else looks for work.
Robert T Kiyosaki

All business people need to strategise and be experts in their chosen field or profession. Online networking is becoming a fact of business life, therefore it needs a strategic approach rather a cavalier approach gaining accidental results. As you create, form and shape your online networking usage, ask yourself the following questions:

- 💻 What are the differences between face-to-face business networking and business networking online?

- 💻 Do I need to consider carefully how I present my business online?

Which Online Networks are Best for My Business?

The online networking culture is in its formative stage and evolving, producing its own mores: attitude, code, etiquette, formalities, protocols and rules. These will be honed as some online networking groups prove successful and sustainable while other networking groups have a short-term season and then disappear. Ask yourself about your online business endeavours. Do you want to:

- 💻 Be a networking pioneer?

- 💻 Maximise online opportunities to increase your business success?

- 💻 Be a business person who influences and shapes social conduct?

If the answer to any or all of these is 'yes', you need to be strategic in your approach.

Reset the Clock

Before lockdown, my diary was empty and I spent a lot of time building up my network. I went to meetings but had little result. I seemed to have a passive interaction with people... and then lockdown happened.

Suddenly, everyone went into a frenzy of *"I need to think about my social media,"* or *"I need to rebrand!"* People had time to think deeper about their business. It is like the clock has been reset. All businesses, large conglomerates and small enterprises, were in the same boat, having identical issues to overcome. Everyone had to hit the reset button.

One positive outcome for me was the speed in which everyone wanted diary time with one another. I hadn't used Zoom calls or online networking before – I've never had so many 1-2-1 meetings! Online also gives us informality, and authority levels changed. Online networking makes it easy to appear as equals to those we previously looked up to.

However, we've created a problem. People are getting worn out digitally from too much screen time, reflected in phrases such as, *"I'm zooming down,"* or *"Wow, that zoomed by!"* It is important to take screen breaks and give your eyes a rest, and to take stock of what you are achieving.

If you are going from one online networking meeting to another, and if you don't take note of the person you want to speak to after the meeting, as quick as you can *'click into zoom'*, you will forget what business you wanted to transact.

People enjoy the social side of networking; nibbles and meals together, because they're able to communicate better in this kind of environment. Personally, I feel networking online has become too quick, too fast paced and, although producing results it has lost some of the *'human touch'* – and I'm someone from a digital field!

Kieran Willis, Social Media Marketeer, Docks Digital Ltd

Online Visibility

Our reputations are important to protect and online we're very visible so we need to include online safety in our strategy. Visibility is not just about being hacked or scammed or fielding unsolicited and unwanted negative comments, it is also in your hands (or mouth) – be careful what you say!

To paraphrase Shakespeare's line from, *As You Like It, "All the online world is a stage and all the business men and women merely players"*. By using online platforms, participating in digital meetings and posting on social media you have put your head *'above the parapet'*. You're visible, recorded and can't hide behind a business card!

Online visibility includes comments you make and interaction you have in groups via the chat box. Online network organisers usually record the session and when you post messages in whatever forum, once posted they cannot be taken down. How many times have you seen someone's reputation destroyed because of a careless remark put up on Twitter? Don't let it be you.

Your reputation and your business brand, are important and it takes many years to establish yourself as credible and an expert in your field. So think of what you type, on ANY site, in light of online safety. It's in your control – you're the one typing the comment after all! Like in Shakespeare's quote, or my paraphrase, online is the 21st century stage - use it for your best performances!

<u>*So Many Online Options*</u>

I love networking online especially while we're in lockdown. My exercise classes, committee roles, and personal socialising have also moved online and I'm feeling very grateful for modern technology right now!

For my business of Tropic Skincare, I have arranged virtual gatherings; to chat, learn, and practice some self-care and pampering – all online.

Ellie Hiam, <u>*Tropic Skincare*</u>

Networking in Times of Crisis

Feature

By Robert Middleton,
Founder *Action Plan Marketing*

This article is being written at the peak of the Coronavirus pandemic of 2020 and the situation isn't good. The economy has plummeted, and a record 26 million (USA) people have filed for unemployment – just 6 weeks into the lockdown. Part of the fallout of this, is many companies and corporations are cutting back dramatically on services; they just don't need them right now.

What does that mean for your business? It means that networking is more important than ever before. It's what you need to generate new business in very challenging times.

The good news is that business people have an advantage. They are small and nimble, able to quickly make decisions and take action. What you need to do is ramp up your networking to a whole new level.

Networking is about building business relationships. You start building relationships by communicating to those in your network about what you do and the value you offer.

This four-step model will give you some insights into how networking actually works.

Affiliation. This is where networking starts, with those you are already connected to. It's everyone you know, people in your community, all the members of professional groups you belong to, business associates you've met over the years, your LinkedIn and other social media connections. You not only need to build affiliations, you need to nurture them over time.

Visibility. All your professional affiliations won't do you much good unless you are in front of them regularly. If you are out of sight, you are out of mind. So, in times of crisis, it's

F continued important to be more visible than ever before. People are distracted trying to put out fires; therefore you need to be a meaningful presence in their inboxes and on social media posts. You need to be meeting people more often.

Information. Even if you are more visible than ever before, it doesn't help much unless you are communicating some real value. What ideas, information, and inspiration are you putting in front of those in your network? Are you sending out a pithy email newsletter? Have you developed a new report? Have you created a helpful video? Right now, there's a plethora of communication like this, but if you don't offer something of value, you will be forgotten.

Experience. Information is tremendously valuable but giving people an experience, a taste of you, is even better. An experience, for self-employed professionals, is a live presentation of some sort. This could be a webinar or other event presented virtually via Zoom video. A report can be useful, but a presentation will be much more memorable. Those who attend a live presentation are often the best candidates for your services.

The whole purpose of these activities is to build the know-like-trust factor. If you have a network of affiliates, stay visible, provide information and offer experiences, then your networking has staying power.

And in ordinary times, this is often enough to stay top-of-mind with those in your network. But in extraordinary times, more is required.

It's all about conversations. I've discovered that the number one activity you should be doing right now is reaching out directly to those in your network (current, past and prospective clients) and having conversations with them.

Nothing really substitutes for this. It's only through conversations like this can you make the depth of connection that will result in something actually happening to grow your business. You can ask questions, you can offer suggestions, you can brainstorm ideas, and you can explore new possibilities.

F *continued* **I usually recommend starting with past clients.** Send them a very brief email letting them know you've been thinking about them and that you have some ideas to share with them. Ask for a meeting by phone or Zoom. That is all. Don't mention any specific services.

This type of outreach emails tend to get a very high response. People appreciate that you are thinking of them and have some ideas to share. They don't get a lot of short, simple, direct emails like this.

When you have the meeting, ask them how they are doing and how they are coping in their current situation.

Don't think of this as a "selling conversation." It's more of an exploration and sharing of ideas, insights, resources, and connections. Be of value in this meeting - be of service. Share something they can use right away. *Give - don't take.*

The majority of these meetings will not result in any new business but you are planting the seeds for the future.

Some meetings will bear fruit. You'll be discussing an issue and something that needs more than a short conversation will pop up. If it does, you can ask more questions: *"How important is that issue? If you don't get that handled what will happen? Is this something that's a priority for you right now?"*

Ultimately, the need for a solution that you can provide may present itself. If it does, I recommend setting up a more in-depth *'strategy session'* to explore how you might be able to offer a service that will resolve this problem for them.

Most networking is passive. You show up, provide information and experiences and hope that they resonate enough that you generate word-of-mouth business whereas this approach is proactive.

Being proactive is not heavy-handed or pushy. You start with short conversations, providing some value and, low and behold, some of those conversations evolve into new projects.

Networking during times of crisis is an absolute necessity if you are going to survive and thrive in your business. So, right now think of who you would like to speak to, pick up the telephone or dash off a few emails **today!**

You are Being Watched!

We use social media to gain more customers and highlight business. As part of this culture, it's good to be 'followed' and build up supporters. In the same way, online mentors attract followers who want to receive up-to-date opinions and to follow their mentor's lead. So, the window of who is watching you is wide and you don't necessarily know who is taking note of what you are saying. You're being noticed, and even years later someone may refer to a blog post you have written or a comment you posted on someone's article. Remember, it's best to keep your guard up, and be on your best behaviour when using these mediums; promote your business and yourself as a successful business person.

The familiarity trap is easy to fall into as social media actively encourages informality. Social media has broken down many barriers - I have noticed a shift-change during lockdown with business people being less reserved and more personable in their messages.

One company, *Nielsen,* reported in their newsletter how colleagues who have worked together for years have now seen another side of one another. Video meetings have meant they've a '*look through the keyhole*' into one another's homes - kitchen, sitting room, bedroom and even under the stairs! They viewed this as illuminating and very entertaining at times, but it also breaks down intimidating layers that higher management roles bring. Managers now appeared more human, perhaps more vulnerable and this has improved staff relations.

This can be positive BUT as a general rule of thumb, don't write or post anything that you wouldn't say to your Granny! This includes tone and language used as well as the words itself.

Never '*badmouth*' anyone – even in fun or as a rant – it'll come back to bite you. This includes being wise in choosing posts you '*share*' or '*re-post*' as the following story will show. The bottom line - you can't afford to lose the respect of existing and prospective customers.

The Human Side of Online Networking

Online networking involved an initial shift in mind-set, as I no longer had completely child-free time due to lockdown. At first I wasn't even sure I could make it work.

It has been an interesting journey, with the kids popping in on some of the calls, and sometimes arguing in the background for good measure. I do think it shows the human side of life and has provided a talking point with other business people who are in the same boat! Despite lockdown, I have used my newfound online networking skills to attract new customers. Working within the health and well-being sector, I was concerned that people would think I was trying to capitalise on the Covid-19 situation and people's fears about their current health. However, new customers have been interested in the MLM approach - it can be a lifeline for people, those who were furloughed for example, which is very exciting.

Rachel Haith, Founder: Inspired Life Group

A Steep Learning Curve

Our group was resistant to online networking, however we soon realised it would be foolish not to join this trend. Despite a steep learning curve, overcoming technical details and deciding upon the best online format, it became clear we could develop meaningful contacts in this new online networking territory.

Melanie Smith-Rawlings, The Happy Foot Clinic

Momentary Poor Judgement has Repercussions

A friend of mine was so disgusted when she received a Facebook post which shamed a famous, rich male singer crying and talking about his mental health. The post compared him, in a judgemental and derogatory manner, to Captain Tom Moore, the veteran hero, who has fund-raised £millions for NHS charities. In her responding comment, she recalled the tragedy of Caroline Flack and the need to be kind and considerate regardless of your personal view of their financial and celebrity status. Then, she took action.

My friend has a sizeable email list for her business and she noticed who had posted this message and deleted them because if this was their viewpoint, she didn't want them as her client or partner. She also saw who'd made a comment, and those who also belittled the singer were also deleted from her list - no longer receiving her services, referrals or custom. A further repercussion was as her tribe agreed with her they did the same with the people in their circle who had shared this post.

What if you were deleted through putting out a similar careless post on social media, on your website, blog or in an online networking group?

It doesn't take much to lose the respect of others and it's very difficult to reclaim this once lost. To quote Warren Buffett, *'It takes 20 years to build a reputation and five minutes to ruin it. If you think about that, you'll do things differently.'*

All the effort, time and money you've spent on branding, networking, building up rapport with people, online advertising etc. can be lost through posting careless comments. A personal viewpoint has crept in, rather than keeping posts business-focussed. You can still be personable in your posts, but wisdom needs to be practised!

Nil Confidentiality Online

Another consideration for online communication is around confidentiality and freedom of speech. Some face-to-face business meetings operate under the Chatham House Rule (anything said stays in the room and is confidential) or you can always deny you said something, but online there are no such rules. Once the send button is pressed, it's in the public domain forever! The Internet is a sharing tool and as such, nothing on it is regarded as confidential it is all in the public domain.

Online vs Offline

**By Felicity Francis,
Founder of Talk Networking &** _Talk Networking Online_

No one could have predicted the immediate halt and upheaval to the majority of our business when the pandemic of Covid-19 hit us all. Those who rely and depend upon networking were put in a huge predicament - not being able to communicate with their prospective leads, referrers and support network.

Thankfully, a lot of groups and individuals saw there was a huge need and have created online networking events; and what a variation of events have emerged, each individual and diverse in their size, frequency, cost and format.

When the crisis happened, I knew I wanted to use it as an opportunity to '_give back_'. My networkers had supported me for nearly 10 years and I wanted to help them keep connected at a time when they needed it more than ever. This meant keeping their businesses alive, trading, referring and most importantly a support network to get them through one of the hardest times we have all had to face.

Talk Networking moved online and is a free service for up to 60 participants per event with the chance to speak for 45 seconds each about their business. What I had not expected was the huge surge of interest and the first two events being overbooked within a matter of days.

A number of my members and ad hoc attendees had signed up, but names and companies I had never heard of were popping up on my booking in list, along with people from further afield, including a lady from America.

I had not foreseen that moving the networking organisation online would open up the chance to meet so many new people.

F continued   I had three big fears about running *Talk Networking* online:

1) Lack of atmosphere.

2) Technology issues.

3) Negative or depressing tone.

I had heard *'networking horror stories'* of how all three points had cropped up and I was going into the unknown.

I planned as best as I could to make sure people understood how to use Zoom and requested words such as 'coronavirus', Covid-19', 'crisis' and 'pandemic' be kept to a minimum and only spoken about in a positive context.

I did not know how to gauge the number of people who would attend. Would a free event be valued, or would it only gain a handful of attendees?

We glided through the event and thankfully the *'networking buzz'* was there throughout the meeting. Together we had interjected fun and laughter and I think after the stressful few weeks we all realised how much we appreciated seeing a *'room'* full of happy faces who understood just what we had all been going through as business owners.

Technology issues were minimal mostly down to one or two participants having poor Wi-Fi. We were thankful for online video conferencing as twenty (or even ten years) ago, networking online wouldn't have been a possibility.

During online networking I have noticed:

- People have gained more confidence in presenting their one-minute pitch online and it has encouraged creativity in how people describe their business.
- A huge shift in more businesses collaborating with one another to target new markets and people are uniting their services to give support and advice to those who are struggling.
- The variety of group sizes. I have seen screenshots of meetings of 6 to those in the hundreds. From small gatherings of advice giving to huge MLM companies uniting teams across the sea.

F *continued*

In all honesty this pandemic has shown a huge shift in not only how we can function but also what working together really means.

I think there has been a big drop in the *'my networking group is better than yours'* attitude. People who were part of one are now willing to venture into other events and try new meetings. Whether that is due to the need to find more business (as other routes have been temporarily halted) or whether it is a change of mindset to see that we are all equals and need to work together to get through this – I'm not sure!

My belief with networking is that it is not a focus for locating new clients or getting referrals, but more importantly it is about building a support network. Having a group of people who know how hard you work and will cheer for your successes and support you at your lowest. They are your guides, advisors and mentors and they are also the ones to become your clients and referrers. This crisis has brought us closer together at a distance and changed the foundations of networking.

I would never wish to end face-to-face networking, but I do hope that online networking has changed the future of how we view our relationships with fellow networkers.

An International Flavour

Recently, there's been an international feel to the online conversations. From my 'almost' next door neighbour in Lincolnshire to Geneva; from Andalusia to Poole; and Sydney to Hull - whoever said lockdown was a restriction to generating conversations and making connections is clearly very wrong.

The future is in our hands – let's make it happen!

Mark Jarvis, Founder: *Referral Partner Community*

Wonderful Technology

Using this wonderful technology to the best advantage for you and your business means you get to show your best image, character and business persona to the world – it's not called the World Wide Web by accident! It can be a great stage/platform to be on, as long as you know the protocols and don't become a complacent, over-confident or conceited communicator – people are taking notice.

You are using a public forum when talking, chatting or writing online on a myriad of apps and platforms. Respect them and remember my Granny's general rule!

The Speed of Online Life

Online culture encourages snap decisions, which is challenging for business people. There is heaps of data on how visitors use websites. For instance, it takes about 50 milliseconds (that's 0.05 seconds) for visitors to form an opinion about your website and determine if they like your site and consequently, whether they'll stay or leave.

It takes 2.6 seconds for a visitor's eyes to land on the area of a website that most influences their first impression and we all know how much first impressions count.

Throughout social media, comments are instant and responses expected within a short window - even emails need to be answered within three days! The relentless pace of communication is increasing without us realising!

It's also addictive, and hours can be lost while replies are crafted and comments made. There's a case to measure how much time you spent on these activities - is it fundamental to gaining customers, making sales and increasing your bottom line?

Online Fatigue

Tiredness and fatigue from too much time spent online may be a new phenomenon, but due to 2020 lockdown, the Internet has become **THE** window for communication. Video conference technology like Zoom has increased with people who have never used the technology forced to use it if they wanted to remain in contact with loved ones. Most businesses have embraced the technology but are we having too much of a good thing?

Networking Lockdown Boom

Virtual and online networking has boomed as a desperate result of the Covid-19 pandemic. Sadly, many online events have actually made networking less effective and more boring. All the stereotypical, negative connotations about networking are doubled online. It is little more than looking at a screen, in turn giving the name and a brief, robotic description of our business, or services.

Thankfully, not all online events have been dull and uncreative. It has been good to see some authentic and natural networking taking place, with people in their own 'home-environments', showing them as real people and not robotic networkers; people in various states of dress, make-up, even only dressed from the waist up!

This time has shown the great resilience of the business sector. It is the self-employed, community organisations and entrepreneurs who are keeping business going in the UK, whilst big corporations have been forced to close.

Our own efforts have resulted in a *'KuKu Cocktail Hour'* - a live online networking connect reception. We dress in our best - drink in hand - and introduce businesses, giving shout-outs for those with great tips, information, free advice, offers and services. We talk about, and to, business people and their services to audiences of hundreds, right across our region.

We all know that networking works on the basis of people meeting and buying into each other, which includes the relationship you build with other people. Standing face-to-face in a room will always outshine a virtual networking world.

Only time will tell how the networking sector evolves in the future of an already heavily digital world.

Stephen Goddard & Philip Brooks-Stephenson,
Co-Founders: KuKu Connect

I heard from one business man who said he took 21 Zoom calls in one day! My means of contacting people has changed from telephone or email to Zoom. During lockdown my typical day can look like this:-

4 - 7.30 am	Writing copy for latest book or creating content for other mediums.
8 - 8.30 am	Online networking group.
8.30 – 9 am	Breakfast.
9 – 12 am	Working on clients' (authors') projects.
12 - 1 pm	Main meal.
1 – 4 pm	Three - four Zoom calls (including at least one prospective client call).
4 pm	Online webinar.
5 pm	Light meal and relax.
7.30 – 9 pm	Online networking group or online social group.

Will the hours spent on online activity change when we start back to face-to-face interaction? For me, I am more productive when using online strategies. I can, therefore, only see Zoom calls continuing, with a few in-person meetings interspersed.

I asked an online networking group to do a straw poll on how many conference calls they make, and my friend, Rob Purle coined it *'Living on Planet Zoom'*. Collectively, we made an average of 30 video calls a week, compared with about five calls prior to lockdown.

I saw a comment by business woman, *Hannah Long* who posted, *"Does anyone else think Zoom fatigue is a real thing?"* This resulted in asking her to write a feature to exploring the topic more (see Chapter 7).

Online and Offline Networking Differences

The easiest way to compare online and offline networking encounters is to put the differences in a table format. The table is not comprehensive, so I've left some blank lines for you to add your own observations. You can also contact me, ladey@ladeyadey.com so I can include your view in the next edition.

Comparisons between Networking Groups

Offline Networking (Face-to-Face)	Online Networking
Confidentiality can be managed.	All comments are on public record, meetings recorded and chat box downloadable by all participants.
Host invites attendees and it's known who is coming.	Host can send out private invitations or there is a general invitation to just turn up.
General niceties as people gather – where are you from, weather etc. which can last for 15 – 30 minutes.	Occasionally, an initial chit chat at the start of a meeting while you wait. Usually, only with a couple of people and no more than five minutes before the meeting officially begins.
Projector and PowerPoint slides are the only technology used.	Technology is more diverse and easier to set up – anything on a participant's computer can be viewed by others through share screen.
Some people dominate a meeting and you can't shut them up!	Mute button is available and it's possible to remove a person!
Usually everyone is in one room and only go into break out rooms in a conference or seminar meeting.	Host can arrange break out rooms for smaller groups.
Background noise is difficult to moderate, and when meetings take place in a restaurant, participants and speakers are competing with piped music!	Etiquette asks for people to be muted to avoid hearing personal background noise: telephones ringing, radio playing, pets barking, children screaming, cars going by, smoke alarm going off etc.

Offline Networking (Face-to-Face)	Online Networking
Members are restricted by travel time to a meeting. Regular networking meetings attract participants from a 25 mile radius from the venue.	Worldwide access to any online meetings. Geography and where you live barriers of travel are removed.
You can read each other's body language when talking with one another (including smell!).	There's a limited access to reading other's body language. Senses used in communication rely on visual and hearing.
It's a person's choice who they speak to, where they sit and who they're introduced to.	All in the online space together – mass introduction – need to use the chat box to engage individually or arrange a 1-2-1.
Etiquette rule: No chatting while others are speaking.	Can text with other people on the call during speaker time via the chat box to everyone or privately (the latter is private between two participants).
Individual note-taking.	Collective note-taking and comments can be saved and distributed or downloaded immediately.
Business cards passed out.	The live screen is your business card. Links can be shared instantly and are clickable if the http:// is prefixed.
Natural physical activity - standing up, and walking around.	Remaining sitting down in front of the screen throughout the duration of the meeting.
Drinks, snacks and meals may be provided by the venue.	Individuals have to get their own refreshments.
No personalised crockery.	Participants can show off their mugs and drink holders!
Always losing pens!	Pen holders at the ready!

Offline Networking (Face-to-Face)	*Online Networking*
Volume is not controlled by the listener and is dependent on the sound system in the room or the clarity and volume of the individual speaker.	Individuals control the sound volume and lip reading is easier as people are directly facing the screen. Where calls are audio only (without video), then more concentration is needed as only one sense is being used.
Etiquette is to give attention to the speaker, and the speaker can see the audience and read body language.	Participants do not need to give eye contact; some put their photographs on instead of video. It's easy to do multi-task when a speaker is on and to listen as if it is a podcast!
If you leave the room for a comfort break or get a cup of coffee, it's obvious that you have left the meeting.	Changing the settings to stop video puts a picture up, and no-one knows if you're in front of the computer or left the room.
The buzz of group conversations that stimulate ideas and 'off the cuff' remarks.	People have to speak in turn so spontaneous talk is reduced. Few spontaneous conversations can occur.
Private conversations in the corner of a room can happen.	Anyone in the room can overhear what's being said.
Choose who you speak to and who you have an immediate 1-2-1 with.	More regulated and harder to do in the meeting – arrangements have to be made for 1-2-1 after the meeting.
Appreciation, and applause can be spontaneous and questions asked at the time, interrupting the speaker if necessary.	Appreciation is more controlled: applause is contained or shown via text reaction/emoji.
Turn up early and meet some people before the meeting.	Participants are only allowed access to the meeting when the host decides.

Offline Networking (Face-to-Face)	*Online Networking*
It's viewed as bad manners to leave the meeting early (unless previously agreed).	Freedom to leave the meeting at any time during the proceedings.
No concern on atmospherics, dependent on the venue and anything the host sets up.	There's a need to check lighting, especially any back lighting, which casts your face in shadow, what's in the background, on the walls etc. that others can see and comment on - or custom backgrounds can be used.
Host tells participants of housekeeping details including fire alarm procedures etc.	No fire alarm practices.
Travel time gives respite from work and time to ponder over conversations.	Little downtime between calls, though this is a time-management challenge.
Instinct and reading the whole body language makes it easier to tell if someone is lying.	Lying and telling untruths are harder to be uncovered.
Easy to move around, sitting for short periods.	Sitting in one place all the time.
Easy to hide at the back of the room and behind more extrovert personalities.	Visible on screen with no place to hide, unless you only have your name or photograph on show.
Leaving with a quiet goodbye.	Frantic waving as the meeting closes and everyone leaves simultaneously!

Networking as an Expat

There is an old joke that says if two Englishmen were wrecked on a desert island the first thing they would do is set up a club and then spend the rest of their time trying to *'black-ball'* each other from it. After working as a freelance for 16 years in Switzerland, I can see the truth in it.

Networking as an Englishman abroad was always going to be a challenge, but little did I realise just how different it would be from the UK. After totally failing to find any use in the local Chamber of Commerce (where only your job title reflected how well they valued you), I stumbled upon the informal network that is expat life.

I was a native English speaker and that was all it took for other native English speakers to help. Well, those who saw me as their social equal that is (class is still exported although money can sometimes trump it).

Over the first eight years, the expats were my network. One English speaker passing me from one contact to another: and from one job to another. Conversations would start with *"Can you...?"*, then explore not just your CV but your skill set outside of it, too. As a result, I worked with everyone from: penniless students (Life Coach), to Autodesk (Training Designer) and Google (Neurodiversity Coach) in my time.

Only later did my Swiss contacts start helping me network too, but by then I was *'semi-Swiss'* to them at least. Over time, I realised that all nationalities network in a similar way, starting with their own native speakers. Russians are very Russian about networking (yes, there's lots of vodka involved); the Italians have their Italian way; Indian people - an Indian way, and so on. It is only when you learn to integrate yourself within the local culture that your network transcends your nationality. If you can integrate with the other expat cultures, all is well and good.

Neil Jones, *Coaching and Consulting*

Use the table below to fill in any differences you have observed.

Differences between Networking Groups

Offline Networking (Face-to-Face)	*Online Networking*

Vocabulary Additions in our Conversations

We're creating new vocabulary as we make sense of living in pandemic, coping with lockdown and migrating to online experiences. I had to laugh when talking with my friend, Nicola Watson, after her daughter interrupted our conversation. She turned to me and said, *"Well, those are words I never thought you'd hear me say, 'Wait a moment, I'm in the middle of a Zoom meeting!'"*

David O'Brien, says the mute button is the most common outcry, *"I think Mike wanted to say something".* Mike does 5 seconds of earnest miming followed by a chorus from unmuted colleagues of, *"You're on Mute!"*

For fun, I have gathered some new phrases. Perhaps you're using them in your conversations?

Lockdown: Common Words and Phrases

Can you hear me?	We've become click-oholics
I think you have frozen	We've got connectivity issues
I'm having a 3D meeting	You're on mute
I've been Ghosted	Zoombombing
Kettle break	Zoom brain
Lockdown hair	Zoom friend
Networking bank account	Zoomland
New normal	Zoom meeting
Online migration	Zoom motivation
Quarantini o'clock	Zoom professional
Shedquarters	Zoomworld
Silent noise	Zoom zombie
Take a Screenshot	Zoomitus

Write Your Online Strategy

Consider your own experience with online networking, is it time for you to think about a strategy for you and your business? How much of your strategy would be intuitive and how much would you have to make direct decisions?

The change in our worldview, in employment and the business environment, reminds us that strategy plans: our vision, mission statement and business plan are fluid. They need to be flexible rather than static, so the strategy can be current and responsive to customer's needs.

Brad Burton - Founder of 4Networking and Speaker

Ladey Adey: (LA): Brad, as Founder of the business, 4Networking, known as *4N*, you were recently quoted as saying, '*4N* online networking is like being in Disneyland'. Could you explain this please?

Brad Burton (BB): I go to Florida every year with my family, and we go to the Disney Parks. If you went to Florida and to Disney, my experience would be totally different to yours. You like different things so you would have a different approach to me; some people go for the food, some people go for the thrill rides, and some people go for the shows. No matter what we choose to do, we both go to Disney, right?

We all have our own style of a Disney visit; nobody sets out to have a terrible Disney experience. If you followed my route of what I do, you might not enjoy it, and if I was to follow your route, I might not enjoy it. In business networking, many people are trying to prescribe what and how you should do it. I think with *4N* you can choose which bits you want, which ride you go on.

You can choose who you associate with, whether you want more raucous meetings, or if you'd like more subdued ones, whether you like big meetings or smaller meetings, or according to the speaker, whose topics can range from the *'four sides of Brexit'* to *'windsurfing!'* It's the whole ability to be able to find what you want within *4N*, which sets this network apart.

I established *4N* in an unconventional way. I'm anything but conventional - I don't look like the archetypal business founder. I have tattoos, shaved head and so forth. This says something in itself, it gives the lead that you can be anything that you want to be in this network. This is a meritocracy - whether you stand or fall is based on your ability and not based on the car you drive or the suit you wear. I think that's what separates *4N*; there's no pomp and ceremony, and none when I turn up either. I certainly don't want that. I've been an outsider all my life and for the first time due to networking, I am now an insider surrounded by all you outsiders!

LA: Fabulous. My Disney rides would have to involve Frozen. So, I'm not sure that'll be your cup of tea!

BB: Well, I have to meet the fantasies of a five-year-old daughter, so on that basis, yes I'd be on those rides!

LA: Terrific. I was really impressed by the way that you supported 4N members by providing the online alternative so quickly. It was amazingly quick. How did that come about?

BB: Well, I've played enough computer games in my life to see what happens in a pandemic. I'm not being facetious here; I genuinely have learnt from these computer games! They start off with some wonderfully sketchy home scene, then within minutes there's police and militia involved - a crisis happens and then it's solved. They all have the same M.O. When I noticed what was happening in Wuhan, I got it straight away. At the start, no one was putting any lockdown or travel restrictions in place. Often 100 flights a day were going in and out, and I thought, *"This is going to get to us at some point."*

I was kind of *'panic buying'* (when the shelves were full) a good four weeks before anyone else considered panic buying! Genuinely, my cupboards were full of beans and toilet rolls! Everyone said to me, *"You're off your head. You're crackers!"* Six weeks later (March 2020), we were standing in three-hour queues to get into Tesco.

So I thought, *"Okay, what does my business look like beyond pandemic?"* For years I've been talking about the *'Now what?'* mindset. People don't ask the *'Now what?'* question enough. The only time people ask themselves this question is when the *'proverbial'* hits the fan - when life throws a curveball, when you've just lost a job or a contract, when you've been cheated on or get divorced? Nobody ever asks the question, *'Now what?'* ahead of time. When I had a nervous breakdown eight years ago, it was this question which aided my recovery.

As the pandemic took effect, people woke up to the reality of it, and they started to panic. Everyone was panicking. I realised the futility of panicking. I'd already done my thinking, so *4N* was prepared. It took four days to create the website for online networking. I made the promotional video from start to finish in nine hours.

I had my guys working like dogs to get it right and get it live. However, my management team didn't know what we were working on. They had no idea. Ordinarily, I'm the kind of guy who can't keep a secret but I had no option other than to keep it secret because I was so busy doing it, I couldn't share with anyone.

The initial system we put in place looked the part, but behind it was Balsa wood and Gaffer tape. Since then, we've developed the online systems, strengthening the infrastructure to support our members online, and they're improving week on week. The reason we could do this is because of 14 years of heritage. An expert is someone that has made all the mistakes in a particular niche field and when it comes to business networking I've made them all but I've learned from them.

If somebody saw what I've achieved and came into the space saying they were going to create *5Networking* online now they wouldn't be able to do it so quickly. Our system looks seamless, so easy, but you don't see what has gone into it. It's like a West-End musical with all the drama going on in the background. Backstage there are broken nails, broken heels, there are tantrums - nobody sees this.

Once the system was up, the management team came on board and it came together beautifully. We bonded by fire in this whole experience. I knew if we didn't move forward in this way there would be no more business, no more *4N*. The business would have stopped. People were saying they wanted to pause their memberships, which would have stopped our cash flow and halted their networking.

I said, *"By all means, you can pause your membership, but it's a bit like me giving you a bag of ice cubes to hold onto until summer - when you come back there will be nothing there. So, you can pause your membership all you want but there will be no network to come back to unless we actively start cultivating business for us all."* This was the approach we took, and it's working.

LA: You reduced the monthly fee and the price of the meetings - how did you decide on the pricing?

BB: We reduced the membership fee by 42% and the meeting fee by 53%. I did it in my usual strategic way: I took a blank piece of paper A1

size, and I mapped out what the future of business networking could look like. (Note: I even dated the paper at the bottom 25/3/2020.)

I did a mind map – considering what networking would look like if I created 4N today. I would be using technology alongside my experience, and it certainly wouldn't look anything like it did back in the day! When I first started, I followed the style of commercial networking and there were no online meetings.

With a new focus of continuing *4N* I wanted to know how we could make meetings more economical and accessible to every business person. There's no excuse not to join anymore! The most common barrier to joining is *"It's too expensive!"* My view is: if somebody doesn't want to pay for networking, what's the likelihood that they're going to want to pay for other members' services? They're not commercially minded.

I asked myself, *"As a business owner, in today's world, what would I want from a business network? I'd want accessibility, I'd want it to be cheap, fairly priced and economical, I'd want speed, I'd want to meet a lot of people at once (not just the same six or seven people each week) I'd want great speakers."* The list continued. My next question was, *"What do we need to do in order to make that a reality?"* This was the format and I worked backwards, deciding where I wanted *4N* to be in the future, what needed to be done to make that happen.

LA: You kept to the familiar *4N* format but made enough changes to recognise differences between online and in-person networking. I thought it was inspirational.

BB: We began with the phone system but changed it within a few weeks as we reviewed the service. Now we use break out rooms. This approach is even better and we know we need to review often to be a business with the ability to change, adapt and survive.

LA: How has lockdown and the pandemic affected 4N business? Have you had to furlough staff?

BB: Yeah, initially everything went wrong and what I mean by that is I had a business that was very fluid, good cash flow etc. and it changed. I've handed in my notice on the office, which we've used for nine years. The reasoning is realising we don't need an office anymore. It's all very nice and very pretty, but is it necessary? Lockdown has shown that we can operate really well without an office; there are no travel costs, no pollution and little cost to maintain a car etc. Having an office makes no sense anymore.

This situation has made a massive impact. Revenue wise, income has dropped by 70-80%. Now, it's about adapting. What is wonderful about this whole situation is, it's not some legislation aimed squarely at networking events - then we would be in trouble. This is a global pandemic which is a global crisis affecting every individual. There are two ways of looking at it: you can sit there and you can cry into your cup of tea, or you can do what I did with a blank piece of paper and say, *"What does this make possible?"* A wonderful thing – what has been made possible is a fresh start. All the mistakes of the past, can basically be pushed under the Covid-19 carpet; we get on with it and start again.

Revenue has been affected massively. I've not been paid for many weeks, but I will say three things to people.

1) Are you going to starve to death? No!

2) Are you going to lose your house, mortgage or property? No! You might get a snotty letter from the bank but it's just a snotty letter.

3) Are you going to die? If you maintain social distancing, wash your hands and behave yourself, then, No.

So, it's No x 3: "No, no and no." What have we got to worry about?

You know, in my life I've lived in times when I had nothing. I lived on the supermarket own brand of beans and waffles for years. I've been on benefits for 4 years. At the age of 31 I was delivering pizza for a living. So I'm not scared. Now, I have every material thing I could ever possibly wish for and a wonderful property in a village, so what's the risk?

It's about having a pragmatic way of looking at life, and even if I never achieved anything more, and Covid-19 caused my speaking engagements and my roadshow to come to a halt, so what? I mean, genuinely I've had a great run, I've done some amazing things; I've written four books, been a speaker at the highest level engaging with some of the biggest businesses in the world - and all through networking. That's not a bad legacy for a working-class lad without any qualifications, and people told me I was destined to be a bank robber!

LA: Obviously, you really believe in business networking. What lessons have you learnt about networking online?

BB: The same rules apply. Nothing changes it's just a medium, whether you send somebody a text message or you send somebody a handwritten note, that doesn't make any difference. It's still the same message.

Online is just another communication tool. Initially, there was a barrier for people to use it because they felt there was something different, or a lot of people wanted to wait to see what happens before going forward. If I'd waited to see what happens in this economy, there'd be nothing to wait to come back to. I think the online technology is an opportunity. 4N will be offering 24 hour networking to members, seven days a week, something that could not have been visualised prior to lockdown.

Recently, I gave a speaking tour reaching 20 networking events online over two weeks. Pre-lockdown, the most I could do was 13 meetings which involved driving 1,200 miles, spending £700 on hotels and £400 on diesel fuel. Now, in the same time period, I can double the amount of engagements - effectively teleporting from home – via online networking.

This new way of working, rather than it being a curse, people need to look at it as a gift. As it happens, I had a blast and presented to around 500 people from the comfort of my home office. Think about it – that's 20 meetings, three 10-minute 1-2-1s that gave 60 face-to-face online appointments.

LA: What's the feedback been from the 4N members?

BB: Feedback from members has been 60% in favour, 40% disapproving, but I don't really know what else people would like me to do other than discovering some way of getting rid of Covid-19! Tell me what else I can do? Some say I should make the online networking free - but there is a perception that it's costing me no money.

That's a really cool idea but how do I pay my people, the staff and other expenses such as the website hosting, which costs around £1000 per month? Strangely enough, I've been more honest and open about *4N's* financial position since lockdown than I've ever been in my life.

We're now through the danger zone, or as I described it recently, it was like the business was in the Intensive Care Unit. I'm going 'all in' on continuing *4N*, and if people want to pause their membership that's their call. I could have closed the network down and all the membership would be gone; in some ways I'd be in a much better financial position, but I chose not to do that. In return, I need the members to support the 4Network too - we need to support one another.

The kind of problems and challenges you face in your business – we do too. The vast majority of our network is in support of the new changes and for us all to continue networking to help our businesses. Networking is increasing as we move into this longer-term scenario; we are beginning to break records, with thousands of people attending 4N meetings each week, which is unprecedented.

LA: What's your vision for *4N* meeting online?

BB: I think we'll have an online arm and a face-to-face arm, which will be amazing.

LA: What's the one thing you'd like people to take away about online networking?

BB: There's more opportunity for business to succeed by going to online networking meetings than there is sat at home waiting for an email or your phone to ring. So many people are waiting - waiting for *Rishi Sunak* (Chancellor of the Exchequer) to give them a bailout. Even if you get a bailout or Bounce Back loan it has to be paid back.

What I'm doing is recognising: there is no magic cavalry to come to the rescue; the only cavalry out there is networking. This activity keeps your mind sharp and away from the boxes of isolation, which is why I started *4N* in the first place. Business people need to keep themselves engaged and moving forward. I'm pleased that online networking keeps them on that journey to heal the business economy.

The Elevator Pitch

The opposite of Networking is NOT working.

Unknown

We may not like it, but the 'elevator pitch' is the heart of business networking – online or offline. It's the only fair way to show who's in the room, yet nothing seems to strike fear into the heart of business people more, than delivering their elevator pitch (also known as the elevator speech or one-minute pitch).

The thought of standing up to give an elevator pitch brings on the fear of public speaking to some degree. The official name for this fear is *glossophobia* and as the actor, *George Jessel* famously said, *"The human brain starts working the moment you are born and never stops until you stand up to speak in public."* However, like it or not, if you're to benefit from networking, it's a fear that needs to be overcome and turned to your advantage!

Some have said that this fear is born from anxiety, lack of self-confidence and the unconfirmed assumption that you will embarrass yourself or be rejected by others in the room. There are two things to remember here:

1) Nerves often disappear when you express the passion you have for your business or profession, and

2) The people in the room genuinely want to be able to hear you (without straining), to know about your business and why you do it. They have a vested interest because they may want or need your business themselves or to help a friend's business. The respect is already there.

The mind plays games with us as nerves take over, but if you can replace your words and thoughts, then your feelings will change too. Swap embarrassment for encouragement and instead of fearing rejection realise these same people will respect you. This will go a long way to calming your nerves and relieving the one-minute pitch dread.

Does that help?

No-Host to Co-Host!

As an employee, I had to attend networking events to represent the company and I hated these events. I found the one-minute pitch excruciating and if I could avoid it I would. When I became self-employed, I thought, *"Hang on, I need to get hold of this networking lark"*. It's one of those things; the more you do the more comfortable you get. Now, I co-host my own online networking platform called *Nudge Network* without any one-minute pitches!

Nudge was planned before Covid-19 and was always intended as an online networking group. It would have been one of the first of its kind, but then lockdown happened and we are currently one of many online groups. It'll remain purely online, and available 24/7 - no early morning starts! We plan to keep the Network 'local' with business people choosing their group based on postcode. The interest has been phenomenal - 160 people registered within the first two weeks of launching the network.

Andrew Kotek, *Nudge Network*

Origins of the Elevator Pitch

The name 'elevator pitch' originated from America. To elevate means to lift up. The popular urban legend is: you are in an elevator (lift) with strangers; by the time you've reached the top floor (about a minute's ride) you had time to regale them about your business!

Imagine: You get into the elevator to discover the one person you've wanted to speak to for the past six months is there. You've tried every communication you could think of to contact this person, failing to get past their gate-keepers and with no response from emails. You now have an opportunity (a minute) while you're in this enclosed space (travelling to your respective floor) to talk to them, tell your story, pitch your idea, and find a way for them to invite you into their office before the elevator doors open.

Think of who this person could be, someone esteemed in your area of expertise, someone famous within your local networks or a business person with worldwide fame such as Sir Alan Sugar, Melissa Gates or Bill Gates! **What do you say?**

How do you ensure you don't spend the rest of the week kicking yourself with, *"I should have said…"* conversations? I once shared an elevator with author, *Nick Hornby*, and I said… absolutely nothing (I was awestruck!) but later, I told everyone that I'd met him!

What can you say that will keep them interested, intrigued or impressed, so they want to continue the conversation? *No pressure!*

Do you have your one-minute story at the ready, which you can give *'off the cuff'* and without notes? Can you smile as you talk about your business in an engaging way?

Crafting your Elevator Pitch

You will find so much good information, advice and 'how to do' your elevator pitch online. In fact, Mr Google has about 30,800,000 blogs and articles, and Amazon has over 150 books to choose from. You can learn from this wealth of material, but nothing beats real-life experience.

If you've written or recorded your biography (bio) this can give some 'golden' material of what to say in your elevator pitch. You may have more bios already written than you think. Each social media platform you use has a profile page in the setup, which gives you a place to talk about your business.

These can be extremely short and are 'nutshell' bios, but those clicking on your social media or reading your comments, like to have some idea of who you are and what you do. Check to see if they need updating and if you can develop them into your one-minute pitch.

Face-to-face meetings usually give a little time at the beginning to mingle, giving you the chance to introduce yourself to other participants. It doesn't take long before a business person asks you, *"What business are you in?"* or *"What is it you do?"* Does this sound familiar?

Perhaps when you ask someone about their business you could change 'what' to 'why' – you'll probably get a fuller, more interesting and memorable answer.

More Than Self-Centred Networking

As a Christian involved in sales, promotions, and building relational links with hundreds of ministries over the past 40 plus years, as well as being a preacher, I have learned some vital lessons about what we term 'networking'. If the primary purpose of our networking is to build our personal profile in order to better position ourselves gaining benefit for ourselves, be it personally or corporately we are no better than 'self-centred' bees floating from flower to flower seeking out pollen.

Whereas, a *'relationship builder'* seeks to build a strong and meaningful link between themselves and everyone (and anyone) they meet - with a heart and vision to impact, impart and input to others - something to help and benefit them rather than us.

Coincidentally, that may (and most often will), mean both parties grow from the connection. In big-picture terms, this is a better approach than everything on a self-centred basis.

When things are only on a transactional process it's *win-win or nothin'*.

Bill Partington, Global Missions

Online there's less time for chit chat as everyone waits in a holding bay until the host lets you in. It's the host who leads the meeting and people usually have to speak one at a time.

Practice Your Elevator Pitch

Practice you must. No one knows your business better than you, or indeed your 'take' of the profession or industry you have chosen to work in. *Dianna Booher* is an international author and communication expert who says, *"If you can't write your message in a sentence, you can't say it in an hour."*

My friend, Ernie Boxall, runs a programme to help people tell their business stories and make their one-minute pitch exciting and relevant. He says, *"You turn up 'mentally' for a meeting 2 days before the event, whenever you rehearse your pitch. The more practice you do for any speech – one minute or more – the more authentic you will be."*

Consider using WWWWH (Who, Where, Why, When and How). Notice there is NO 'what'. Yet, this is the trap we fall into when explaining the work we do – telling our listener a list of features, which is forgettable, not engaging. As mentioned earlier, when you next find yourself asking someone, *"What do you do?"* change it to, *"Why do you do the work you do?"* instead. The 'why' is where the stories lie, it holds your audience and everyone loves to hear a story!

- 🖥 Why are you passionate about your business?
- 🖥 Why did you start your business?
- 🖥 Why your heart breaks at some of the behaviours in your industry and why your business is different?

Wouldn't you like to know the answers to these questions when talking with others?

Elevator Pitch Tips and Hacks

When crafting your one-minute pitch, try to take the word 'I' out of the pitch. Focus instead on the potential clients and their interests and use of your product or service. It will help you if you leave out the detail such as when the office was opened, number of staff, how long in business (all yawn-worthy) and use stories instead. The old adage, *'Facts tell, stories sell!'* is worth remembering.

Concentrate on one aspect of your business at a time. If you have more than one business – talk about them one at a time. When a speaker talks about multiple businesses, *"I do this, this, oh and this..."* This is **not** a good advert for any of the businesses. In fact, the mixed messages confuse your audience. Your listener and potential client is unable to hear any clarity but the message they receive is that you haven't decided what your main business is. So, stick to the 'Rule of ONE'. *Joanna Weave*, a long-time copywriter, teaches, **'Use the rule of ONE – one message, one promise, one target'**.

A nice rule of thumb when writing out your pitch is 150 words equates to one-minute of speaking. *Sandra Garlick*, recommends, *"Think of the Power of Three and put three short points into your one-minute pitch"*.

At the end of your one-minute pitch, always give a Call to Action, give people something to do to contact you. This continue the conversation. The final piece to add is your kiss-off line!

Elevator Pitch Format

Listen to how other business people give their elevator pitch, especially those people you admire or are in the same industry as yourself. What do they say that you like? Note their style and rhythm and then copy it – just replacing your information and your own story instead of theirs. Later, when someone compliments you on your elevator pitch, you can say who it was who inspired you!

Mental Well-Being Online

I benefited significantly, on many levels from the online networks. I gained business connections but also online networks aided my mental well-being. It has made me feel connected and part of the bigger picture, rather than being too isolated - which happened in the first weeks of lockdown.

Robert Drury, Mortgage Advisor:
Andy Wilson Financial Services Ltd

Customer Data is King

by Nathan Eaves,
Founder: _The Art of Selling_

Networking has been a game changer to so many businesses. As I am sure you have already picked up on from this book, the arena has changed and will continue to adapt, too. Does that mean you need to change your attitude, style, and brand? Or worse, alter yourself to allow the new change to dramatically impact your business for the better? I am a sales trainer devoted to make sales, 'easy peasy lemon squeezy' for small business owners. My mission is to positively impact the core of the business so that it will be passed down through the business or assists the development of the business as it grows.

First of all, we need to define what success we gain from attending a meeting. I don't want you to rush and say 20 new sales from the first meeting either. For me, 'success' means meeting new contacts or developing an existing contact relationship. This is what I call my **'Most Wanted Action'** **(MWA)** but my MWA must align my actions to my goals.

The goal is to build my network to be able to call anyone I have met for a conversation about breakfast cereal.

Breakfast cereal?

Yes, if I can talk to a member of my network about breakfast cereal, it means I have the confidence to talk to them about anything. Try it. Go through your contacts and find out how many you could call to simply ask them.

"What's your favourite cereal?"

Success in networking means being able to build up contact relationships and having the confidence to talk to them.

What is a Follow-Up?

A follow up is a conversation with a contact about a need, want or request. The key word is conversation. Following up is not selling, it is relationship building which may turn in to a sale (maybe even a sale during that conversation). I could meet you at a meeting and hear something that I wanted to know more about. I would simply communicate with you as set out below and request more information. Follow-ups are, in their most basic form, the task of data gathering.

Data = Sales.

The more data you have, the more sales you can make. Period. GDPR may put people off here, but if the data is secure and only used for the agreed usage then *'Data (not cash) is King'.* The core of any business is its Data.

The information you know about your customer and potential client is data. You were not born able to change a light bulb – this is learnt data. Following a YouTube video for instructions to change a bulb is also data. Everything we know, memories, habits, tendencies, cravings and dreams are merely data.

I train businesses to make sales easier than ever before by the transfer of data. If you have never sold or purchased a business I will let you in on a big secret – you are buying or selling data. How it was run, the processes, the products or services, where they can be sourced, what has been accounted, and much more...data.

What Data do You Need?

EVERYTHING! You want reasons to communicate. What they have, what their 'itch' cycle is, their birthday, anniversaries, other symbolic things like, the car they drive or the watch they wear, where they shop and why. You need to be able to look at the Data to be able to communicate with them.

If you can communicate, you can be present, if you are present – they will think of you! **Ask:** *"Hey Sue, I thought I would give you a call to say, Hi, to catch up, and ask you about how you are getting on with your son being at Leeds*

F continued *University. Have you adjusted to life at home being completely different?"* Or, *"Hey, I thought I would give you a call to say, Hi and catch up!"*

The difference is simply - data. But, the impact shows care, honesty, and authenticity; it showcases how kind you and your brand really is – yet all it is, is data.

Why do I call People?

To communicate with them, to play out my script; to see if there is an opportunity to close a sale. I won't push - I will ask questions. The conversation will land on a problem they may have which a product of mine can solve.

Types of follow up.

Communication can be undertaken in many ways. This is where your preferred method of contact can be used. What stops most of the communication is non-action. There can be a number of reasons people fail to communicate *(yes, fail)* which can include: lack of confidence, self-doubt and overthinking.

This is why I refer to it as failure because I want to help them build their business. If a product or service is going to take away their problem, fears or concerns – you need to communicate with them. It would be wrong of me not to communicate with people, to help them.

'Food for Thought' Questions.
- What do you need to know for them (or their company)?
- What is their preferred method of contact?
- Who could introduce you to them?

Ways to Follow-up:
- You can write a letter, note or card and send by post.
- You can send a small gift.
- You can send them an email or a message on social media.
- You can phone them.
- You can meet them for an in-person or online 1:1 meeting.

Try the above actions and notice the difference it makes to your business and customer relations.

Simple Elevator Pitch Format

In the main, keeping it simple is best. Here are some outlines for you to use:

For _____ [who], I offer _____ [service/product], so you can _____ [why]. To get it, _____ [how] I'd like to ask you to _____ [put in your CTA and Kiss-off line].

The Call To Action is essential as it tells people what to do next and where to go to get the help or offer they need.

The Screen Between

Networking is a popular means for businesses looking to connect and market themselves. In this new age of limited time, digital platforms have propelled networking to a new level via the screen.

These platforms have made it easier for people to research and connect with the 'right' person saving on countless phone calls and getting nowhere after battling with the *'gate-keepers'*.

It has allowed us to do business with people without an in-person meeting. Does it take away from the phrase, *'people buy from people?'* Do you really get to know people with a screen between you?

Networking has now seen another twist as pitches are delivered on a screen in front of others sat behind their screens in real time. Personally, I think on-screen one-minute pitches, as an initial introduction are great, then you can arrange for that essential face-to-face meet up. It gets rid of all the awkward talk for people who perhaps feel uncomfortable approaching others for the first time.

Online networking has now become a major way for us to connect and market our businesses, and ourselves. Every form of networking has its place, not one format will suit everyone.

Hannah Thompson, *The Development Partner Network*

As mentioned earlier, revisit your online bios or profiles and rewrite them. Often you have a one-liner to convey exactly your business purpose within a restricted word count. Build on this for your elevator pitch and time in the 'spotlight'.

Most people give their name, business name, profession or job title, who they are looking for as a client and then run out of time.

Be prepared to experiment and mix it up. Include in it phrases such as:

When I'm not helping people _____ *[service/product], then you will find me* _____ *[where].*

This gives the element of surprise and is memorable. Use questions to help the listener identify more quickly with your business or offer.

Be confident and unafraid to craft many one-minute pitches. See how many different versions you can make for different groups – especially as you meet the same people at local events (even online). It's important to be memorable and adapt for different products or services you have.

Here are two I use quite regularly and after I've spoken, I'll place them in the *'Chat'*.

Are you an ambitious business person? Did you know that writing a book helps to raise your business profile and brand, gain more clients and position you as an expert in your field? Let's talk more about the book inside you and start you off with some free PDFs to help you achieve your goals. Download the PDFs from my website ladeyadey.com *and arrange a 1-2-1 with me. My links are in the chat. Remember there is a book inside you.*

For the Little Unicorn Book Series, I use the following:

Are there any 2-5 year olds in your family? Do you enjoy reading to them and helping them to know their colours, numbers, and days of the week, or even names of dinosaurs? My daughter and I have written a series of children's books featuring a Little Unicorn who helps children learn to read. We are told that adults love the books too. To get your signed copy visit our stand or go to the website, www.ladeyadey.com. *Buy the books and you will become the most popular person in your family.*

Networking Grew My Business

by Graham Todd,
Founder, <u>Spaghetti Agency</u>

I regularly say, *"Networking meetings made Spaghetti Agency what it is today."* This is because my business was born from organising Tweet Ups. In 2010, Karen, Christy and I set up Tweet Up, which is a networking meeting for a range of people who know each other through Twitter. It's like Internet dating, but you're getting people from the Internet to meet up in a business environment rather than a date!

This was my first ever networking meeting. I was working for a wine merchant at the time and had never officially networked before - so it was pure accident that I later fell into organising events with these two ladies.

We ran five or six of these Tweet Ups and they had anywhere between 50 to 100 people. Through this I attracted the attention of Jo, who is now my life partner as well as business partner. This was where we fell in love and also where I fell in love with social media. I used it to come up with networking and content marketing using the law of attraction. Looking back now, it was like it was meant to happen. Today, I'm here at my office with a team of 10 people and we're cruising through an economic downturn and it all came from meeting people we chatted to on Twitter.

We've just re-introduced the Meet Ups, every quarter, which really did grow organically, purely by accident, from what was known as WarwickTweetup. This is how I grew my email list. I did social media training in the back of a pub, and people booked in through Eventbrite. We started to email people when we launched our business and it all started there.

F continued We now have a following of over 2,000 people in our Facebook group, *Spaghetti Besties*, and more followers across social media and I'm often asked, *"How did you do it?"* People want the secret. While I would not claim to be an expert, the secret to growing your business is... Hard Work. That's it.

The Facebook group has been going for a number of years and is very small in comparison to other groups but I know pretty much everyone in there. They continue to engage with me because the content is good and it's a supportive place, but it takes a lot of work to keep it like that. Last year, I moved from another big networking group where I spent a lot of time, creating content and building up my connections. Now, my concentration is genuinely just helping business people who join me as a *Spaghetti Bestie*.

I suspect I spend way more than half of my time online helping people for no cash reward. I'm just there answering people's comments and questions for no reason other than I enjoy doing it. That was my strategy during the Tweet Up phase too.

Now, I do the same in Spaghetti Besties, I'll post stuff in there to keep people talking, tag people and generally support people there. It's taken a lot of effort and a lot of time. I write a blog a week with smaller posts sprinkled all over the place. It continues to be enjoyable, albeit hard work and effort, and I don't see that changing.

For me, the transition to online networking is not new because the Tweet Ups were from online to real life, so it was reverse lockdown. It was the opposite of lockdown. It was like, *"We're online but let's get into real life."* I've been doing that for over 10 years, networking online followed up with meeting people in real life. I spent three to four years in 4Networking, which is real life networking and I made sure I connected with every person I met in real life networking online too, reverse engineering of what is happening now. I've carried on networking with them online so I haven't struggled to transition with online networking during lockdown.

F continued

I see other people struggling with online video calls and I admire them for being willing to give it a go, but I don't see it as the future of networking. Human beings need connection, and they need it in real time/life. I see the future of networking meetings happening where you can have breakfast (or meals) together. I still think it's important and it's my personal view despite being a digital guy!

I go to a 'real' pub a couple of times a week, and during lockdown I've missed the social interaction. I was on Facebook Live when *Chris* jokingly said, *"Wouldn't it be great if we had a virtual pub?"* and I said, *"That's going to happen, I'm going to make it happen."* I kid you not, as soon as I switched off the Live video and opened my Facebook there was a message from my friend *Jay*, (who is an affiliate representative for Remo). His email said, *"You've got to see this app."* I clicked the app open and when I saw it on my screen I thought, *"Wow, this is cool."*

So, I created Social Saloon, The Virtual Pub for Besties on Remo. The difference with Remo and apps like Zoom and Messenger rooms and others is the flexibility Remo gives. It allows you to network with five other people, then move on, whenever you want, to another table of five (six including yourself). It's as though you are at a real life conference, you can move around to meet others; it's pretty stable as well. It's cool and fun to use and who knows where virtual pub conversations will lead!

I use online a lot but I'm missing people as do my introvert friends that I speak to! Recently, I had an interesting chat with someone whose business does personality profiles, and she said, *"Even the introverts are struggling with lockdown."* That puts it into perspective; we need to be around people, even for a little bit. The group 4Networking has the catchphrase; 'business networking is 50% business and 50% social'. I'd argue with that ratio, as in my experience most people who go out to networking meetings want 80-90% social.

F *continued*

It gives them something essential as a human being and they get a business connection as a bonus. Other networks are slightly different, but they say the same thing; to have the human connection and to build relationships. As good as online networking channels are - Twitter, LinkedIn, Instagram, Stories, YouTube - they do not replicate a real life conversation. You don't get that closeness, seeing the whites of the eyes stuff. You just don't!

I think networking online will continue as an element but it will be every now and then rather than the only way for business people to connect. True, more people have been getting involved with online networking meetings using apps like Zoom, Facebook Live, Reno, but I think people want, and need the face-to-face contact and people will want to go back to 'traditional' business networking.

The Time Limit

Networking organisers arrange their meetings in different ways and will set the elevator pitch timing according to their agenda and the number of people participating. They range from 10 seconds to 90 seconds, often run as a round robin system, with participants taking turns at the start of a meeting. Depending on the time you are given have the *'best'* pitch ready (adapted to the time-limit).

10 seconds:

A one-liner is expected. Most people give their names and business name. If you're wearing a badge or your name is on-screen, the information is already there, so you can save yourself a couple of seconds.

A 10 second pitch can be broken down into two 5 second pieces of information:

First 5 seconds: Today my offer is _____ or,

What I love about my profession is _____ or,

My business gets me leaping out of bed in the morning because

_____

Next 5 seconds: The CTA. You can join me by _____ or,

Take action today and receive _____ from the website_____ or,

Kiss-off line _____

30 seconds:

Utilize your one line bio and expand it. Use your **why**. Why you have chosen your business or profession, why it benefits others and give a CTA & Kiss-off line at the end.

Tell Your Story

For the best networking experience, on or offline, relationship building is key. To speed up the connection between people, the one-minute pitch comes into play. Whenever you are asked to speak about yourself, you need to make it memorable.

The more you share about; why you do what you do, who you are as a person and how you can help others, the more people will engage and remember you.

If you just *'talk business'* they will only hear you if they are looking for what you do. It might even be that business people who have known you for years may say, *"Oh, I didn't know you did that in your business!"*

So, tell your story. Research shows that 80% of business can come from people you have already met and, in my many years of experience, I know you can do business with 2 out of every 12 contacts in your database by staying connected and by being more personable.

Kim Penney, Founder: Advantage 80/20

One-minute or longer: You can engage with listeners with a surprising amount of content in this time frame. Stem the terrifying feelings by practice. If you're familiar with what you are going to say, you can go on autopilot and give a great, engaging one-minute pitch without nerves affecting you.

Take the format above and include a thank you to someone else in the room and why you're thanking them, so it becomes a quick testimonial or referral. The Athena Network®, has a useful form to create a one-minute pitch, which is reproduced with permission (see Extras).

The Kiss-off line

After the Call to Action, finish with the kiss-off line. This has nothing to do with chat up lines but is your strapline, slogan or catchphrase. A very simple sentence which raises a smile and people associate with you. After a while, they may even join in with you as you say it. We see the kiss-off line all the time on TV adverts, if I say, *"Just Do It"* and mime a tick – you know I'm referring to *Nike*.

Match Your Tone to Your Kiss-off Line

You've probably heard the saying, _'It's not what you say; it's the way that you say it...'_ this is all about tone of voice. Tone of voice is important in speech but how it's used in written and spoken communications says a huge amount about your brand! Have you considered the tone of voice in relation to your spoken communications, including your elevator pitch?

A fellow networker once told me, _"Your content is better than your delivery."_ What he meant was the information I presented was good, but I wasn't matching it to the right tone of voice; the language, speed and intonation I was using were at odds with the content.

One way to come up with a tone of voice is to think about what your brand would be like as a person. Would they be funny or serious? Are they formal or conversational? Do they speak quickly or slowly? Once you've nailed this down, you can weave these brand characteristics into how you deliver your Elevator Pitch.

Imagine you run a company that hires out bouncy castles. Your brand personality is going to be fun and vibrant. So, when you're talking about your business, make sure you come across as fun and vibrant, too – no one wants to hire a bouncy castle from a formal, serious or humourless person!

By matching your tone of voice to your brand values, you'll find it easier to connect with your audience, so they really 'get' you, your brand and business proposition.

Create a 'kiss-off line' to close your elevator pitch. Used consistently, this will help people remember you and your business. In time, people may even chant it back at you!

You could use your existing strap line or come up with something new. Just make sure your kiss-off line matches your brand personality and tone of voice.

Faye Stenson, Copywriter: _Black & Write_

My favourite kiss-off lines:

Make your Sales, Easy Peasy, Lemon Squeezy - Nathan Eaves

How to Shine instead of Shiver - Ernie Boxall

Everyone needs a Wing-Woman or *Everyone needs an Admin Ninja* - Nicky Armstrong

Succession and Exiting Planning – So Make the Most from Your Life's Work - Paula Finch

It's not just a Good Idea - It's GENIUS! - Tony Smith

I Make People Cry with Math - Katya Bozukova

Enabling others to Thrive not just Survive – Emma Rose

Making GDPR a Sweeter Pill to Swallow – Cristina Vannini-Goodchild

Make a date and we'll make you look great – Paul Tompsett

80% of business comes from people you already know – Kim Penney

Changing your Thinking, Changing your Doing, and Changing your Forever – Mark Jarvis

So, Who are You when at Your Best? – Nicola Ellwood

Remember, Our service is 'On Point!' – Jason Spering

The Key to Winning Bids – Dewi Hughes

Distilling your Ideas into Knowledge – Bruce Roberts

Tomorrow's Materials Today – Lyndon Sanders

Brilliance in Resilience – Neil Wainman

More than Just Words on a Page - Faye Stenson

Making Menopause Mainstream - Bev Thorogood

Keep Smiling... You've got a Beautiful One! - Niraj Agarwal

Changing the World - One Book at a Time - Ladey Adey

By having a kiss-off line your one-minute pitch could be less scary as you know you are going to end on a great note and make people smile.

As *Sandra Garlick* said, when she replied to my LinkedIn post of over 1,000 views on the subject of kiss-off lines, *"I hear kiss-off lines regularly at the networking events I attend. They are definitely worth trying out. It makes you memorable for all the right reasons"*.

Keeping to the Agreed Time

Online meetings start quicker than face-to-face meetings as there's no need to hand round a microphone or stand up and sit down again as people introduce themselves and try to be visible in the room. Your picture is already on screen and becomes highlighted when you talk. This also encourages people to be very prompt at the start of the meeting time. The organisers, online and offline, take the scheduled timings really seriously, even if you don't. They find ingenious ways to make people keep to the time: stopwatches, count-down clocks, flags, hooters, whistles and if they could produce the Vaudeville 'hook' I'm sure they would!

Etiquette demands that the time limit is respected; those who go over are not appreciated! Online there's the mute button, of course, but this seems a little harsh.

"I am what I am
I am my own
special creation
So come take a look
Give me the hook
or the ovation"

— *La Cage aux Folles*

Disrespecting the time limit is the one thing you do NOT want to be remembered for. If you're a habitual over-time talker or state that the time limit does not apply to you (for whatever reason) behind you, there will be lots of eye-rolling and dread when you stand up! It sets a very bad example, especially if others follow your lead and then the organisers get stressed!

Perhaps this isn't quite so noticeable in other countries or when there is a relaxed culture of come when you are ready. However, in the UK time-keeping can be particularly rigid! It does seem that online calls encourage good starts and the majority of people do arrive at the stated time - they know the meeting won't wait for them!

Tools to Back-up Your Elevator Pitch

In face-to-face meetings, your business card and various promotional materials will be part of your marketing arsenal. The equivalent online is the *'Chat'*. Here you can post messages and comments to everyone on the call.

You have to suss out the way the organiser wants to use the *'Chat'*. After you've introduced yourself, paste your introduction (similarly, but not identically worded) and links to your website and social media. Aim for a maximum of 150 words. An emerging etiquette is to post details or links to your website only when;

1) It's your turn to speak – it's bad manners to do this when others are talking, or

2) When the organiser invites everyone to do so.

Here's a thought, which could avoid pitching panics and nerves. At the end of the day, NO-ONE remembers what you said with the exception of a CTA or kiss-off line! Try it out, can you remember what others have said? Think back to the last networking event you attended and from memory pick out someone who was there.

- What did they say?
- Can you recall the exact words?
- What can you remember?
- What did they wear?
- Did you 'like' them and the way they 'presented' themselves?

The same might be what they remember about you too! This proves there is no need to give ourselves such a hard time over the elevator pitch! Relax and let it develop naturally.

From my perspective, I love the one-minute elevator pitches – it's the best introduction I can have of YOUR work and how you spend your time from the *'horse's mouth!'* I enjoy learning about you and working out if I want to speak further with you, or if I know someone who would be a great business partner for you. I know many other networkers (many mentioned in this book) who have exactly the same viewpoint – so be brave and work on your elevator pitch today.

An Emerging 'New Normal'

Online networking and online working hasn't changed that much for me. Of course, the time of lockdown has meant I am unable to meet clients face-to-face. Covid-19 is forcing us all to think how we develop and conduct business. I rely on Zoom and other on-line collaboration tools more than I have done previously, but as a supplement to meeting in person.

For me, there is little difference in working online as offline; you still have to let other people speak, to give them time to reflect and think before they respond. You still have to ensure that you understand people's perspectives, ideas and contributions.

In my profession, we have networks who know networks who know networks. So, the skill is finding your way through to individuals or companies who need your skills and expertise and vice versa. LinkedIn is a great tool for me.

I've built a network throughout my 30 plus year career and I can recognise and welcome newcomers quickly - a new tier, the next generation. Good networks can expand to accommodate new people and new faces; it's important so as the network widens, it stays healthy, introducing new ideas and experience.

With Covid-19, networking online will be the future of business networking. If you're far away from your office nexus and know the health risks then you have less incentive to travel. Remote working has also encouraged *Continued Professional Development* training to be more accessible online.

It has been good to see public bodies and cultural organisations going online to communicate with their audience. Institutions such as the Royal Society of Medicine, Royal Academy of Dance, the National Theatre and museums have created video tours and inspirational interactive activities. All well received and I think will be part of the future new 'normal'.

Sarah Coleman, Director: *Business Evolution Ltd*

In **C**onversation **W**ith

Jacqueline Rogers - Founder and CEO The Athena Network®

Ladey Adey (LA): Jacqueline, we first worked together in 2007 when I bought the Lincolnshire franchise for <u>The Athena Network®</u>, your business network for female executives and entrepreneurs. I'd like to explore with you the role of women-only business networks and their relevance today. Do you think there is a need for women-only networks today?

Jacqueline Rogers (JR): I don't think the need has gone away. What I do think has happened is, women's realisation that they do need a women's network, whereas, at the very beginning, they were unsure; it was a relatively new concept. You may remember, there was a bit of uproar, and we were often asked, *"Who did we think we were setting up an organisation for women?"* Back in the day, we were accused of being sexist and segregating genders.

Whereas now, women networks are taken for granted. They have their place in the continuum of business networking. In fact, the desire for women's networks has grown. The backlash has settled down, giving business women a comfortable and safe place in which to network.

Over the years, we've demonstrated how well women-only groups work, creating: business leads, collaborative working and referrals.

LA: Why are women-only networks so popular?

JR: Women are social-minded creatures; it doesn't take long for these networks to become a club and have their own community. Women make a real commitment to each other; they turn up consistently and deepen their relationships.

At first, I genuinely thought it was about women preferring to be in a room with other women and not feel uncomfortable or under pressure in predominantly masculine networks. Now, I recognise that women-only networks have different dynamics and inner culture to traditional networks.

We've moved away from an emphasis on the one-minute pitch and, as one of our key cornerstones, I expect members to understand one another's businesses and be willing to help and support one another. This deepens the relationships and my members tell me they cannot find this community spirit anywhere else. When they arrive, they can relax, breathe and then talk about what's going on in their life as opposed to launching straight into business talk.

LA: Do you think women bring something different to the networking scene?

JR: I believe women are natural communicators. They bring the community element; it's what makes them 'tick' and they're in it for the long game. It's not just about their business; they're genuinely interested in those of other members. Some will lay awake at night thinking about somebody else's business as much as they lay awake at night worrying about their own.

Even with online networking, it's the personal connection that counts. Women see the bigger picture and are gifted at looking further than what is presented directly in front of them. They're looking at the kind of referral a fellow business woman says she wants and then maximises it with, *"Has she thought of x, y, and z, because that could really make a difference to her business growth."* Women are usually inclusive with one another and aren't just there to network. There's so much more going on.

LA: What's been different for women's groups since coming online?

JR: I'm not going to lie; initially, we noticed huge resistance. Women like and want the physical aspect of networking - where they walk into a room, they hug each other, and ask; how's the family? How was your time on holiday? etc. and that's okay. They can have that kind of conversation at the start of our meetings and then they dive into, how has it all been working in your business? There was some trepidation that this would be lost when we went online.

One of our cornerstones is to support each other and our businesses. To this end, we made the online networking roll out as slickly as possible. We documented how this would work, via videos as well as through the handbook. I personally created videos, ran workshops on how to use Zoom (the platform we've chosen to run our meetings) so members could feel comfortable and familiar with the new means of meeting.

Of course, they've missed the personal connect-touch element, but then so has the whole planet. We introduced Huddles, a separate meeting time where all personal issues can be shared, and to be aware of any mental health issues needing our support.

Online groups mean there's more movement by members now visiting groups in other parts of the country, which builds up their networks. We're attracting more people and having larger meetings, which benefits all business women. The biggest difference from a management point of view is now all Athena Regional Directors meet online at 10am every day for an hour. This is to check in with one another, build up our knowledge base and ways we can reach out to the members in the most compassionate way. Any decisions to be made, which affect the whole network of over 130 groups, are made collaboratively. We have lively discussions before rolling out any meeting changes. This internal, inner network circle means we can give a seamless service to our members.

Honing Online Networking Skills

Networking is marketing.
Marketing yourself, your uniqueness, what you stand for.
Christine Comaford-Lynch

The purpose of using networking to market your business is to raise the visibility of you and your brand. Two wonderful quotes by actor, Garrison Wynn are, "It does not matter how smart you are if nobody knows what you are talking about" and "People buy into what they can understand quickly. If it takes you a long time to make your point, most people think you don't have one!" These quotes relate strongly to the time and effort you put into honing your networking skills.

Firstly, does anyone know you're in the room? If you're taking time out of your business to participate in online or offline networking, you need to make it count.

To be memorable, you have to stand out, and it has to be more than a jazzy tie, which one accountant told me was his claim to fame! You want to be remembered for the right reasons – for someone to think, *"I want to know more about what they are selling"* or *"Hey, I don't need what you are offering right now, but I know someone who does."*

This doesn't mean you have to be; all *'rah-rah'*, overly extroverted and stand on chairs (though I have seen this!), but it does mean you need to be engaged or intentional in your actions. To test how you are coming across, check out the tone of your voice and body language when talking about your business. Be brave and record yourself via online video, then analyse your mannerisms (kindly). When networking online, it's about contributing via the *'Chat'*, looking into the camera lens and not looking sloppy! In other words, be interested and interesting!

As mentioned in Chapter 3, your elevator pitch needs to be practiced, as this is your verbal calling card. Just as a CV is designed to attract the employer's attention and offer you an interview, your elevator pitch is designed to attract the attention of a potential client or partner.

It's expected that you will appear on the screen in a *'live'* video, therefore throughout the meeting you are being watched. It might feel like a goldfish bowl as you see yourself on-screen with a myriad of faces; the problem is you have no idea who's watching you, as eye-to-eye contact does not exist. You can (*and I recommended that you do*) look directly into the camera lens so it seems you are looking directly at people – but it's not the same as face-to-face eyeballing!

Your Screen is Your Business Card

Your picture and live video is on view for the duration of the meeting – this can be from half an hour to 3 hours – so turn your screen into your best business card. Help other business to find you easily or *'stalk you!'* on other platforms such as LinkedIn. When I am in a networking meeting, I have LinkedIn open and type in other participants' names and request a connection adding a note about which network I've met them at. It builds up my connections quickly.

At the very minimum your screen should display your FULL name, then either what you do, company name or website. Make the changes each time you enter a meeting (*see Chapter 5, Name or Rename*). It gives a very professional image and shows your expertise using video communication.

Your Avatar, Biography (Bio) and Profile

To be visible online includes posting and being present in meetings, but it starts with what people can know about you straight away. This is shown via your individual avatar, biography and profile.

Your **avatar** is your picture which has been uploaded into a specific area on your platform, or you can use an avatar symbol, which is a computer generated, graphic image representing you. These can range from cartoon like and pictures without faces! If you do not tell the platform which picture to use,

it will automatically put a faceless icon in that place. My advice is to keep your avatar consistent across all the platforms you use, make it 'on brand' and recognisable as you – a very nice professional head and shoulder photo is ideal.

Your **bio** is a history detailing your achievements, passions and who you work with. It's worth having a number of versions of these to pop into the *'Chat'* when it is your turn to speak.

Your **profile** is requested by each social media app – it can be a one -liner and appears below your picture. Keep it short and on-brand.

Overall, think about what your ideal client wants to know about you via your avatar, bio and profile. Make people want to contact you.

I Miss People

Business Online Networking has been a Godsend during this time of lockdown when we can't get out to see people in real life. I miss people! So, to see everyone, virtually at least, is the next best thing.   **Belinda Roughton, Founder: *Invoice Finance Solutions***

Surprised

The online video networking has really surprised me. Initially, I thought, *"This can't possibly work with 20 to 30 people in a meeting."*

How wrong could I be?

I have found Zoom and MS Teams work brilliantly for business networking.

Chris Moody, *ASL Computer Services*

Will Online Networking be Rubbish?

I love meeting people in person so I thought, *"Online networking is going to be rubbish"*. However, once I got past my fear of the unknown; of hosting online and using technology, it was a lot easier than I imagined. Already, it has proved popular, drawing women from further afield and we now need to limit the number of participants in our meetings! In the future, I can see both online and offline networking being offered to busy business mums.   **Marie Elizabeth Edwards Founder: *Made by Mee, Mee and You Networking***

Speaking at a Networking Meeting

There are many levels of talking with people. For instance, do you communicate with clients and potential clients in the same way as talking to your family? Most probably not, but if you were to describe your business to your favourite relative, how different would this be to your standard pitch? Sir Richard Branson said, *"Picture yourself in a living room having a chat with your friends. You would be relaxed and comfortable talking to them, the same applies when public speaking."* Your elevator pitch is a form of public speaking albeit for a fraction of a time, so breathe life into it just like talking with friends and family.

When you get an opportunity to speak in your network meeting, please resist the temptation to hide behind a PowerPoint presentation. It's your time to share WHY you are in business and the stories of WHY you get up in the morning and serve your clients.

What can you do when giving a Zoom talk to stop people from *'ghosting'* you? Admit it, how many times do you check your emails, put a comment on Facebook or check the LinkedIn notifications when the speaker shares their screen, putting up a series of slides, or you engage your 'Stop video?' *(I'll hold my hand up here.)* You may still be listening but you're not *'present'* for that speaker. This is called 'ghosting'. It's a shame because it's a disincentive for the speaker – who feels they are alone and talking to themselves. However, the audience will only remember how they felt, what they've learnt and the speaker's passion.

I believe, online speaking is more difficult than in-person as all communication takes place *'above the keyboard!'* The senses used are hearing and sight showing only what's visible on the screen. All other senses usually utilised when speaking in-person are not engaged.

So, how can you make your speaking slot sizzle and sparkle online? **It has to be interactive.** If it is structured to involve the audience, by asking them questions they can answer in 'Chat', 'Unmute' the mics, ask for a raise of hands – be creative, so just sitting passively looking at the screen is not an option. Use their names, they are there in front of you at the bottom of the screen, not to embarrass but to involve. This wakes them up and puts their attention back on you – the speaker! Isn't this what you want? The reason you agreed to speak in the first place?

Leave behind the fear of being judged, it's the fear of being ignored and unmemorable which is the danger here!

The Entertainer and
The Wallflower

Dr David Cliff, MD of <u>Gendanken</u>

Lockdown, home working and other factors have increasingly resulted in the use of online technology which in turn facilitates networking. This is a good thing both ecologically and systemically as it allows people access to networks that hitherto would have been inaccessible by geographical and logistical limitations. It involves more than the simple transposition of proximity based interactions into virtual ones.

How we network is a reflection of personality. **Face-to-face business networking has its entertainers and wallflowers, (extraverts and introverts)** and online networking produces a new dynamic for both to consider.

Online networking, whether it is for business or other functions, requires discipline. Qualities of liveliness, humour, dramatic entrance and the like that make an extrovert the 'life and soul' of the networking group on a face-to-face basis can be positively disruptive in an online environment.

Online networking groups require clear discipline, mutual respect and organisational management by hosts as many of the normal social cues that govern our interactive behaviour are stripped away and have to be managed by proxy.

For the more extrovert style, this poses the challenge of achieving greater sensitivity to other people in the room, whether that is a literal or virtual room and reconsidering their relationship with these people, whilst finding self-expression. In this context, the extrovert may not like a meeting host managing ebullience by simply moving on or, as may happen, using the mute function, periodically.

F continued

For those more inhibited, especially those where networking is perhaps a trial, networking by online means can generate a bandwidth of reactions. These range from; the online medium being seen as yet another inhibitory factor for them to surmount; through to being a form of shield, which limits their exposure and thereby enhances confidence. Uninhibited by the more extrovert, due to the reasons already stated above, for many, the online world can be an amazing leveller.

Qualities of introversion and extroversion are of course not fixed labels we can or should place on people or ourselves. They are conditional to the social environment we find ourselves in. This environment involves: the raison d'être of the encounter, context, local and organisational culture, custom and practice, social rituals and conventions, amongst many others. This interaction between perceived personality traits and the social environment gives rise to the archetypal stereotype of the quiet office functionary being the party animal at night.

Just as we possess extrovert and introvert traits, social environments often provide what might be termed "exhibitory" and "inhibitory" factors that interact with who we are. There are several key issues for functioning well in online networking for both groups are to remember.

Firstly, online networking is a unique social environment that has necessary rules so people can interact fairly.

Secondly, the online environment mutually shields people from some aspects of self-presentation normally experienced when face to face however, it reveals others. For example, we often can see into people's homes, their fittings, fixtures, décor, home apparel, even children and pets, offering a unique, information rich, subliminal, alternative view of who they are and reciprocally, who you are. This is not a non-intimate encounter!

Thirdly, networking in a business context is the promotion and propagation of business. It is easy to lose sight of this on an online basis where complex social interactions go on, suffused with the remote aspect of the technology, separate us from the core function of the meeting in the first place.

Finally, despite all of the above, people are pretty equal in the online world. For the extrovert, there is an opportunity to show a more thoughtful and perceptive side and for those less so, there is an option for considering carefully the messages to be delivered and the connections we are seeking to make. In real terms, this means jumping on and off the online environment to connect as readily with colleagues as if they are in the next room. Social skills are not innate, they are developed and honed by practice.

Just as with any other encounter, successfully networking online involves the management of the social environment, cognisance of people's performance within it and self-awareness. In common with all networking, it needs to be carefully thought through in terms of the desired impact, objectives sought and the agendas of those participating. Lose sight of these and your results are inhibited whatever your levels of self-expression!

Introverts Find a Place

As a more introverted person, who finds it a struggle to fight for air time when networking in a big room full of ego's, online networking provides me with a calmer environment to meet people.

I can hear everyone's story with clarity; can contact them through the 'Chat' immediately and it feels more natural to me.

Online networking allows me to put more focus into the individual in front of me.

I love the following quote by *Bob Burg*, (it's always been one of my mantra's), *'The single greatest 'people skill' is a highly developed and authentic interest in the other person.'*

Jon Davies, Managing Director:
Get the Edge UK Training and Consultancy Ltd

Make Yourself More than a Screenshot

Be as attentive as you can be. Often, the smaller the meeting, the more attentive you need to be – but then there is informal relationship building going on. In the larger meetings (12 plus), in my view, there is less obligation to be *'attentive'* as each screen is so small, so relax. Take a break from staring into the camera and select 'stop video' to prevent fatigue and online overload. *'Stop video'* changes the live picture of you to a still picture or a blank screen with your name on it! It doesn't stop you from hearing what's going on or force you out of the meeting. Seriously, engage this function whenever you need to, like when you feel a cough or a sneeze coming on because it's not nice seeing someone blow their nose on screen!

It's funny, but in face-to-face contact, someone can scratch their face, flick their hair, pull all sorts of strange faces and you hardly notice! Unless it's particularly constant we ignore it, filter it out and can't recall it BUT online with the small picture right in front of us, bodily habits are seen. We see the head scratching and other such whether we want to or not! It's not particularly great viewing.

Be Visible During Calls

You can stand out at an in-person networking meeting by helping the host by putting others at ease, and being someone the organisers can rely on to lift the atmosphere and aid the running of the meeting. Identified helpers are appreciated and often find themselves invited onto the group's committee.

Online is different. Whilst the host is the one who directs the meeting, controls the mute button, and monitors the break out rooms. It's still important to be a great guest and participant. Voice communication is so quick that pertinent points can easily be missed, so a helpful participant can type pertinent points, quotes or links mentioned into the *'Chat'*.

Use the *'Chat'* to comment positively on what others are saying – it shows you're being attentive to what is being said and not just waiting for your turn to speak. Interact with others without judgement or criticism.

A good mindset is to treat all online video calls like a real meeting – giving your full attention and staying for the whole meeting.

Social Media is Real Life

Lauren V Davis Founder: <u>**Lauren Davis Creative**</u>

Think of your social media like hosting a warm and inviting party, and if you do, it will be your best relationship-building tool.

Imagine you are invited to a party. When you get there, everything is a little too perfect. The furniture is perfectly in place; it looks like the sofa may just be for decoration. The conversation in the kitchen is polite but impersonal, the music is a little too quiet and the host is generally cold and uninviting. Sadly, you're afraid to pour yourself a glass of wine because you may drip some of it on the perfectly vacuumed white carpet.

You find a person to chat politely with and stay an hour and then you head out. You think to yourself, *"I so much appreciated this invite, but I am probably going to think twice before committing my whole evening to this particular person's party in the future."*

Now imagine the opposite. You are invited to a party and when you get there, the host warmly throws open the door and greets you with the kindest hug. They proceed to connect with you over recent events in your life. You walk in and see pictures hanging on the wall. The pictures represent the host's life - some with family, and some with friends.

There are a few pillows out of place, and a couple of dog toys on the floor when you walk in. It's almost as if the environment is saying what the hosts haven't said out loud. *"This is our home, we live here, and you're invited into our home. Please feel comfortable."*

You walk into the kitchen, see an array of things to drink and eat, and find a few of your other friends are already here. Your favourite song comes on. You laugh, drink, eat into the night

F continued

making memories and creating bonds through conversation and this experience you wouldn't have otherwise had.

This night will have those memories that years from now you say, *"Remember that one night at the party..."*

When you get home, you let out a big happy sigh that says, *"This was a great night."* You check your phone and you have a text from the host that says, *"I am so glad you came to the party tonight. Your presence made it that much better, and I can't wait for you to come back next time."* You drift off to sleep with that satisfaction that tonight was a perfect night.

All of Social Media is Real Life.

Even as near as 5 years ago, Social Media didn't play such a big role in our lives. Now, people report using social media as a source of where they keep up with current events, where they stay connected with friends and family, where they find humour or have comic relief from the seriousness of their days. Some go to social media to learn, educate themselves and find inspiration or encouragement.

Doesn't this sound a lot like a really great dinner party with your intelligent, hilarious, and empowering friends? Now, it's time for you to let out a sigh of relief.

Social media doesn't have to be scary. It can be a place to develop real relationships for you and your personal brand, which turns into your biggest support system. Your cheerleaders, biggest encouragers, and connections will translate into conversions and growth if you are genuine - *and if you are reading this, I know you are.*

You are the fun party host and you have guests waiting on your invite. Invite them into your house.

Your house = Your Social Media pages

I tell people to choose one platform they love to be on that gets them excited about social media, and one platform where it will serve their audience the best. You don't have to do them all. Start with two platforms.

Welcome your guests. Acknowledge the people who connect with you as your guests. They will feel great when you

F continued remember and chat about relevant things in their lives, your social media followers feel great when you engage with them. Spend time connecting with your audience and they will bring their friends. Pay attention to the people who are already at your party instead of those who have yet to arrive. Know the psychographics of your audience and show up for them.

Give your guests a genuine experience. Build bonds, and show them who you are. Don't be afraid to be yourself on social media, be just as your guests would find you the moment they walk inside your house. Include little pieces of you, your life, and what makes you who you are – the expert in your field. You are worth more than your work! People love following you because they love YOU and how you present the information.

Send your guests home feeling happy and full. Get them wondering when the next party is. Keep your audience coming back for more. When you provide your audience with a great experience, when they feel loved, acknowledged, and engaged, you build trust with them. This will be the foundation of your success on social media and best engagement in business networking online.

LinkedIn is My Best Networking Tool

By using LinkedIn as a networking tool, I've found I am meeting more people, or different people, than I could ever meet at a networking event. For instance, I read the Financial Times at the weekend; names come up and I think about the kind of conversation I'd love to have with this person. I look up these influential leaders on LinkedIn and I asked them to connect with me and sometimes they say, _"Yes!"_

Kathryn Colas, Founder: _SimplyHormones_ and Author: _How to Survive Menopause Without Losing Your Mind_

Managing Your Talk and Participate in Q & As

To be asked to give a talk is the biggest honour in any networking meeting. The talks are usually business-related, and relevant to the culture of the group. When you're speaking, people know you're in the room and your delivery, style and information is appreciated.

I have given more networking talks *'than I've had hot dinners'*, but online talks give a different dynamic. This is due to the impossibility of direct eye contact with listeners and the constraints of the technology.

If including a Q & A session as part of your talk, you will have to unmute people so you and other participants can hear them. If everyone is unmuted you run the risk of people talking at the same time.

I love the way *Nigel Botterill*, in his *Entrepreneurial Circle Clinic*, invites members to send in questions a few hours before the meeting, BUT if you're not on the call, then your question is not read out or answered! However, if you aren't as prepared as this, then watch the *'Chat'* (or give someone this role) for questions, either from the *'hands up'* icon pressed electronically or by people physically holding up their hands, which can be seen on the screen.

Organisers need to watch for participants with questions, as people can feel ignored if their hand has been missed and their input haven't been responded to.

From the networker's point of view, asking questions is a great way to be present in the room; it reminds people that you're there. When asking a question at an in-person network, it's always good practice to give your name before stating your question. This doesn't work online because either the host or speaker reads out your question or you are unmuted and everyone can see you when you begin to speak.

Who Else is in the Room?

Online there is so much more you can do: you can take a screenshot of who's in the room. This shows the names of people on the call, and you can look them up later on LinkedIn or Facebook and begin a proper conversation.

I repeat, make sure your name is showing on your screen with your first and second name, so others can find you easily via social media to follow up with you after the event.

Unity for Business Networks

The 2020 lockdown gave me the opportunity to develop my existing networking group. In this way, *lockdown has been the gift of time, the gift of thinking and the gift of opportunity.* I've been able to strategise my networking business.

My vision was to connect business people across regions and to expand networking by franchise and finalise the networking format, which is like a dating agency but for business people. In the same way people utilise a personal introduction agency to help grow personal relationships, I'm looking to facilitate introductions for business people so that they can grow business relationships.

My events feature Afternoon Teas, Golf, Cricket, and themed dinners etc. and could be considered business dates. It gives a common subject to talk about, something more than business. Business people don't have the pressure of the immediate sales pitch as the first introduction to others, which I think puts people off. As somebody using the dating agency analogy once said; *"You know, you don't drop your trousers on the first date!"* which is sometimes how sales pitches can feel!

I'm a strong believer in networking to build relationships. You might be looking for a financial transaction but there are other way for business - by some kind of collaboration, or using your own network for referrals, which is referral currency.

Online Networking, forced by lockdown, is changing the engagement between business people. There is a community feel developing, with kindness being outwardly shown, CEOs are appreciating staff and customers more. Whatever Brexit did to us in its division, lockdown has done the opposite; I think it's pulling us together now as an economy and as a market. Maybe our island mentality is coming to the fore again, resulting in good business networking online and offline.

Claire Bicknell, Founder: <u>Catena Network</u>

Grow Your Network

Boost your list by contacting those who were on the online meeting with you and ask them to connect. This can vastly increase your list, tribe or connections. An example using LinkedIn is:

- 🖥 In the *'Chat'*, give your LinkedIn address and ask for participant's LinkedIn details to connect or,
- 🖥 Search for the name of the person you have met online and request to connect.

It's good practice to send a message or note with the request to connection. Simply remind them where you have met (the networking group) and why you'd like to connect.

Invite Tom to connect   ✕

Build a quality network by connecting only with people you know.

Message (optional)

Hi Tom - I believe we were on the same webinar/ network with Robert Middleton last night would love to connect

190 / 300

▣ PREMIUM

Don't know Tom? Send an InMail with Premium to introduce yourself. More people reply to an InMail than a connection request.

Try Free for 1 Month

Cancel   Send invitation

The characteristics which need to be honed whilst using online communications are:

- 🖥 Kindness.
- 🖥 Thinking of others even when promoting your business.
- 🖥 Conscious of your tone and body language.

Keep the above points in mind and take on board the words of Franklin D Roosevelt, *"I don't care how much you know until I know how much you care."*

At the end of the day it's all about authentic relationships and deepening these kindred connections.

Lessons Learned from Lockdown

We have learnt a great deal about online networking due to lockdown including the fact that there is a definite need for it - something we'd dismissed as unimportant in the past. For me, I like to meet people, I have a very busy lifestyle, I travel the world and I have five children. So more than ever, I understand the need for connections and the opportunities given by online networking.

Online networking is very, very powerful.
We've learned that while people sometimes don't want to leave their home and they prefer to network in their pyjamas. People still are looking for connection, they are still looking to grow their businesses, they are still looking to be with like-minded people.

Leona Burton, *Co-Founder of MIBA* and *CEO MIB International*.

be the
most important
person in the
zroom

In Conversation With

Mike Kim

Ladey Adey

Mike Kim - Marketing & Brand Strategist and Speaker

Ladey Adey (LA): Mike, it seems the business world has migrated to the online world and it is fascinating see how networking is working online now. How has it been for you and your business?

Mike Kim (MK): My business has been mostly online, or when engaging offline, the marketing is always done online, so I actually haven't missed a beat at all. Due to the lockdown, I've been missing out on the speaking income but it isn't a big deal because this isn't my primary business but a strategic platform to continue to build my list and build my brand.

By my *'brand'*, I mean, my reputation in the US and my visibility. Visibility and publicity are really important parts of any marketing plan. It's necessary to raise your profile to the degree that someone has heard of you; they don't even need to have met you! They just need to have heard of you. This makes it much easier for doors to open up. It's like the publicity factor. I do a lot of events, speaking wise, other people's events, often unpaid, just having my travel expenses covered. I do this because it's such good publicity, the more people have heard of you, the better it is for you - hands down, all the time.

LA: How do you use networking online?

MK: For networking online, I mainly use social media. This is how I use it; I'll tag other speakers, and I will post on their stuff. That's really the new networking for me. It's my way to stay in their minds or at least not go completely dark with the people who I've met at conferences - either as speakers, entrepreneurs or attendees.

I'm consistently active on social media. I don't have an in-depth social media plan, but I will regularly post on social media because I think the new networking is really about visibility.

At a face-to-face networking event, you meet a person who you don't really know and have a stilted conversation trying to find common ground. The alternative is when a friend introduces you and says, *"Oh, Ladey, this is Rachel and by the way, Rachel is a friend of Mike Kim."* It's immediately different, right? The tone of the conversation changes and flows easily because connections have been made. This is why it's so important to have a high visibility, to make sure you've been heard of.

LA: Is having a high profile easier online or offline?

MK: Online definitely. How many networking events are people going to offline? Not very many. The easiest thing to do to get heard of is to go on virtual stages, podcasts, interviews, webinars etc. It's really that simple.

LA: Do you think more people are going to move their business online and find new ways of engaging with customers?

MK: Some, but not as many as you think. I think people talk a big game, then they don't execute. I think they are idea-rich but execution-poor. As soon as the government start reopening the economy, people are going to go back to doing what they did, because that's what they know. Learning a new skill is often really difficult for business owners who have been entrenched in a certain way of doing things for a long time.

LA: Have you been surprised at how online communication has transformed people's lives?

MK: I think there's been a learning curve for a lot of people. People have been surprised that a lot of work can get done without having to go into an office.

LA: I know you run mastermind groups, how do these work for networking?

MK: In my groups, when people first join, I encourage them to have 1-2-1 conversations. The first week is getting to know other members, just to 'shoot the breeze' or touch base with them. They get to know one another because when you're in the trenches with other people, you just get to know them.

It's all natural - there's no forced networking. I actually don't use the word 'networking' very much. I prefer to call it 'relationship building'. It's getting to know other people. It's making new friends. I do think that networking for business people who aren't doing good work is a complete waste of time.

You should be doing work that's getting you noticed, not networking per se. This attracts people to you and your business, which is a fundamental shift.

Most of the folks who bring me in to speak at their event have never, themselves, heard me speak. They know I've spoken at other events, or they have heard of me because other people are talking about me as I've been helping people and producing work that's worth noticing.

LA: Do you think there's a skill in referring people, introducing business people to another business owner?

MK: I think referrals are common sense and something we do in life all the time. I think gaining a referral is a skill because you have to be intentional about the work that you're doing, what you're known for, how you're presenting yourself. Are you pleasant to be around, and is it clear what you do? What are the values associated with you and your brand?

A brand is what people think about you or feel about you when you're not there. If it's not known what you do, perhaps you're always changing your mind, you're taking a really long time to find your footing to establish yourself, then it's going to be hard for people to refer you to others. The longer a lack of clarity over your brand exists, the harder it is for people to change their perception of you, even when you land on your final brand!

LA: How are people using referrals in the mastermind group?

MK: Having clarity on your brand is a fundamental goal in my mastermind group. If someone in my group cannot explain what they do, that's a problem. It's either they have a branding problem, or I'm not paying attention to them. We work on their message because it's my job to know what they do.

I've been in other people's mastermind groups and sat in on calls with others for three months and I still don't know what some participants do. They seem like a nice person. I just don't know what they do. I can't tell you what they do. Then all of a sudden, they say, "Oh, by the way, I'm a copywriter."

Now, they're clear they want to be a copywriter but I can't refer them to others because in my mind they've been continually changing their mind. They've created a brand of confusion, as they seem to lack conviction.

Does that make sense? I have folks who have come through my coaching course and various programs of mine for three years and every year they have a different brand. One year - they want to be a leadership coach, the next year - a marketing consultant, the third year - an author trying to write a book on this topic.

They don't have clarity and seem to lack the entrepreneurial edge. If all they do is jump around and try wearing different hats or trying to find their footing that's fine, but until they know who they are, what they do and become 'on-brand', I can't refer them to others.

LA: One of your training modules I've enjoyed the most has been the importance of the bio and its relationship to branding. I see the bio being similar to the one-minute pitch, how do you see them crossing over?

MK: It's the context that matters. As a speaker, for instance, your goal is to have the shortest bio possible. The shorter your introduction, the more authority you have, for example, *"Ladies and gentlemen, on the stage tonight is Mr Bill Gates."* In fact, you don't even need to explain his background as founder of Microsoft, etc. It's a simply a simple announcement because he has a brand, a reputation and everyone has heard of him.

A lot of folks out there are passing themselves off as experts in fields and industries that they've never actually done anything in. I don't hire copywriters who don't write good copy for themselves. I don't hire marketing consultants who can't market themselves.

In this day and age, if you're one of these folks who have a reputation, then I will follow and subscribe to your work. I'm not saying you have to be on social media, but you have to have a reputation, and that reputation is the brain of your business.

LA: I can see why it's necessary to get clarity, particularly, as you never know who's listening to your message.

MK: That's right and that's on you. It's not someone else's job to figure out what you do. It's your job to clearly communicate what you do.

Embracing Online Technology

Pulling a good Network together takes effort, sincerity and time.
Alan Collins

As the migration to online communications grows the use of technology has taken the world by storm. People who have never bothered with social media, online conferencing or telephone systems turned their attention to them during Covid-19 and lockdown. Plato's phrase, 'Necessity is the mother of invention' happened before our eyes! Business people had to:

- 🖥 Engage with the online technology to keep their business alive.
- 🖥 Learn, and master, digital systems to make communications with their customers easier.

Those in the business world, and older people, were using the technology for the first time, needing to learn the physical use of the apps and the etiquettes surrounding them leading to a *'brave new online world!'*

All is good - as long as we remember that all online communications are public, as there is no such thing as confidentiality when utilising social media or online business networking events. Many of the applications (apps) have a recording function, which organisers of networking event switch ON. Anything you comment on, or type in, is there for public viewing. If you accept this and monitor how you represent your brand and yourself, then usage of the technology can complement and increase your business.

The online business networking scene has embraced many apps, and the list continues to grow. Admit it, how many of these online tools have you used, more than ever before, since lockdown?

New apps are coming online every day, including ones which will enable businesses to keep control and have ownership of content (beware of content ownership being claimed by the app masters!).

Applications and Platforms Most Used			
B-Connect-D	Caffeine	Convertkit	Facebook Messenger
Google Hangouts	Houseparty	Instagram	iTunes
LinkedIn	Mailchimp	Mentimeter	Microsoft Teams
Otter	PayPal	Pinterest	Pod
Reddit	Remo	Skype	Snapchat
Steemit	Survey Monkey	T4S (Traffic 4 Sales)	Temi
TikTok	Trello	Tumblr	Twitter
Vimeo	WhatsApp	YouTube	Zoom

The Human Factor

In my view, networking online is effective but not as effective as face-to-face networking. Face-to-face offers that 'human factor', which is essential to build successful connections. Perhaps the future will be, that we will use both face-to-face and online networking.

As with the face-to-face networking events, we must be prepared in what we say, how we act and look. With online networking we still need to be pleasant, competent, knowledgeable, and professional.

To look good in front of the camera, we need to be smart or casual looking but never messy. The background must be clean and tidy, it's best not to use personal areas such as bedrooms to broadcast and where possible, to limit background noise.

In addition, we must ensure that our laptops, ipads and mobile phones etc. are in excellent working order.

Stav Melides, _Glyvolution_ and Reg. Director: _Catena Business Network_

To access these apps and tools you need a decent Internet connection and up-to-date equipment. It's your choice as to which device you are the most comfortable with - computer, tablet or mobile phone. From this point, the quality of your camera and microphones will become a huge factor in how easy it is to communicate.

Microphones (mics) are usually installed in the devices, but some people find it easier to add on external microphones. A headset works well because it directs the sound straight into the device; limits outside noise and you look really cool wearing them!

Cameras are also installed on most devices and the skill is how you present yourself in front of the camera!

A-Z of Mastering Online Apps

I could give a *'how to use'* lesson on particular apps, but there are many videos and lessons online covering this *(just search YouTube)*. Instead, I've taken the common features which are necessary to master effectively presenting yourself and your business in the most professional manner - they apply to all video conferencing apps currently on the market.

I have referenced Zoom in examples and pictures, but the features are interchangeable with other video conferencing apps. Why Zoom has come out 'head and shoulders' above other apps during and since lockdown is an unknown phenomenon. They hit their tipping point and quadrupled their sales. Their branding has formed part of common parlance - phrases such as *'Being Zoomed out'*, *'Suffering from Zoomitis'*, *'Join us in Zoomland'* and *'Having a quick Zoom'* to name a few. Who would have thought it?

Every app used for online networking meetings has its own way of operating, but in the main they have similar features and the protocols work across all the platforms. By understanding and mastering these you will:

- 💻 Enhance your business networking skills.
- 💻 Show your online professionalism.
- 💻 Make online interaction easy and enjoyable.
- 💻 Improve your relationship with other business people.
- 💻 Gain advantage over your competitors.

Avatar

Your avatar, profile and user name are equivalent to your business card. Ensure they are professional and accurate, not a fun or frivolous name. Have your ten-word bio on view if possible and a good clear headshot picture.

Ladey Adey

I help ambitious business people write their books, increase their brand and be acknowledged as experts in their field.

Have a short bio at the ready, and save it in *'sticky notes'* or a 'Word' doc to copy and paste into the *'Chat'* as you introduce yourself. Have more than one so you can rotate them and keep what you do fresh. This is particularly important for any networks made up of 80% regular networkers. Reveal a little more about you and your business to those you meet most weeks. Ask yourself, could those regulars tell someone else what you do and nail it?

Backgrounds

Conference calls give us the chance to see inside your home. As curious beings we want to see into each other's houses and rooms. It gives a more personal side of you - whether you are messy or tidy, what pictures you have on the wall or books in the background!

We notice everything - all the time. I was on *Mark Jarvis'* early

Ken Marshall

morning business network (PURE), and in the background of businessman, *Ken Marshall*, was a wall of books. I knew someone with that number of books couldn't be anything other than a lover of books and had probably written one (or needing to write one!). This led to a conversation with *Ken*, buying his first book and talking with him about writing and publishing his second! Business was generated because of the home background.

Be cautious when using generic, manufactured pictures such as the *Golden Gate Bridge* in San Francisco, waving palm trees or cartoons that move *(I'm not an advocate)*. Ask yourself, what is your background communicating about you, your brand and business?

117

Your logo in the background is *'fair play'* and uploading pictures can work – especially if linked to what you do. Sometimes, I may change my background for a limited time to illustrate a specific point.

One of the most professional backgrounds I've seen is *Kayleigh Nicolaou's* screen.

Her business logo is very clear and she fits on-screen without obscuring any detail in her background.

Kayleigh Nicolaou – www.kakad...

You can change your background at any time during a call as the app sets up the background on a *'green screen'*. Green screens have been used for years, allowing images to be behind actors, particularly those presenting the news and weather reporters.

One issue with the computer-based backgrounds is without a plain background behind you the camera gets confused, and it seems as though you are a hologram, or only parts of you are in focus. This worsens when you move or shift position or when you hold something up to show. Interestingly, there is less problem with paid versions  than the free ones! The solution to this is investing in a freestanding green screen or one that attaches to the ceiling.

Somehow, I don't feel 100% authentic when using a false background – *but that's probably just me!*

BOT

Initially, I thought bot was short for robot – but actually it's an acronym  - *'back on track'*. Social media bots are used to engage with you in social media via an automated programme. They mimic human users, so you think it's a real person responding. It's very clever technology, and I can see the attraction in using them. Like most automated software, it saves time, and you can comment on other people's posts - raising your profile without having to do it yourself. BUT... isn't the point of social media to engage and have direct conversations yourself?

Recently, I contacted a speaker and, as I was impressed with his attitude and knowledge, I hoped to be part of his tribe and to grow a networking relationship. His reply was encouraging and he sent me a link to his next webinar, all very nice. I then went back with a secondary question and guess what? He thanked me nicely and sent me a link to his next webinar. This seemed odd, so I went back a third time with a very specific question and, yes, back came the link to his next webinar. He had a bot running. *Guess who won't be going to his next webinar?*

I believe there needs to be transparency when using a bot; the website should let you know, via a pop-up message, if using a bot.

I am a bot, but I would love to help you with our platform. Would you like to schedule a demo?

My interest in networking is in the personal interaction that can build, leading to surprising and genuine engagement, so a bot response cheats me of this. One of the most recognised bots is the really annoying 'pop up', asking if we accept cookies before continuing on a website.

Apparently, bots are recognised in over 250,000 users. They can also be known as spiders, crawlers or even as part of malware, and as trolls. We've accepted Google spiders as a compromise to raise our ranking on Google and as part of Search Engine Optimisation (SEO) management, whereas the malware bots are quite concerning.

A more positive word for these bots is *'algorithm'*. Algorithms are mathematical calculations and are part of the programme in all apps. *Simon Goodchild*, of T4S, helped to explain it to me; he said, *"Social media platforms (such as Facebook) use algorithms to monitor how accounts are used. Based on actions and monitoring, risks may be automatically raised. Social media platforms may then do a variety of things, ranging from restricting your ability to post right through to pausing, temporarily banning or even closing your account down."*

Mike Luxford, of MLCS Ltd, also gave me some insight, *"A bot is an algorithm which monitors your posts. For example, on LinkedIn if you have created a new 'post' and 'share' a post, then the new post will get a higher ratings than shares and therefore more coverage.*

Whereas, if you put a website link in the post, you get a lower score than if you put it in the comments. This is because the website link takes you away from the platform (LinkedIn, Facebook et al) and, of course, they want you and your audience to stay on their platform."

Breakout Rooms

Virtual communication platforms have been priceless in enabling me support learning and skill development with my clients, when I can't get meetings in-person.

I run online training sessions to teach concepts, explore models and up-skill people. Once we have covered the core content, being able to utilise the break out function on the platforms means that my participants can practise what they have learnt. They can share their learning experiences with each other, more privately and with better context.

As a facilitator, the break out function helps me to ensure their learning is valuable, in context and applied to themselves.

Nicola Ellwood, Executive Coach: *Communication and Culture Specialist* and Chair of Lincoln Business Club, UK

Breakout Rooms

Breakout rooms (also called callout rooms) are where the technology allows the organiser to put a small number of people into a separate *'room'* for a set amount of time. This is about the only feature which is currently not possible to be recorded and therefore could have some element of confidentiality! In the breakout room, you're

able to share your viewpoint with a smaller number of people and they with you. It helps to expand your knowledge of each other.

The breakout room shortcuts the *'getting to know you'* process, especially in a crowd of people attending the online event. Some would say it's serendipitous who you are (randomly) placed with; I like to call them *'Godincidences'!* If you find a like-minded person you want to know better, then it's time to follow-up, link up on social media, exchange emails and keep in contact.

If breakout rooms are part of the meeting format, you'll be invited to join them. This is optional, and if you don't click to join, you'll remain in the main room with the host.

If you're put into a breakout room and you suddenly become tongue-tied – then it might be worth starting with some *'ice-breaking'* questions:

1) Is this your first video call?
2) How are you enjoying the world of online networking?
3) Why are you in business?
4) What are you working on at the moment?
5) Who do you need introductions to?

Breakout rooms usually last 10-15 minutes, but might be longer. You can leave either the breakout room or the whole meeting at anytime. Be careful - it's easy to hit the wrong button when wanting to return to the *'main'* room and find yourself outside the whole meeting and having to rejoin!

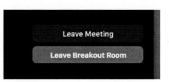

Free to Breakout

I'm in the 'love-hate' camp with Zoom. Recently, I have attended video calls with a high number of participants which have been torturous because the sound booms around, the host doesn't show up on time, the flow of the meeting is lost as people join late and my worst bugbear, talking to a group of people where many participants stay off-camera.

However, when a Zoom meeting is run well it's an excellent substitute for face-to-face meetings enabling effective discussion and connection.

I recently attended a *Women of Impact Book Club* meeting. The host is an experienced Zoom facilitator which made a huge difference. She split the meeting into three segments.

Segment 1 – 90 second introduction plus book review.

Segment 2 – Zoom breakout rooms.

Segment 3 – Plenary - in main Zoom room.

I had never experienced breakout rooms before. We were split into groups of three people. The computer randomly generated the group selection and we each received a pop-up invitation to join our breakout room. Our small group conversations were confidential and unrecorded, and the host *'dropped in'* to join us at various points.

It was fascinating to go from the big group meeting where I felt conscious of not interrupting and stayed on 'Mute'. The breakout room allowed the intimacy of a small group discussion and we were able to talk together in a more natural way. We got surprisingly deep in our conversation even though we didn't know one another.

In summary, breakout rooms are an excellent feature. It's quick, (no scraping of chairs) and furthermore, the countdown and rejoin is ruthless so no lagging behind can occur.

Jackie Forbes, <u>Drawn To Learn</u>

When staying in the breakout room, most people find that time flies and would like longer. It's useful when someone takes charge or is the breakout room *'monitor'* to keep people to time, especially if they have a minute to introduce themselves. A more laid-back elevator pitch is useful here – as it's a relaxed conversational style of engagement, encouraging queries rather than the usual one-minute pitch format.

Those in the room are usually notified when there's one minute or less left before automatically returning to the main session. Sometimes a countdown clock is seen.

Breakout Rooms

Breakout Rooms will close in 50 seconds
You will be returned to the main session automatically.

Return to Main Session

It's at this point that the room host or participants often realise that not everyone has spoken or someone has spoken too long - invariably in response to questions and interest in their work shown by the other breakout room members. It can result in some funny messages in the *'Chat!'*

If sharing needs to happen from the breakout rooms, it's possible for someone to be the designated note-taker and post a summary into the *'Chat'* as people are speaking. To encourage full participation, everyone needs to have the option *not* to have their conversation relayed in this way.

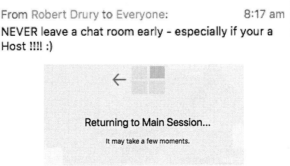

From Robert Drury to Everyone: 8:17 am
NEVER leave a chat room early - especially if your a Host !!!! :)

Returning to Main Session...

It may take a few moments.

Camera Use and Abuse

I see many camera mistakes everyday in networking groups. They're easy to correct once you're aware of them. Prior to the meeting, check to see how you look on camera, and be prepared to move your camera or change the computer angle if the camera is built into the device.

Here are a series of pictures of what NOT to do in front of the camera while participating on business networking calls online.

Camera Positioning

Problem: Camera set too high.

Solution: Adjust the camera or move the angle of the computer screen.

A New Comfort Blanket

In this ever-changing world we live, work and play in, we have all had to make adaptations to our normal activities in one way or another. Many of us have now begun to take part in online networking and embraced our new way of interacting with other businesses, connections, friends and family. I was never a big fan on being on camera – so the thought of Skype, Zoom etc. had me banging on my comfort zone door.

After a couple of weeks of hitting the *'Join'* button, I find I quite enjoy networking in this new way. I am making more connections, learning new skills and enjoying the virtual coffee meetings arranged from online networking.

Amazing things happen when we step over the comfort zone threshold! I now look for more online training, webinars and networking events to build my brand, my knowledge and create strong collaborative partnerships.

Embrace the new way of networking and its possibilities!

Jo Keen, Founder: *Rainbow Consultancy*

Problem: Camera set too low.

Solution: Adjust the camera or move the angle of the computer screen.

Problem: Too much light behind you (backlighting) means you're in darkness and shadow (we do want to see you!).

Solution: Move the computer around, so you're facing the light or invest in a lighting ring and place this in front of you. This prevents you from looking like one of those silhouette images when a person is hiding their identity!

Problem: Getting up to reach something or getting out of the chair to leave the room (empty chair syndrome).

Solution: Use *'Stop video'* and have your favourite still picture shown instead.

Problem: More than one person sharing the screen.

Solution: Check your image beforehand to make sure you're both in plain sight and as near to the centre as possible.

Feature

Smart Use of
Networking Technology

Tony Smith, Director, Genius Technology Solutions

When it comes to using technology there's no 'one-size fits all' solution. As the saying goes, "Different suits for different dudes." This is certainly true for the digital world of online networking.

The principles of networking remain the same – you need to build rapport, engage with people, create relationships and help people where you can. The good old adage, *"Know, Like, Trust"* needs to be implemented but where do you start with knowing, liking and trusting the technology?

The popularity of video conferencing has soared during the Covid-19 pandemic. As lockdowns are imposed in many countries, millions of people have started using such systems as Zoom, POD, HouseParty, Microsoft Teams or BlueJeans for work and leisure. These systems allow multiple video chats but each come with limitations and benefits including concerns over data security and privacy.

In many cases, due to the rush to develop a working from home operation, people have cobbled together a mish mash of different technologies, systems and platforms to maintain their operations. This includes strategies for networking, maintaining and building relationships with existing customers, suppliers, partners, colleagues, staff and as a means to develop new business.

It may be that NOW is the ideal time to take stock and actually consider how to create a unified communications system? Covid-19 has focussed the mind of companies and workers across the world on business continuity planning, yet it's still one of those things that people think won't affect them!

F continued

We have all witnessed the disruption to *'business as normal'* as a result of hurricanes, floods, snow and a myriad of other disasters, many of which disrupt the lives of people and business. Whether due to a fire or flooding which damages the telephone & broadband network or merely weather conditions (or pandemics) that prevent people getting into their normal place of work. Even transport disruption causes problems!

All of these problems could be overcome, though, or at least mitigated, by a unified communications system.

Whilst some of the technology to support this relies on public infrastructure such as; broadband, mobile networks and software, there are elements of choice available to those who want to maximise their independence to ensure business continuity as far as possible.

Online networking and communication rely on three key elements:

- Connectivity to a communication network, e.g. broadband or wireless connection.
- Devices to connect to the network, e.g. mobile device, laptop or desktop computing.
- Compatible software.

At each stage there should be adequate security including firewalls and virus checkers to maintain the security and integrity of the system, and the information being shared across it and the users of it.

The connectivity may be through traditional routes such as fibre or cable, but that comes with the risk of disruption due to accidental damage. A mitigating option might be, the addition or alternative provision of a 5G or 4G system, which would allow fail-over if the main system drops out providing a seamless continuity of signal allowing the user uncontended use of their broadband i.e. no one else is accessing the signal and diluting the speed of the connection.

F *continued* With the advent of the UK analogue phone system being switched off in 2025 the likelihood is that in due course 5G will become the medium of choice to provide broadband to both homes and business premises.

There isn't the space to provide a thorough comparison between all systems here but using POD as an example illustrates the advantages to look for in a unified communication platform.

POD offers a simple uncluttered approach. All anyone wants is a better way to connect and do business including networking.

POD is a smart unified system that works around you and your business, allowing you the freedom to take your office anywhere. It links seamlessly between all your devices and is tailored for all business types from; a one-man band, to complex set ups such as a market leading call centre.

The system has a powerful user experience, allowing easy connection and online networking via chat, call, text or video meetings. During a call with one person, you can easily switch to video, share screens and invite others to join the conversation – all simply at the touch of a button, without putting the original call on hold.

During the design process, careful considerations were made about how to meet carrier-grade security and data privacy requirements. As a result, many of the normal security issues reported to date do not affect a POD Meeting.

The security of a product, however, is only as good as the ongoing effort applied to continually improve, and the speed of response to address issues that do emerge.

There will always be some risk with technology and its advances, but whilst we are all still learning, clever technologies allow us to incorporate their application into our business (while on the look out to improve our business delivery), enabling us to network and connect online safely, easily and effectively.

Human Mannerisms on Camera

Some of our natural behaviours are filtered out when meeting face-to-face, but oddly, once online they *'stick out like a sore thumb'* and aren't very nice to watch. A list follows including sneezing, scratching etc. but my *'pet hate'* is eating while on screen. When you feel the urge to cough for example, take a moment to *'Stop Video'* it will automatically show your picture or name in place of the live video. Ensure *'Mute'* is on, and you

 can come back when you can be more attentive. It's easy to *STOP* your video and then START it again; so don't worry that it will force you out of the meeting.

Giving 100% attention 100% of the time

Online networking organisers are increasingly encouraging participants to devote their undivided attention to what is happening on-screen. As someone who attends 15-20 networking meetings per week, the more I observe, the more I'm beginning to disagree with this. In the previous chapter I mention that attentiveness can be dependent on the number of people on the video call. My feeling is that we were not created to stare for hours into a small camera on the computer – so we need to use the tools to suit us and not feel guilty about being *'attentive'*. Seriously, no one remembers, and the online networking police will not come knocking on your door!

I have no problem with multi-tasking on a call, with some moments of attentiveness. When taking part in a video call there are times to be active and times to be passive. The passive times are when there is a speaker who is not interactive with the group (this can be like listening to a podcast or a radio programme) and it's during those moments other tasks can be done whilst still listening.

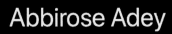 Often, I use this time to take a screenshot and to connect on LinkedIn with those who have put their full name on the screen. If you're worried about not looking attentive, the press **'Stop' Video.**

BIG No-Nos

Problem: Bored or Yawning.

Solution: Use *'Stop Video'*.

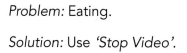

Problem: Distracted.

Solution: Use *'Stop Video'*.

Problem: Eating.

Solution: Use *'Stop Video'*.

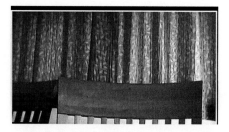

Problem: Hair Brushing.

Solution: Use *'Stop Video'*.

Problem: Leaving Room.

Solution: Use *'Stop Video'*.

Problem: Scratching.

Solution: Use *'Stop Video'.*

Problem: Sneezing or Blowing Nose.

Solution: Use *'Stop Video'.*

Problem: Animals.

Curiously enough, most people don't mind animals or children in the frame for a short while, but howling dogs or noisy children can be annoying – so use *'Mute'.*

Camera Best View

People still like to have eye-to-eye contact; I know this is much easier in-person, but via the screen it means looking directly at the camera lens. This is the view of you that other guests or your audience (if you're the speaker) are seeing. It's how you connect with them, so they know you're talking to them as individuals (just like TV presenters).

Ladey Adey Publisher for Your Book

To find the buttons needed to fully participate in a video conference call, they are usually at the bottom of the screen. Here is the panel from a Zoom call.

Captions (Subtitling)

Using Google Meet as an app for networking, I was delighted to see

it was possible to enable Captions or Subtitling. As each participant spoke, a text bar appeared at the bottom with the words. An excellent feature especially when there are many in accents and audio quality.

'Chat'

For me, the *'Chat'* is a huge boon to the online networking experience and gives freedom within the meeting to talk to others on the call. It gives an interactive feel without having to wait for your turn to speak. Organisers can *'Lock'* it to prevent you from using it though! You do have to concentrate, so as not to mix up people! You can use it to build up your LinkedIn tribe by searching people's names and asking to connect.

Use the *'Chat'* wisely and you'll make friends. Used unwisely, and it could prevent people from doing business with you! Only make comments pertinent to what is being said, and use it to put in a brief bio (a virtual business card) at the time you are asked to introduce yourself.

Be careful what you put in when someone else is speaking – though it helps to build up relationships when the comments are constructive to others.

```
                    chat 27-4-20 Woman Who.txt — Edited
09:41:52        From Ladey Adey : https://www.linkedin.com/in/ladey/
09:42:51        From Lesley Brown : https://www.linkedin.com/in/lesley-brown-5b2764138/
09:45:06        From TJ: Hello All - lovely to see/meet you here
09:45:49        From John Cleary : Hi everyone. As Sandra said I'm the official Woman Who photographer. I'm pivoting during the
lockdown. If you need help with making your Wordpress website work harder for you; memberships, courses, building a list, or
booking appointments, please do contact me for a chat. https://www.linkedin.com/in/johnclearyphoto/
09:46:35        From Lee.Osborne : Our coronavirus hub can be found here fsb.org.uk
09:46:37        From Jane Hooper : I'll raise a glass to you all on Friday
09:46:51        From Andrea : That's kind Jane
09:48:41        From VO: I forgot to say most importantly that although our offices are physically closed we remain open for
business - our staff are all being fantastic and operating from home!
09:50:43        From Anne Birch : Lorraine - amazing woman, proving yet again that women can achieve anything given the right
support, confidence and resilience
09:53:35        From Cheryll Rawbone : Hello I'm Cheryll Rawbone from Gallagher Insurance and charity Friendship Project for
children my twitter is @GallaghCovChes and linked in is https://www.linkedin.com/in/cheryllrawbone
09:54:22        From Jane Hooper : https://www.linkedin.com/in/jane-hooper
09:54:43        From Cheryll Rawbone : Lorraine very inspiring your resilience and get go intiative
09:55:41        From Ladey Adey : How nice to have the true meaning of giving - inspirational Lorraine
09:56:06        From Sandy Ameer-Beg : such an inspiring lady!
09:56:23        From Wendy Harris : You're helping so many people Lorraine
09:56:30        From Jane Hooper : Not a small difference - a big difference to them
09:57:00        From Socially Shared : What a wonderful thing to do for people Lorraine. You are a true inspiration! x
09:57:09        From RMS: what a really lovely thing to do.. such an amazing story. You should be super proud of yourself xx
09:57:09        From Ladey Adey : Can you pop in your LinkedIn link Lorraine Please  - I might have missed it earlier!
09:57:20        From Patricia Howard : Wonderfully thoughtful and inspiring.
09:57:49        From Andrea : Sharon Louca sends her apologies Sandra, she is having technical issues
09:58:18        From John Cleary : Lorraine for fundraising, have you heard of EasyFundraising? It's a great way for people to
donate without it costing them anything through online purchases.
09:58:24        From Victoria Prince : Amazing, thank you Lorraine! xx
09:58:28        From AMP  : Well done Lorraine. Inspirational!
09:58:52        From Andrea : You are a total inspiration Lorraine! Thank you for sharing!
09:58:54        From Andrea : You are an amazing lady!
09:58:56        From FP: Very inspiring Lorraine - such an invaluable service especially during these difficult times
09:59:10        From TJ: Very inspiring, thank you for sharing. x
09:59:10        From S: love it, amazing Lorraine.  I would love to be a part of this
09:59:15        From Lesley Brown : So interesting and well done inspiring about your determination. Would be nice to have this
in my area Derby
09:59:24        From KPJ: Lorraine is also very generous with her support to other charities
10:01:04        From lorrainelewis : Thank you everyone for your lovely comments and support!
10:01:32        From lorrainelewis : Thank you John I will check this out.
10:01:38        From lorrainelewis : https://www.linkedin.com/in/lorraine-lewis-bca-736b5b195/
```

You can save the *'Chat'* at any point, and it's very helpful to keep the details and links from other participants. The screen shot (at the bottom of the opposite page) shows a ten-minute segment of a two-hour online call. It was taken at a *Woman Who Inspire Academy* networking meeting. It covers a time period in which, *Lorraine Lewis*, Founder: *The Lewis Foundation*, is the keynote speaker. *Note: it begins with sharing LinkedIn details, as encouraged by the organiser, Sandra Garlick. Attendees left comments related to Lorraine's talk, and shared links to keep in contact.*

Lorraine appreciated the comments and left this message: *"I am very passionate about what I do and I do it because I love it, feel challenged and know the difference it makes to others. To see the comments from participants saying what I do is inspiring; and getting this feedback makes all the difference means the world to me and boosts my self-confidence. Thanks everyone."*

At 09:57:49 – there is a note to the organiser about someone experiencing technical difficulties, which is helpful to the organiser if they are watching the chat.

Private or Public Chat

Within the *'Chat'* you can make comments to *'Everyone'* and/or you can chat specifically to one person, known as *'Private Chat'*. This is really useful, as you may want to comment to someone without everyone else seeing your conversation. The picture below shows *'Private Chat'* in brackets (Privately).

```
●●●           📄 BNO 1-5-20 robert Middleton private chat.txt — Edited ⌄
21:13:32        From Tom Huberty : You can use your phone as dictation tool to capture
the idea and then send the info into your email to sort and expand.
21:16:23        From Ladey Adey : then put the mp3 audio file into otter.ai for free
transcription and you have your doc or text file
21:17:22        From Charles Kovess : Thanks Tom and Ladey for sharing good ideas
21:17:49        From Tom Huberty : Thanks, Ladey
21:18:36        From Elaine Schuhrke to Ladey Adey (Privately) : that is thinkin!
21:19:04        From Elaine Schuhrke to Ladey Adey (Privately) : Thanks for coming up
with the idea!  Do you do this?
21:19:48        From Pat: Or when you have the sensation that there is nothing you can do
to solve the pain, either yours or somebody else's.
21:20:32        From Ladey Adey to Elaine Schuhrke (Privately) : I do it all the time.
When writing books or my video blog I record myself in Zoom - take the audio - pop it into
otter (free) or Semi (paid) and for my book I'm writing at the moment I've had interviews
with people recorded in Zoom, then put to otter and within minutes I've got a text file to
edit -Brilliant
21:21:45        From Elaine Schuhrke to Ladey Adey (Privately) : I'll say BRILLIANT!
Thanks for the info....I'm gonna give this a try!
21:22:02        From Ladey Adey to Elaine Schuhrke (Privately) : Can I give you my otter
referral link?
21:22:36        From Elaine Schuhrke to Ladey Adey (Privately) : Please!  It will act as
incentive to get me into it sooner than later!
21:24:07        From Ladey Adey to Elaine Schuhrke (Privately) : whats your email?
21:24:29        From Pat:| looking forward to the recording as I lost the meeting several
times. Thanks for doing this for us!!
21:24:45        From Ladey Adey to Elaine Schuhrke (Privately) : https://otter.ai/
referrals/CN67TQTK
```

Security   Manage Participants   Chat   Share Screen   Record

Michael Heppell · Following
I teach people how to be brilliant   ...
5h · 🚫

Clackers

5 · 39 Comments

Ladey Adey 00:48   ...
I help ambitious business peo...

Ohhhh a new 17 challenge!

Reply

Add a comment...

Poor Postings Equals Bad Manners

You don't just shake hands, ask people what they do and then move on, that's not how networking works, not if you are a good networker. So why do people think there's any value in the _'like and comment'_ posts?

"Let's grow together! Please 'Like' this post and comment below. I connect with all who comment."

To me, it's not a good way to make connections, there is no value here - almost a LinkedIn equivalent of shoving a business card under someone's nose and then walking off. We all want to share our message with more people but there's only value if those people want to hear your message otherwise it's a vanity metric. I've grown my LinkedIn network by posting and interacting, it has happened without contact collecting!

Chris Rose, Founder: Electric Innovation

However, you need to pay attention – it's very easy to mix up the two, creating a potential embarrassing situation if you send your message to the wrong person or to *'Everyone'* when it's a personal or cryptic comment to a friend on the call! This is illustrated here by *John McHale* in the following *'Chat'* message (reprinted with permission, of course).

```
11:07:00  From John McHale to Ladey Adey Publisher for YOUR Book (Privately) : That's way too many shots for both nines, Giles.
11:07:12  From John McHale to Ladey Adey Publisher for YOUR Book (Privately) : Oops !  Wrong person !!
11:07:28  From Ladey Adey Publisher for YOUR Book to John McHale (Privately) : You hit me – needs to be Giles!   Easy to do lol
```

Save 'Chat'

It's good to save the *'Chat'* to your own computer – this is easy to do. At the bottom of the *'Chat'* is *'File'* and three dots - click on the dots, and the *'Save Chat'* button appears. Click this and the *'Chat'* will be saved onto your device.

Some organisers disable the use of *'Chat'* or disable it for part of the meeting, such as when the speaker is presenting, or they will only allow *'Chat'* with everyone and not *'Private Chat'*. It's all in the hands of the organiser! If you're desperate to talk to someone in the meeting privately when locked out, use LinkedIn to message them – this is in fact, safer than the *'Private Chat!'*

Comments

Comments on social media apps are open for the public (or a limited to the group if in a private Facebook group). Anyone can respond to comments and start a new post. In some apps such as LinkedIn, the more engagement via *'Comments'* you get, the higher your social selling indicators become. The *'Comment'* has been designed for engagement and dialogue between people. Remember, if you're going to say something controversial, ensure it's not going to hurt your brand or indeed the other person. The comments can be seen by anyone in the world and are outside your control to retract!

Use *'Comment'* to support someone - your comments will mean a lot to the person who has taken the effort to post. Likes and thumbs up are OK, but the most valuable feedback to someone is via the *'Comment'*.

People post their viewpoint for a reason: to know if others agree, have an alternative point of view or are willing to contribute to the conversation.

Kim Penney **mentioned you in a comment**
"I like that analogy Ladey. I'd be very happy to visit Mo time and time again."

Do you love to hear people's success stories? I do, and...

33 Reactions • 57 Comments

You can use *'Comments'* to build your business networking by being pro-

Ladey Adey
I help ambitious business people write their books, increase their brand a...
3w • 🌐

Do you use # hastags in your posts - why and which are your favourites?
#onlinenetworking #networkinggroup #businessnetworking #businesswomen #businesswomen #networkingtips #networking #businessconnections #networkingevents #linkedintraining #authors #authorslife #womeninbusiness #writing #writeabook #publishing

🕐 10 • 23 Comments

👍 Like   💬 Comment   ↪ Share

📈 996 views of your post in the feed

active with online posts. One of my posts asked a couple of questions and received 996 views, 10 reactions and only 23 comments! BUT the quality of those comments were second to none and increased my network.

One comment (4 hours after posting) came from *Tony Walton*, who wasn't a connection of mine - he is now! In it, *Tony* referenced *Pete Davies*, Senior Director of Product Management at LinkedIn, USA.

Tony Walton • 2nd   17m ...
██████ training | social media | lead generation >>> digital ...
Only use three hashtags. No more. Straight from the horse's mouth (Pete Davies at LinkedIn).
👍   💬 • 1 Reply

Tony and I continued our online text conversation and discovered some mutual interests. Tony runs a networking group, and his comments appear in Chapter 7. Tony never expected to be mentioned in a book simply from a comment posted on a Sunday afternoon!

Only a percentage of the 996 views will look at my profile and ask to connect. I'm able to continue the conversation with those who left comments; it builds relationships, knowledge of one another and puts money in our *'networking bank account!'* This is the power of online networking, which is fun, not onerous.

Comment on the Comments

When someone comments on your post, respond to continue the conversation – ask another question. This is how posts go viral. You post or respond to a comment with a comment, share it, tag someone and a group conversation begins. All of a sudden, a stranger becomes a connection and that connection can become a friend or business buddy. The technology is all there – it only takes a click on a person's name to send an invitation to connect with one another.

Emojis

These are small digital images or icons which expresses an idea or emotion, such as the smiley face, thumbs up etc. They're often used when you've known someone a little while, although some people feel that they're unprofessional and have no place in official business communications. On social media, the rules are more relaxed, emojis are widely accepted in posts, replies and comments.

GIFs

GIF stands for Graphics Interchange Format and is an animated video file or video version of an emojis but with a bit more punch. Often a file is a 2-6 second clip from a film. Interestingly, GIFs are subject to copyright laws, but as of 2020 there are no cases of lawsuits being enforced!

Try to be selective how and when you use them. One person's humour is another person's insult!

Hashtag (#)

Hashtags (#) were created so content would be easier for people to find. The symbol # is placed in front of a word or phrase without spaces. It's a recognised system used on all social media sites. They draw attention to those interested in the topic and enable them to contribute to the conversation. Events often have hashtags linked to them so participants can find comments easily. When using a hashtag, all related comments are relayed in one place.

What is your favourite hashtag? #onlinenetworking #authors #businesswomen

You can use up to 30 hashtags, but that's a bit much - and any list which is bigger than the actual post looks like spam. Three hashtags work well and is the advice from *Pete Davis*, *"Use hashtags (we recommend no more than three) to help other members find the conversations that match their own interests."* All my future postings will be cut down to three hashtags!

If you want more eyes on your post, then hashtags will boost your message. It has been proven that posts with hashtags receive over 12% more interaction than posts without hashtags.

You can create your own hashtags very easily - choose a word or a phrase and check that it's not already being used. Use sites like Twubs or Hashtags.org to check and register your hashtag. Hashtags are often used for events and reference the name, time and place (of the event).

An interesting fact is you cannot copyright or own a hashtag like you can a website domain name, for instance. By registering a hashtag, it stakes your claim and adds the hashtag to a directory. *(I have just registered #worldonlinenetworkingday for 29th October - pop the date in your diary!)*

Hashtags are evolving, like apps and technology; they can now be used as Calls to Action, questions and to incite urgency or emotion.

For those interested in the *'hashtag genealogy'*, Twitter began the # system. The first post was in August 2007 by *Chris Messina*, a social technology expert, with his first hashtag '#barcamp'. The post asked, *"How do you feel using #for groups?"*

There is plenty of information about hashtags on the Internet, and I've referenced a couple. Interestingly, most were written a number of years ago, which would imply that we've got used to them now and they're a natural part of our online language and communications!

Leaving the Meeting

The two minutes between the end of the meeting and people leaving

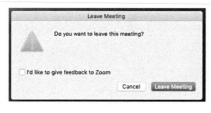

have been described as the worst and most awkward online social moments. People are unsure what to do, or manic waving takes place with a cacophony of *"Bye and Thank You"*. Make it simple – hit the *'Leave Meeting'* button and go.

Lighting Rings or Ring Lights

To see you properly you need to face the light. Lighting ring equipment previously used by the photography world are excellent to improve your home lighting. Photographers use them to give an attractive catch light on a subject's eyes, and they help to eliminate shadows. Business people use ring lights for social media posts.

They're a great idea for serious online networkers too. Place the ring light beside the computer, or fit onto the mobile phone (see References).

Mute Button

During online networking meetings, it's usually a case of *'only speak*

Ladey Adey *when you're spoken to!'* You can mute yourself, but the control of the *'Mute'* button is in the hands of the organiser as they can mute and unmute all participants simultaneously.

Name or Rename Yourself

There are two places for you to name yourself. The first is in your profile or settings, and your name will immediately appear on your screen. It's really important this features both your first and last name. How else will people be able to contact you after the meeting? Remember, your screen is a live business card.

If you don't change this name, the computer will automatically allocate you a name made up of capital letters and numbers such as ZX32NLA. If the organisers of the call have the 'waiting room' set-up, they will only let people in who have registered or who they recognise. Random letters and numbers are unrecognisable as a real person and organisers generally will not let them in!

Once an online meeting like Zoom is underway, check your name – at the bottom left of the screen under your picture (if this is not your business name check your main settings). At the very least, it should be your full name – this way people can contact you easily on LinkedIn or Facebook. Now, for the fun part, you can add your business name, a short slogan or strapline next to your name.

This name is changeable inside any meeting; you can change it to anything, so people have quite a lot of fun giving themselves superhero names. Though, I'd say don't leave it on there for the whole meeting unless people already know you really well! Others do need to be reminded of your real name.

I ensure my name is updated at each meeting to Ladey Adey,

Ladey Adey Publisher for Your Book

Publisher for YOUR Book. This serves as a reminder of who I am and what I do, and for it to be in the forefront of people's minds. I want them to think, *"Yes, Ladey will help me to write my book as she believes there's a book in everyone."* It's subliminal messaging, but think about it, your picture is on other participants' screens and it stays in front of them for the duration of the meeting (up to two hours).

'Rename' - the Easy Way

The easiest way to *'Rename'* is to go to the bottom of the screen, click on *'Participants'*, and the pop-up window appears showing you the list of people on the video call. Your name will be at the top just above the host of the meeting. Alternatively, you can click in the small dots on your picture at the top. Click the arrow next to your name and select

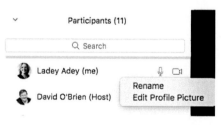

'Rename' in the dropdown menu. A box appears for your choice of name - keep it fairly short as it may cut off on other people's screens, depending on whether they are on computer, tablet or mobile. *Simple!*

Password

You can be creative when creating your password. When scheduling a call a password is automatically allocated for security. It's a password randomly chosen by the computer, once more, using a mix of letters and numbers - for example, u2YP52x. Totally unmemorable! You can change it and it's worth doing as a subliminal way of reminding people of your values or business brand.

It needs to be a short phrase or one word. Use a shortened version of your company name or a message such as *'be safe'*, *'wash your hands'* or *'the book in you'*.

The password will remain the same for every meeting you schedule until you change it. Like any password it's good practice to change it regularly, though don't forget to notify your attendees when this is done.

Posts

Nowhere else can you give your opinion as quickly and easily as on social media. It's a brilliant platform to contribute, let people know your view, pass on hints, tips and hacks, get a discussion going and even help to expand your own knowledge or gather research.

Posts are usually short, up to 300 words, including hashtags, tags and links. Recording it first and transcribing it relates to only 3 minutes of talk! A larger word count falls into the *'Article'* or *'Feature'* category and is a more formal type of writing.

When you receive a comment, *'Like'* and *'Comment'* back respond and ask further questions - it keeps the discussion going. A simple *'thanks'*, or *'I agree'*, are conversation enders.

Schedulers

By scheduling social media posts, you can write posts in your own time and decide when they should be sent out. Apps such as *Hootsuite*, *Later* and *Buffer* help to manage your time and automate regular posts across numerous platforms quickly and at a time you specify.

Screenshots

A screenshot can be your next best friend in lots of ways, so get into the habit of taking plenty! Take a screenshot of each and every meeting you attend. Online networking groups rarely issue a registration list or list of participants, but you literally have them in front of you on the screen. At the top, switch to *'Gallery View'* so you can see as many people as possible and take a screenshot. Rename the screenshot with the date and meeting title, then file. Create a folder which also includes the saved transcript of the *'Chat'*.

Use the screenshot as a reminder of who was *'in the room'*, believe me, a few weeks later, when you suddenly think, *"Oh yes, someone said..."*, but you can't remember who said it, you're able to check your files with the screenshots. The visual picture of them will trigger your memory. When someone contacts you and you can't quite place them – find them in the screen shot or search for their LinkedIn profile to jog your memory.

Sometimes the *'Chat'* is disabled by the host, so you cannot access it. Organisers may activate a Q & A screen instead, which can't be saved to an individual device. Take a screenshot of the Q & A.

If in doubt, screenshot it – you can always delete it later, but you can't recapture the online moments!

Protocol is that this screenshot is for your personal use only, so don't share it on social media (unless you've asked for permission first from each and every person). Later, follow-up with those who've left comments, they're active participants. Find them on LinkedIn or Facebook and connect. It's all part of your follow-up strategy!

The Plus Side

Louise Third, Founder: <u>**Louise Third PR Consultancy**</u>

Networking should be about respecting one another and having a genuine interest in fellow guests, and their business as well. It's also an opportunity to encourage people to learn more about our own business. While attending large networking gatherings, I have often observed a hierarchy across guests, which can make some business people feel lost, overlooked and unimportant.

A good host will make sure the VIP or keynote speaker circulates to speak to as many people as possible; when this doesn't happen, those close to the VIP will form a huddle making it very difficult to break into the conversation. I got round this on one occasion by making the effort to talk to the VIP's wife who seemed to have been left on her own. We covered a number of matters I thought she might be able to pass on to her husband. It worked.

Online networking seems to lessen the 'I'm not worthy' factor. Maybe it's because we all have the same size video box around the screen, giving a sense of equality. We can all use the *'Chat'* and *'Comment'* to give our views, as well as ask questions at any time. If one person dominates the questions, it's starkly obvious in black and white and leaves a poor impression. Online networking, well hosted, can achieve greater equality no matter your background or business experience driving the fundamental belief that everybody has value.

Best online business networking can cultivate a culture of sharing and collaborative working; competitiveness is kept at arms length. The organiser's ability to unmute individuals and enable turn taking is more equable with less opportunity for one person to dominate the meeting. There appears to

F *continued* be a democracy about the screen whereas the plus side of face-to-face networking – inspired improvisation and is not possible online.

In October 1999, I was handling the public relations (PR) for the Institute of Business Advisers (IBA) at their annual conference in Coventry. I was given the job of chaperoning the Minister, Patricia Hewitt MP, to the ladies bathroom ahead of her keynote speech. Literally relieved to have a moment in a female environment, the Minister chanced on around six senior female business advisers as she and they washed their hands. After quick introductions, we spent ten minutes discussing how we might work with the Government to get more women into starting their own businesses, and more female adviser role models. Action agreed, we dried our hands and headed back into the conference throng. A couple of years later (2003), I was covering the PR for a *Women in Enterprise* conference in Leicester where *Patricia* was due to be the guest speaker.

Strangely, my phone began to buzz at around 6am that morning, and whilst I think I'm good at PR I wasn't expecting interest from the World's media! It transpired that the previous evening on *BBC Question Time*, *Patricia Hewitt*, now Secretary of State, had openly disagreed with *Tony Blair*'s decision to go into Iraq. So, a quiet morning turned into; instant reputation management, crisis-handling, liaising with the Minister's office, liaising with my client and fielding media interviews.

Good PR relies on building relationships. The chance conversation in the Coventry Hilton, Ladies Bathroom with *Patricia Hewitt* meant I could quickly do my job to help her and her Department, as well as my client, through the media frenzy that day in Leicester. Win-Win all round.

Patricia continued her career and during that time, whenever I met her, we would remember the few minutes in the 'Ladies' and reflect on the progress we were both making in encouraging more women into business.

Obviously, online you are stuck in one place for the duration of the call, so this kind of spontaneous networking and conversation cannot happen!

Statistics

The only way to measure your social media activity is to look at statistics whenever you can - compare them and draw conclusions for your future activity. We're used to tracking on websites (via Google Analytics) to measure user activity, but it's useful to see your social media trends too.

Each social media platform has its way of doing this - number of *'Likes'*, *'Views'*, *'Comments'*, or on business pages, formal statistical information.

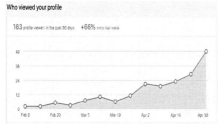

The free version of LinkedIn, for instance, gives a trend of people viewing your profile in a 90-day measured period.

It's always worth checking out the statistics to ascertain if specific social media platforms are enhancing your networking profile. By reviewing the statistical evidence, I could see that I had connected with considerably more people during the 2020 lockdown period than previously. This showed a monumental growth for my brand during this time with data that I could use to continue this trend.

LinkedIn has a Social Selling Dashboard which shows your Social Selling Index Score, measuring how effectively you are establishing your personal brand, finding the right people, engaging with insights and building relationships.

This is updated daily, here's the link: https://www.linkedin.com/sales/ssi or Click on the *'Me'* icon, view *'Profile'* and you'll find it below your top card information. Click on one of the numbers, and it will open the *'Dashboard'*.

Tags @

Tagging a person means putting the symbol @ in front of their name. The name has to be the same one they use on social media. The magic of the technology means that the name will be recognised and that person will get a notification in their social media account.

What's the benefit? It's a shortcut to contacting people. If you have a post talking about an event and you tag someone you know, they get the same information without you having to email them all the details.

> **Mark Jarvis** `Author`   1d ...
> Better business leads by unlocking the real power of your network re...
>
> Fantastic start to a Friday and the start of a new month, great to hear from Jon Davies Eddie Palmer Kerry Lummus Rob Purle Chris Rose Alex Harrington Richard Holtom Nicky Thomas ♡ Lisa Davies Catherine McHale Ana San Segundo Sheila Stamp Ladey Adey Helen Millington.
>
> Look forward to seeing you all again on Monday morning 8am

If you mention someone, it's a way to *'big them up'* - recognising that they may have a valued comment and opinion to add to the conversation. It can also be a quick means of referring one person to another. Tagging someone means they are more likely to comment on your post. It's possible to stop someone from tagging you by changing the settings in your account, though in the world of networking why would you want to do this? For me, it's a great compliment to be tagged *@ladeyadey* – so feel free to tag me in your posts, and I will comment.

Time Limit

Some apps only run for a set period of time, and close down automatically when the time has expired (especially if using the free versions) so be aware of your timing. Keep to the scheduled time, people do like to know the finish time. If it looks like the meeting is going to overrun – negotiate more time with participants. An automatic warning comes up letting

> ⚠ Remaining Meeting Time: 09:43 `Upgrade`

you know if you have a limited time and when the app will close (invariably with an option to upgrade!).

Video

To communicate, we sit in front of the computer and use the video setting. Previously, few businesses used video as part of their business. Now, we're all becoming used to and speaking to many people at once or having 1-2-1 conversations through the computer. Video is a powerful tool in engaging with our audience, and a website is now thought to be lacking if it doesn't contain a video on the home page! To quote *Nigel Botterill, 'Video is the new normal'.*

Do you have to use video? No, you can choose to have a still  photograph or just your name displayed instead – but people like to do business with real people, and video shows potential customers, and partners, the face of your business.

Be brave, and start your video for conference calls and take control of your own *'Mute'* button too.

A Painful Realisation

It pains me to say this, but the future of networking is online.

 As a prolific networker who signs up to all the groups I can, either paid or free membership, it pains me to come to this realisation. Why does this hurt? I am a people person, who wants to meet people, look them in the eye and have a handshake.

Noticeably, weekly networking events have a fundamental problem in their diversity and the chance of quality time with that one person in the room that can make a difference.

There is nothing more frustrating than sitting on a table sandwiched between someone who has a window cleaning business and someone who is a dog walker, and across the room, is the Head of HR who you are desperate to speak to. Listening to the one-minute pitch from these lovely people with only half an ear, you are focused on how to get a couple of minutes with the HR honcho only to watch your quarry hastily leave the room just before the end of the meeting.

Online networking is more focussed and disciplined and allows niche breakouts that suit everybody. The time and money saved in travelling means you can invest in being more professional online and use the time to follow up properly - and talk to that illusive head of HR!

Tim Ladd, Founder: *Red Umbrella*

Video Stop/Start

This might feel slightly misnamed, as some people think it means you leave the meeting, or it stops the main speaker. This doesn't happen – it simply means others in the group/meeting can't see you on your live video. This is an incredibly useful function, and it's a quick click with the mouse to activate it. It's great for those moments when you need to hide, such as a family member wants some attention. It's also perfect when you want to pop out for a 'cuppa'. Clicking *'Stop Video'* is good practice and avoids unsightly views or empty chairs etc. You don't have to be on view 100% of the time in a large meeting. Starting up the video again is another simple click of the mouse, this time on the *'Start Video'* (it's a toggle function).

Tips for Organisers of Online Networks

Those brave organisers who are facilitating our online networking meetings (some for the first time) so we can actively continue in business, have many strands to the job. They need to:

- 🖥 Use technology well, including allowing people in and out of the meeting, assisting participants if there are technical issues, starting on time and keeping the meeting running.
- 🖥 Ensuring the meeting delivers effective and enjoyable networking.
- 🖥 Participate as a business person themselves.

Here are some other points for organisers to consider.

End of Meeting

Hit the *'Leave for all'* button quickly to avoid a lot of embarrassed waving!

Mute Button

Currently, most organisers keep the mute button on or ask participants to keep themselves on *'Mute'* until it's time to speak. This is all good meeting etiquette. Yet, sometimes it's good to have an open mic session. People are generally considerate and try not to talk over one another. When people are listening without speaking it's called *'silent noise'*. All participants can gain a lot if the organisers are brave and not heavy-handed on the *'Mute'* button.

Managing People and Time

Invitations and notification of the event are key in ensuring people attend. Emails with links to gain entry into the event are useful, and they need to be sent out regularly, including on the day of the event – making it easier for people to join and not have to trawl through their never-emptied inbox.

It's up to the organiser how many people enter their calls (sometimes this is limited by the app they are using). How people are allowed to join the meeting is set by the organiser. This is useful to protect the meeting, so only known people can enter and stops any *'Zoombombing!'* It also lessens the disrupting effect of latecomers. Often a lockout after 10 minutes is set and this needs to be communicated to people when inviting them to the event. The downside of this is if the technology fails (it happens to us all at some point!) and a user 'drops-out' of the meeting they may have difficulty re-gaining entry.

As organisers, you have the power - the power of the *'Mute'* button and what your participants can or can't do on the call. However, there may be a conflict with using the technology securely and giving your participants the best experience you can - after all, you want them to come back, right?

Managing the call starts by having a unique ID for the meeting and requiring a password. Be savvy with the password – remember to make it relate to your meeting and your brand – rather than boring numbers!

You can make the meeting an invitation-only event and create a waiting room, so participants can't come into the meeting until you're there. For added security, you can also choose who's allowed in - anyone you are unsure of, don't let in.

You can choose if it's only you who can Screen *'Share'* and prevent what goes into the *'Chat'* etc. You can also disable someone's camera and *'Private Chat'*. Personally, if the latter were disabled I'd be less inclined to join a future meeting!

With power comes responsibility; you can lock the meeting which stops latecomers from joining and you have the ultimate control and can remove someone from the call or put them on hold. This can be done without other participants being aware – which could never be done without making a scene in a face-to-face meeting!

Online Culture

Be aware of the kind of ambience and rules you'd like to create as this sets the culture of your group. Remind participants if the meeting is being recorded and the use of the mute button etc. It's equivalent to the hospitality and fire exit information at the start of a face-to-face meeting. The best description I've heard was by *Adam Davey*, who said, *"Online culture is like the wind. You can't see it; you can feel it. It's hard to explain it, but you certainly know if it's blowing in the wrong direction!"*

Polls

These are a great way to be interactive with the participants. They provide information you may need or can be used as a fun icebreaker. Organisers need to remember to give out the results to the participants before the meeting closes. Here are some examples from the first Lincoln Business Club online meeting.

Raised Hand

The idea behind this function is to show the organiser that you wish to speak and be taken off *'Mute'*. There's a *'Raise Hand'* icon at the bottom of the screen. Click on it and the icon will appear

at the top of the screen. Unfortunately, it's so small it can get lost on the screen. If there are lots of participants, with screens on multiple pages there is very little chance of it being seen. A better chance of being noticed is to put up a physical hand or comment in the *'Chat'*.

Ladey Adey Publisher for Your Book

Recording

In consideration of people's privacy and data protection law, organisers

need to tell their participants if they're recording the session. Best practice says this needs to be pointed out at the start of EVERY meeting along with any information of its use, such as in a membership area, closed Facebook group etc.

What happens to all these recordings? Does anyone actually listen to them after a month? I imagine the recordings eating up the ether! It's this kind of thought, which wakes me up in the middle of the night (not)!

Waiting Room

Switching on the *'Waiting Room'* in your settings means that participants have to wait until you manually admit them into the room. As mentioned previously, if you don't recognise a name, or it's made up of letters and numbers (XJ32NN) don't let them in. It could be a scam or a *Zoombomber*! Remind your participants the importance of using their real names when sending out the reminder link.

Webinars and Large Conference Calls

It's helpful to have others to assist with managing a webinar or large conference call which involve a large number of people. This way, questions to the speaker can be noted and easily replied to, keeping the event running in a smooth and professional manner. Consider asking others to help, rather than doing everything yourself.

Conference and Other Software

I've had limited exposure to *Remo*, which is a piece of software used by *Graham Todd*, who hosts a virtual pub for *Spaghetti Besties* and *Felicity Francis*, for some *Talk Networking* meetings. It's a fascinating experience; it's as though you're at an actual conference. Participants find a table and chat with the five other attendees on that table. They can swap to another table where there's an empty chair, have conversations with those on that table or listen to the organiser or speaker. The software hosts up to 1,000 participants and it's easy to use.

On the topic of getting the best out of online networking, *Jo Ciriani*, *Director of Spaghetti Agency*, has put together a great blog: Online Networking Events – The 'New Normal?' (see References).

As I finalise this book, with only 36 hours away from going to print, I am contacted by *Anne Lauvige* via LinkedIn who has heard that I was writing this book and she asked, had I put anything in about Speed Networking?

It turns out the *Anne* is the facilitator for a digital platform called *B-Connect-D*. This app makes speed networking possible online and I for one can't wait to try it! It enables one-to-one networking to happen. Anne sorts out all the technology reaching out to your networks offering a new and different networking experience. This is speed networking online with benefits, such as not being in the environment with too many voices talking at once as associated with the in-person version.

Final Technology Thoughts

We're now in a period of history where resistance to the Internet, apps and video calls has been dissipated due to the necessity of communicating with each other during lockdown. I enjoyed researching the online technology and how best to use it. This chapter is as comprehensive as I can make it, if you know of an omission, error or a brand new app that has come onto the market since the publication of this book, let me know *(ladey@ladeyadey.com)* so I can update this chapter in the next edition.

Mike Luxford - Founder of MLCS Ltd, The Hosted VoIP Company

Ladey (LA): Mike, were you surprised to see Video and video conferencing become so popular?

Mike Luxford (ML): There was a growing trend for more video and 2030 was the anticipated year for it to become more prevalent in business. Now, this is the reality for many – 10 years early. It's not just working from home, but remotely; it's about being able to work where you are, on whatever device is to hand. Due to Covid-19 and lockdown, video has taken off and I guess the controls have been relinquished.

Previously people said, *"No, I can't do this"*. Now, consumers are impatient. They are at home and start asking different questions such as:

- How can I do this video conferencing?
- How can I keep in touch with people?
- How do I make it happen today?

LA: What Equipment is needed to access Online Networking?

ML: Devices can vary; you need a desktop (*Windows* or *MAC*), laptop, tablet or mobile. If the device has no inbuilt video camera, or it's of poor quality, then an external USB camera is a great option. A headset is another option to improve sound quality.

Note: If you are using older equipment you should expect that you might have issues for various reasons. In particular, Windows 7 is now at end-of-life, so you either need to upgrade the software or it's time for a new device. Windows 7 is also a security risk now, so for that reason alone you need to upgrade.

LA: How do I join the meeting?

ML: Generally speaking, if you are invited to participate in a video call the link will be sent to you. Simply click the link or follow the instructions. Instructions often detail how to hear and see during the meeting. Some have the option to use a telephone to dial-in for the audio. If the audio and video do not automatically start, check the instructions or look for the toolbar on-screen as sometimes you have to *'click'* on the video icon and the audio icon to activate them. Invest in a good headset with a microphone.

LA: I've found that if the video conferencing doesn't start up right away, it's always worth checking the email, if there is a problem at the organiser's end they sometimes issue a new link! What do I need to remember to do?

ML: I am not an expert in video meeting etiquette, but the following seem perfectly acceptable rules:

- Get your webcam set up so that you are looking directly into it, we really don't want to see your nasal foliage!
- If using a mobile device, use a stand so that the camera isn't wobbling around.
- Try to stay still and don't fiddle with things and stay focused on the camera.
- Lighting from the front is best as backlighting can turn you into a silhouette (but often we have to settle for the best we can manage) – you can always experiment for yourself to see what works best on a video call with yourself.

LA: What about the Internet connection?

ML: This is going to be the Achilles heel of video meetings, for several reasons. Internet speeds range from none at all, woeful, to the nirvana of full fibre (up to 64Mb throughput). The UK's average Internet speed figure seems to be around 50Mbps download and 7Mbps upload. Here are a few typical technical details on Internet speeds:

- Basic ADSL broadband speeds are quoted as up to 24Mbps download and up to 1.5Mbps upload.

✍ Superfast broadband speeds are quoted as up to 80Mbps download and up to 20Mbps upload.

Generally speaking, the faster your upload speed the better your video experience will be. For Zoom to work, they recommend a minimum download speed of 1Mbps and upload speed of 0.8Mbps. You can see that people with basic ADSL connection and very slow connections are going to struggle with video before they even start!

LA: Is there any time of the day when it operates best?

ML: On what was a normal day with most people out at work, and the kids at school, assuming you had that 7Mbps upload speed all would work well. In the UK, around 3:30pm when the schools are out, you would see a decline in speed which would result in more frozen screens, jerky video and voice plus video becoming unsynchronised.

However, with everyone at home (all of the neighbours at home as well) you can expect that your Internet speed will be slower than normal just because so many people and devices are accessing the Internet at the same time. I just counted how many devices I have in my house of 4 adults – there are over 20 devices! If you start to multiply that out in your street, you can start to understand the huge demands being placed on the Internet and why it's running slower than usual.

Note: Some consumer Internet connections have data download limits with penalty charges if you exceed the data limit. It's only small additional cost to go unlimited.

LA: Are there any tweaks, which will improve the Internet experience?

ML: If your device has an Ethernet port, plug it into your Internet router (if possible). Wired is always superior to wireless. If you don't have enough ports on your router, you can buy a device called a switch, which increases the number of available ports. A4-port Gigabit switch costs approx. £15.

Perhaps you are nowhere near the router and have to use Wi-Fi. Wi-Fi has several challenges, which can be easily overcome.

Keep the router up high and in the open. A common mistake is keeping the router under the TV; the signal cannot escape the Lounge (never mind anywhere else in the house).

Most people just use the pre-set Wi-Fi settings, this means every device in the house connects to the same Wi-Fi. If everyone is trying to use the Wi-Fi whilst you make a video call, it's likely to receive poor quality of call. There are things you can do to combat this.

Wi-Fi uses two bandwidths 2.4Ghz and 5Ghz, your devices normally decide which is the best one for them. The 2.4Ghz bandwidth has a longer reach than the 5Ghz one. You can manually change these if you want to and see if transmission improves.

Visit the Internet router management page (they should all have a simple step by step guides) and create a new Wi-Fi network with a new password. This means your device is no longer competing with everything else for Wi-Fi bandwidth.

Or, you could configure 'lock-outs' on certain devices (such as games consoles) so that they cannot access bandwidth during specific hours. However, it's important to be aware that some apps like *Snapchat* can generate huge amounts of traffic too.

Wi-Fi signal strength can be adversely affected by many things: plants, people, shiny surfaces, including tiles, water, microwave ovens, thick stone walls and foil backed plasterboard. Water absorbs the signal and shiny surfaces reflect it, essentially confusing the signal.

Using powerline Wi-Fi extenders can lessen these issues. These use your mains wiring to deliver signal coverage via local repeaters, which are plugged into mains sockets. You may require more than one unit but these do work well, even providing wired connections on some models. Wi-Fi extenders only work across a single mains fuse board therefore if you have an office with separate fuse board it won't extend there.

Another option is to use MESH Wi-Fi units, which connect together using Wi-Fi and boost the signal in the local area. You must ensure that each unit has full signal strength otherwise the local Wi-Fi signal won't be good enough. This system requires trial and error in the set-up but they do work well.

LA: What about 4G and mobile connections?

ML: If your Internet connection is poor or saturated by users, there is another option assuming you can get a 4G signal; dependent on your network and coverage at your location. The 4G capabilities will also be subject to the number of devices connecting where you are.

EE claims to be the fastest 4G network, boasting speeds of between 20-90Mbps download and 8-50Mbps upload - comparable to Superfast Internet). This is great if they cover your area!

You'll need 4G data on your plan for this to work and you'll need to ensure you have a big enough limit that you don't incur extra charges. *Note: Some consumer Internet connections have data download limits with penalty charges if you exceed the data limit. It is only small additional cost to go unlimited.*

You could use your 4G enabled phone placed to get maximum signal strength and tether your PC device to it. However, a better longer-term option may be to buy a 4G router (cost approx. £65) and then add an unlimited data-only 4G SIM (cost approx. £25/month on 12month contract). Position the router so it gets the best 4G signal and then connect via Wi-Fi to the router and thus out to the Internet. These 4G routers also offer wired ports.

It's pertinent to mention that a one-hour zoom call will require around 0.5Gbps of data, so a 4Gb data limit equates to 8 hours of video calls.

LA: What is the difference between Office and Home connections?

ML: Perhaps the biggest difference between office and home (business and consumer) is security and something called, *Quality of Service.*

Quality of service means ensuring that voice and video quality are high. This can be difficult to achieve on *'consumer'* internet connections because the providers have a very different idea as to what is the most important, for instance, Sky think it's Sky content, not your business or leisure choice.

Quality of service also includes security. It has been proven that as consumers we are far more lax with personal details, we willingly surrender important personal data on a daily basis to the likes of Amazon, Facebook, Apple and Zoom without a second thought. Who actually reads the terms and conditions? No one. Well, very few - we want it and we want it now. There is a well-documented case of an app whose terms and conditions stated you would handover your first born to the developers and countless thousands of people downloaded it. In business networking, business rules apply. Is it secure? Is my business data safe? Who keeps the information and where? At home we are more likely to go with *'try it and see'*.

In business, if a video call continually drops in and out it's frustrating and potentially you could lose business, especially if the client, or you, needs to repeat themselves. Also, many online networking events have a lock-out policy on late arrivals, so if you drop out of the event halfway through you may not be able to rejoin. At home, if you are calling Granny, you can simply hang up and try again.

If you need business grade at home then apart from installing a dedicated business Internet connection, the simplest solution is to subscribe to something called an SD-WAN. This is a very technical solution that delivers; encrypted security, quality of service, management and speed improvements to even the most basic of Internet connections. As it's a managed service, all you have to do is plug in a couple of cables and turn the power on; the rest is done for you. Your business traffic is identified and prioritised over and above everything else. It costs just £20 a month on a rolling three month contract, which can be scaled up to support multiple internet connections operating as one, so you get increased speeds plus resilience, because if one connection fails it just keeps on working.

LA: Do you think there will be an appetite for more home working arrangements?

ML: It's funny how quickly people adapt and change. Individuals are finding out which times for working is best for them. I know some will have to go back to nine to five working hours at an office or factory but many people have discovered that they can work when it suits them without a loss in effectiveness and productivity.

LA: Can this change the culture of how we work?

ML: Absolutely. The genie is out of the bottle, isn't it? Although we haven't really been tested in terms of a normal working day as yet. However, if you do your normal working week, in three days, what is the issue? As long as the boss can see you're actually working and there's all sorts of tools to check this. Why not embrace it as a new normal or modern work/life balance?

Note: Prices/Costs mentioned are accurate in 2020.

Your Online Networking Success

The successful Networkers I know,
the ones receiving tons of referrals and feeling
truly happy about themselves, continually put
the other person's needs ahead of their own.
Bob Burg

Business networking is the life-blood to every business or profession at every level, and there's a myriad of ways of doing this, from mentoring 1-2-1, to the organised monthly meeting (and everything in between). Let's remind ourselves of the three key motivators for business networking:

- 🖥 To find new clients.
- 🖥 To meet with like-minded people, and keep updated.
- 🖥 To attract partnerships and contribute to the business world.

Choosing Your Networks

In life, there are choices to be made. It's the same in business and particularly with networking. It's impossible to attend them all and you need to find the ones which suit you and your business. Choose between five-ten groups you want to engage with on a regular basis, be known and recognised within those networks. Ultimately, business networking only works if YOU are active and engaged. Time, energy and money are always in short supply, so there's a need to be strategic when working out the best network to attend – offline and online. You need to decide:

- 🖥 Who would you like to meet?
- 🖥 Why do you want to meet them?

⌨ Where do they network?

⌨ What do you want to achieve from the networking group?

⌨ How is your contribution to the network going to benefit others?

The answers will give you a clear guide to knowing your best network.

Choosing Your Network

At networking meetings, I often ask business people *"What are your networking goals?"* In return, I'm usually met with a blank look. They've identified a need to do some networking, plucked up courage to walk through the door and have settled on a group that they like. Yet, they aren't exactly clear what they are trying to achieve. Picking the right meetings and using the right tactics is the key to networking success.

Networking leaders will tell us; *"networking works"*, *"you're selling through the room"*, *"you've got to give it time"* and BNI's *"Givers Gain®"*. While these are true, networking doesn't just magically work because you keep showing up. It is vital to have a clear picture of what your goals are in order to choose the right networking groups for you and to make the most of your investment (time and money).

The first question to ask is; *"Are my target customers at this meeting?"* If they are, you will be working to build trust and make sure they understand what you do including how and why they should buy from you. If your direct customers aren't in the room, then you need to sell or market *"through the room"*, to ensure people can explain what you do to someone else!

A lot of trust-building happens outside the room. Your networking plan should be 40% preparation, 20% meetings and 40% follow-up. The 40-20-40 continuum is a good guide to follow. The key to networking success is choosing the right meetings and using the right tactics.

David O'Brien: _Business Doctors Lincolnshire & Rutland_

Your Ideal Customer and Avatar

It's useful here to think of your ideal customer and create an avatar of that person. You need to create an image in your mind of your ideal customer, giving them a name and even finding a picture on the Internet of what you think they would look like.

I join networking groups which attract businessmen and women as they are my ideal customer for the writing of business books, consequently building their brands and setting them on a speaker's trajectory.

My ideal customer when looking for contributions to a children's author anthology is parents, grandparents and schools. I can only attract the children's contributions through networking in groups containing mothers, fathers and those who can give referrals to their personal networks such as teachers, governors, scout/guide leaders and family members.

Depending on your service or product, your ideal customer (or those who have contact with your ideal customer) will network in different places. It's your job to find where they are and engage appropriately with them to build up trust and rapport.

If you're in the wrong network, then you are wasting your time. For instance, someone selling pillows and candles needs a *'feminine'* networking group, and someone whose business is fitness for busy dads needs a *'masculine'* networking group. It might sound obvious, but it's surprising how often business people are trying to break into a mismatched market, then wonder why they can't get any contacts or sales leading them to proclaim that, *"Networking doesn't work"*.

Sometimes, people stay with a network due to misguided loyalty - they genuinely like the people in the group, and it has become a social function. If your business is not receiving an obvious return, increasing your bottom line, leading you to attract more customers or clients, or improving your knowledge or social life – then find another networking group. Online networking groups are easier to pop in and out of. Somehow there's less peer pressure to turn up every time!

For each product, service or market you have, you may need a new avatar to describe your ideal customer.

Anti-Avatar

This is the customer you'd rather not have – the one whose calls you dread, and when you see their email in your inbox, your heart sinks! They're not bad people; there has simply been a mismatch between their values and expectations and yours. It might be that you took them on as a customer because you needed a sale (possibly offering a discount to secure it), rather than looking deeper, having confidence in yourself, your services and price point.

The good thing is these types of clients will teach you more about your business, the processes, procedures and practices than any other experience can - albeit the hard way! I've learned more about contracts via this route than I expected. Work out your *'anti-avatar'*, in addition to your avatar, so you know who will benefit from your expertise and those who would be better served by going to another company.

For my publishing business, I need to have clients who are social media savvy for the marketing of their book and are willing to have mentoring calls via Zoom. These are two of my non-negotiables for taking on a new client to ensure I can serve them well.

Overall, you need to know who you want to have as a customer. As *Mike Garner* says, *"Knowing who you are NOT selling to is just as important as attracting those who you'd like to sell to. Avoid those you don't want to work with."*

Commit to Connect

Making the initial connection with people is hard for a lot of people, but is actually the easy part. Fostering relationships and helping them to grow over time takes a lot of patience and hard work.

If you can commit to building not just the number of relationships but the quality of those relationships then any kind of networking you do is going to be a lot more successful.

Bryan Cohen, <u>Best Page Forward</u>

The Six Degrees of Separation

It's said, there are only six degrees of separation between you and the person sat next to you on the train, or chatting with over the Internet! The theory is that we are six or fewer social connections away from one another, and you can actually connect to anyone within six steps. You may have even played the 'Six Degrees of Kevin Bacon' game!

Online connections may decrease the number of steps from six. It's certainly given us a more 'contracted' world - there's more connectedness between humans than ever before. If we're connected in many different ways, it follows that some connections can be those of a timely nature; people flow in and out of our lives and appear at auspicious moments.

My favourite referral story is when I became reconnected with *Kathryn Colas* by a mutual friend, *Kris Cavanaugh Castro (Begin to Shift based in the USA)*. Kris spoke the wonderful words, *"I think you two should link up as you have some things in common and could help one another!"* It worked out to be one of those circular moments. *Kathryn* and I had met and spoken many years back at a conference. The timing was right; *Kris* knew something about me, which *Kathryn* didn't, as we'd lost touch. Now, fast-forward two years, I'm *Kathryn's* publisher, and her book, *How to Survive Menopause Without Losing your Mind*, was launched in March 2020.

Chris Rose, author and engineer who loves to turn ideas into products pointed out the mathematician, *Paul Erdös* numbers theory, to me. Using *Erdös'* numbers, *Chris* could be connected indirectly to *William Ewart Gladstone*, former British Prime Minister by three handshakes! *Chris* went on to make the following point, *"Connections and connections-to-connections matter. The trick is to turn those tenuous links into genuine connections. That's what networking is all about, though I admit William Gladstone isn't likely to be available for a chat any time soon."*

What's your six-degrees of separation story? We do need to connect and to connect others to one another. This means taking some action, perhaps working together, socialising together and taking time to get to know one another. One of the first things to do is, check out someone's biography, profile and people in their circle of influence to find the connections! Are you and I connected? What are the six people of separation between us? Contact me and let me know.

Know Your Ideal Customer

Simon Goodchild, Founder T4S
(Traffic for Sales)

Think of your favourite book, film or TV character, I bet you know them well? You know:

Their history, their family and friends, where they work, what triggers them, what they wear, where they go their favourite foods, drinks, activities, where they go on holiday, what they read, how they relax, what social media they use (or don't), what car they drive, where they live, what they earn, how they spend their spare cash, what they love and hate.

This is how you must know your ideal customer, give them an avatar. You must be able to describe your perfect customer and know everything about them. Even give them a name.

By knowing everything about them, you know where to find them (online or in real life) to offer them your product or service. You know which groups they belong to - you know where they look. How do they spend their time and where do they get their information from - Facebook, or Instagram, or LinkedIn or reading newspapers?

By understanding your customer you can strategise and sell to them. Without this client research you are simply guessing. Doing your research means you can confidently invest in the most appropriate advertising, Facebook Ads, influencer marketing, business networking or an insert in a local newspaper.

The right advertisement on the right platform saves time and money and gets the sale. So, understand your target audience and then engage.

F continued

Engaging with your ideal customer

Working out your pitch and marketing messages can be done with confidence when you know your customer's triggers.

This quote by *Blair Warren* summarises perfectly your tactics needed for engagement with your perfect customers:

'People will do anything for those who encourage their dreams, justify their failures, allay their fears, confirm their suspicions, and help them throw rocks at their enemies.'

Apply *Warren's* five points in your marketing messages and you will have very satisfied and happy customers.

Your Biography (Bio)

You want to be noticed and stand out, and you want people to relate to you. This is what your bio is all about – YOU – but it's also your calling card. Your online business card is on view in so many online places that it's easy to forget about it! Regardless of the platform, it needs to be up-to-dated regularly and be *'on brand'*.

Business people spend more time designing their business card which is a disposable item than they do their bio, which is constantly being viewed. Even your name on a video can be customised to maximise the opportunity of repeatedly letting people know what it is you do. My video name is *'Ladey Adey – Publisher of Your Book'*. It's the constant message I want to put out there. When there's more room, I add my logo with the question – *'Is there a book inside YOU?'*

Bios are a way of never missing an opportunity to get in front of people - consciously and unconsciously! The most memorable ones use emotive language and leave the reader curious about you.

How do others decide if they want to connect with you? They check out your profile, which holds your bio, and listen to what you say and how you say it. They also look at your comments and interactions with others and how you respond directly to them.

Your bio is also the root of your elevator pitch as it gives the heart of what you do and why you do it. Often, it's part of a media pack or speaker information, which people use when they introduce you, and they may want to know your background and achievements.

Think of your bio like a series of sound bites. Create different types of bios – a humorous one, one full of quotes, a straight one, and remember to update regularly.

A bio can range from a short book to a one-liner - and anything in between. It needs to give people some knowledge of you, your history and your personality. It needs to be enough to make people think, *"Oh, I'm curious about you - and yes, I'd like to know more."* This way a conversation can begin at some point. This communication (if it occurs) builds your network and relationships, so you become their client or they become yours, or you refer each other to your networks.

The Purest Form of Marketing

Networking has always been a part of business, but in many ways for me, it's felt like a necessary evil. That was, until I found what I consider *'a right way'* to do it. Networking fits for me nicely in the 'awareness' stage of marketing - letting people know you exist in the first place. What it does beyond a click on a site (a view or an advert) however, is create something far more meaningful: actual human connection. It's low pressure, but high touch.

The point here is when you look at your own business, particularly in the Business to Business sector, it can often feel like your customers are also those who are your friends, or have been recommended by someone. This magic here makes it the purest form of marketing, and also part of a process that doesn't feel like marketing at all: it's just a need which has been satisfied.

Whether it's online or in the real world, networking will always continue to be vital for how marketing is done - that is, until the robots take over!

Joe Glover, Founder: *The Marketing Meet-up*

Writing Your Bio

Ultimately, the feel you get from a bio determines whether a person is somebody you feel you can trust, whether they seem like somebody you would like very much to spend some time with. Do you think, *'I want to give my business to this person?'* This is what you want to create for others to read.

Adding something unusual or unexpected often creates a spark of concentration. It could be, *"My name is ... and I'm a heavy metal fan. I live off the grid in rural Lincolnshire with a cantankerous drummer."* If your hobby is sailing you'd say, *"When I'm not dodging icebergs you'll find me sailing the Internet and making your social media count."*

You can talk about your family - having boisterous sons and daughters who actively lead you astray! Or, that you had to learn business principles and build a business without doing stuff which might embarrass your mother or your grandmother.

I use the phrase, *"When life threw a whole load of bananas at me, I had to pivot, switch my life around and start a new business."*

Like all copy advertising, all writing on your business and your bio needs to be interesting. It will be referenced by others and used by them to ascertain your brand and worth.

Your first foray into writing a bio might have been a curriculum vitae (CV). The whole purpose of a CV is to get you through the door to an interview. The whole purpose of the bio is to get you through the door to have a conversation with a prospective client or partner.

Tell them about your life. If you keep it very straight: my business is..., my business mission is..., my qualifications are..., my skills are..., it may sound very 'salesy'. Does it inspire and stand out amongst your competitors?

Your bio needs to scream, *"Look at me - engage with me. Don't go to anyone else you don't need to, because I've got everything you need. I'm different, I pay attention to your needs and I've that unique selling quality you must have to make your life more fulfilling and you can't live without it."*

Be inspired by looking at other people's bios and identify any phrases you like; customise these and make them uniquely yours.

Be Curious

I called my networking group, *The Curious Marketing Club* as this sums up everything about me; my view on life and how I feel marketing needs to be conducted. As children, we have a natural curiosity but adults get fed up quickly and tell youngsters to stop asking questions. I was always that kid at school - always in trouble for asking too many questions; it's even on my report card as a criticism!

My mum, my greatest supporter said, *"That's how she learns"*. Without this, I'd never have begun a marketing career - originally I studied engineering! Networking is a huge part of marketing and the more curious you can be, the easier it is and the more enjoyable it is.

It was already in the pipeline to take my network online but the lockdown situation brought this forward. I wanted to bring together different industries and have a crossover of expertise. My differential is that it's all about mindset and to be naturally curious about one another and our businesses.

When conducting business online, it is necessary to be as natural as possible, so you are the same on screen as off screen. I see some people behaving in a robotic way, talking in the third person and talking in a language that they would never use in any other situation by being on a computer screen.

I've also noticed that many people start with the pitch and forget about the key things you need in order to build a relationship - listening and allowing the other person to talk. This is where the best information lives; we need to be curious about other people, their challenges, their current situation and how they feel about it all. Not everyone you speak to will want to buy from you so you want to make a good impression and be memorable - you never know - they may know someone that is in need of your services!

Charlie Whyman, *The Curious Marketing Club*

If you write a blog or an article, your bio needs to go at the end along with links EVERY Time. Don't assume people know about you (they don't!) or that they don't want to know about you (they do!).

How long should your bio be? It can depend on how long an average person's attention span before they zone out is or it can depend on the character length allowed in a profile box.

Bios increase your visibility on the Internet, feeding your SEO ratings and making you memorable in people's hearts and minds too! Here's a fun check: type your name into Mr Google and find out what comes up. I've an unusual name which helps, so when I do this exercise, I find 4,010 pages for my name and 236 video results.

All platforms or apps - LinkedIn, Twitter, Facebook, Pinterest, Skype, Instagram, Amazon, Networking group pages and membership pages, start off with a profile to complete. Use it well, and include a real picture, and not the standard avatar. Skype call their profile a 'mood message'. Anytime you can give your message – take advantage of it!

Make Your Bio Powerful

A tip from my mentor, *Mike Kim* is, *"In your bio add, 'It breaks my heart when...'".* What frustrates you in your industry? For me, it breaks my heart when I hear of people having a garage full of unsold books. These are books which are not on Amazon, as they don't have an ISBN number. These authors think they are a published author but all they have is a printed book, not a published one - there is a difference!

Liven up your bio story by putting in this phrase, *"When I'm not doing... (add your main business activity), then you will find me... (add an interesting unexpected fact here)."*

You can write your bio in either the first or third person. When writing in the first person, you use 'I' statements, I say, *"I am an author first and a publisher second."* It sounds informal and relaxed. Whereas using the third person is more official and uses your name instead of I. For example, *"Ladey is an author first and a publisher second."*

Be creative and use emotive language such as, *"I'm constantly amazed when..."* or, *"What makes my blood boil is ..."* Notice the number of places your profile appears; you never know where your next customer is going to come from or who is looking at you - and being online opens a window to a continually watching world!

Use your bio to give a strong viewpoint appropriate to your industry. It's been said, *"If you don't have a viewpoint, you're a follower, not a leader!"* Which do you want to be?

Here's an example of one of the funniest LinkedIn profiles I've seen:

all the boxes say, *"Blabalblabla"* (who hasn't wanted to say that at times?) BUT, it fits because this bio reflects the brand and message from its owner. Curiously though, when I approached this business person he'd forgotten writing this in his *'About'*, *'Specialities'* and *'Experience'* sections of his profile. He was slightly embarrassed and asked not to be identified! It still amused me, so I wanted to use it to show you, as an example– he gave his permission for it to be shown for this purpose.

The Follow-Up

Follow-up means just that – continuing a conversation with a business person you've just met or spoken to at a meeting.

In every meeting you'll have met someone who you want to talk further with. It might be something they said in their elevator pitch that resonated with you, something you want to pass onto them or ask them, and someone you genuinely want to develop a business relationship with. If you come away from a meeting not wanting to speak with or meet a single person ever again – it's time to move on and go to a different networking group. Assuming you do want to talk to members, it's not a time for shyness. Synergy is always at play. If you have a fatalistic outlook, you may conclude there was a reason you were both in that room or on that Zoom call, precisely at that time and on that day.

So, make the most of the initial connection with the follow-up.

It needs to be done quite soon after the meeting. If you leave it a couple of weeks or longer, that person will have forgotten the conversation and possibly give themselves a headache trying to remember you. This is not personal; think how many people can you remember from their elevator pitch you heard last month?

Follow-up can be great fun. You both have something in common; you have just attended the same meeting and have exchanged details. People will take your call, answer your email, and arrange a 1-2-1 online or face-to-face. It's time to be genuine and interested in knowing more about them and their business. It's not a question of opening the door, picking up the phone and using the follow-up to direct sell to them. Remember the long game!

The follow-up is about building and maintaining your own network. Be selective on whom you contact. It's a strategic and deliberate action.

This isn't only for new prospective business people you want to get to know; it's also a timely reminder to keep up-to-date with your existing contacts and an efficient way to get in touch with them.

If you choose not to follow-up after each meeting, be aware your competitor will be making those connections, building up rapport, and they will beat you to that next contract, partnership, referral or sale!

Follow-up can be motivated from other things you notice about a fellow business person just by looking at the screen background, what is on the wall, or types of books on their bookshelf etc.

A final point on following-up is summed up in this quote from *Michelle Moore*, author of *Selling Simplified*. She says, *"Not following-up with your prospects is the same as filling up your bathtub without first putting the bath plug in the drain."*

No-Show

Having booked a 1-2-1 and sent through a Zoom call invitation, you need to prep for the meeting in the same way as if it was an in-person meeting. It might be that this is set up on your Zoom account or the person you're meeting might prefer it to be set up on an account of their choice. Either way, there's a unique link which is used to access the video call.

Here's a personal plea to everyone using virtual meetings – if you can't make it, let the other person know. Waiting for someone to turn up and having a *'no-show'* wastes time, is frustrating and damaging to the relationship when there's no explanation given. Invariably, one party has to chase around to find out if you're coming to the meeting. Give the same respect to unavoidable cancellations of online meetings as you would to an in-person meeting.

A relationship killer when asking a person why they missed a meeting is to receive the response, *"Sorry, I forgot!"*

Breaking Barriers

I've been deaf in my left ear since birth and have about 10-15% hearing in that ear overall. Over the years, I've developed strategies to pick up what is being said in a face-to-face meeting but the most I can 'hear' is about 50%. This increases if a person looks directly at me or I am sitting at the front near to the presenter and there's no background noise.

The difference using online video-conferencing such as Zoom is transformational. I wear headphones so I can have the volume as high as necessary and background noise is cut out. I set the view to 'speaker' mode so I can always see their full face. As people talk one at a time, I can lip-read easier; I can see the lip and mouth movements, which aids my hearing. Even the breakout rooms work very well.

I now catch about 90% of what is being said; so online networking is a boon for me - and others who have hearing problems. Online networking has increased the number of potential clients to my training and coaching business.

Bev Thorogood, *Floresco Training & Coaching*

The Referral

The ultimate compliment and best introduction is the referral - either giving or receiving one. The best part of networking, and there's nothing nicer, is to receive a call or email saying that a mutual contact has referred you to them. It means someone you know has understood enough about your business to tell another person you're good, and they trust you enough, that they're willing to pass on your details. It's the equivalent to word of mouth advertising and is priceless.

This is a natural way of conducting business and building networking relationships and much better than saying to someone, *"Can you give me their email?"* Ask instead for an introduction.

When you like a product or service, you *'wax lyrical'* about it to anyone who'll listen. You might talk about how great this product is or how great a film or book is to your friends and family – you'll say, *"You MUST try/watch/read this."* Imagine somebody's so impressed with your services or products that they can't help themselves and enthusiastically talk about you to their networks.

Passing business in this way is centuries old. My friend *Sheila Stamp, Travel Counsellor*, knew I needed some public insurance so I could run a workshop at an event. She referred me to *Melanie Jackson, ARC Broker Services*, who had exactly the policy I needed. *Melanie* goes the extra mile in her relationship building with her clients. Out of the blue, on a grey, lockdown day, I received a card from her in the post which contained sunflower seeds and an invitation to plant them and be in her fun competition for growing the largest sunflower.

This is going the extra mile. Thinking *'outside the box'* and bringing kindness to your clients is when *'referral marketing'* goes into *'relationship marketing'* and brings huge benefit to those businesses who make this part of their networking strategy.

Viral Referrals

We love it when posts, videos and pictures go viral (just think of *Captain Sir Tom Moore*). Suddenly thousands know about our business, brand or something about us. This can be done by following-up on links, sharing them, then creating more, with others passing the information onto everyone on their list.

Relationship Marketing Online

Mark Jarvis,
Founder: Referral Partner Community

As a specialist in *'Relationship, or referral marketing'*, I'm often asked what this term actually means. It's very easy for each of us to understand what we do in our own business, but trying to explain it to someone else can be tricky.

Let's define the term *'Relationship or Referral Marketing'* in as simple a way as possible. Relationship, or referral marketing is a business strategy to attract new customers through a process of building relationships, which results in a flow of personally recommended business.

If relationship marketing is about creating a flow of business referrals, why do business people settle for waiting for referrals to happen? The simple answer is, they don't have a marketing plan for referrals, which seems rather strange particularly as every business owner acknowledges the value of referrals.

Let me pop this idea in your head, imagine yourself reviewing your last 12 months in business and when looking back you note that you have doubled the number of referrals you received and that each one of those referrals resulted in an ideal client. What would your bottom line look like in 12 months time if you achieved this?

That's all very well, but let's bring this back to the scenario we are discussing today, and that is online meetings. Earlier I mentioned that relationship marketing is about creating a flow of personally recommended business and this starts with a pipeline, a pipeline of people. Joining an online meeting is very similar to a face-to-face meeting or networking event. The same truths hold, be true to your values and don't sell.

F continued *Theodore Roosevelt* once said *"I don't care how much you know until I know how much you care".* If we transfer this concept into a meeting, the premise is: *'I don't care how good you think you are, if I don't think you care I won't buy into you'*. And just to be clear, that's not buy from you that's buy into you. Relationship marketing is a tactical strategy: meetings within that strategy (whether online or face-to-face) are a tactic to grow your network.

Now, more than ever, it's not what we know, neither is it who we know, by far the most important aspect of relationship marketing is how **well** we know people and how well they know us. It's not how well they know what we do – I can testify to this because I know people don't care what I do!

How can I make my meetings a more effective tactic within my relationship marketing strategy? Simply be yourself and show that you care, be interested in others and show you have the interests of others at heart.

Zig Ziglar once said, *"Help enough people get what they want and they will help you get what you want."* If you are not yet getting what you want, perhaps you're not helping enough people get what they want.

When joining in with an online meeting, my top tips are:
- Be yourself.
- Listen to others.
- Don't be distracted.
- Be in the meeting and not elsewhere.
- Know what you want to say and why you want to say it, (not because it sells your product or service but because it informs people about how you help).
- Be prepared to follow-up.

The final point, and the one to my mind, which is the most important - make sure that you follow-up. Not trying to promote your product or service but simply to help someone, make a connection and begin the relationship journey.

Meetings, whether online or face-to-face form part of our relationship marketing strategy and the way that we begin filling our *'relationship pipeline'. Note: Different to the sales pipeline!*

My friend and fellow author, *Glenn Salter* (his pen name is *Simon Fairfax*) posted a note in *ALLi* (*Alliance of Independent Authors*). He spoke about his experience being interviewed on an independent radio station, and generously gave the link for other authors to contact the broadcasters at *www.chatandspinradio.com*.

I was one of many authors who took up this information and passed this onto other authors. This is the start of viral referrals as there's the possibility to reach hundreds of people as we passed on this information.

Buyer Beware (Would I lie to you?)

I was having a chat with *Neil Jones*, an HR and Mental Health Consultant who mentioned to me the ease of lying and deception when relying only on video communication.

How can you know if someone is being 100 per cent truthful online? It's almost impossible to discern with only a limited view. When face-to-face with someone who tells a lie or is avoiding being open and honest there are tell-tale signs in his or her body language. The feet can be a giveaway, for instance. However, this is part of the body never seen on video calls as the screen only shows an *'above the keyboard'* view - the top half of a person! There are other signals which we instinctively pick up when we meet face-to-face through seeing a person's full body language – alas not possible via this technology.

Neil reminded me that it's essential to be wary of entering into negotiations relying solely on digital meetings, regardless of how *'quick'* it appears. In other countries, such as Norway, the culture demands that negotiations are worked out with in-person meetings.

Good Organisational Skills and a Good Memory

It's easy to think there's no need to worry about organisational skills and just rely on a good memory when networking online. I find it's much easier to get mixed up if you don't get a handle on organising your online meetings.

As a comparison, when arranging to attend a face-to-face networking meeting, I'd have a diary entry, stating where and when and the name of network. I'd go to the meeting, collect business cards and once home follow-up before filing the cards or putting them in the bin.

Online, I've to know where the link is to get into the meeting. I record this detail in my computer calendar including the link and put a note in my paper diary. Sometimes, I copy the email the organiser sends into a folder called *'Online Meetings'*, so I can find it easily. Otherwise, I'm trawling through my packed inbox two minutes before the meeting is about to start, desperately trying to find the link. This impacts on my stress levels and is the equivalent of rushing late into a meeting feeling all flustered and frustrated!

Zoom calls have become such a regular occurrence and an essential part of follow-up. Simply recording who the call is with is not enough; it's a good practice to add a note indicating what the meeting is about. This saves embarrassment and confusion when on the call. I've learned this the hard way. I once had a call, which I told my family was with a gentleman in Australia; when on the call I quickly discovered it was actually with lady in New York, USA!

We're exchanging a lot of information to a vast number of people via online interactions, so we do need prompts to engage our memories. My friend, *Ben Wright (I Want Fish & Chips)* – yes, that's the name of his marketing company! - told me an interesting story. He was with a woman in a breakout room and he asked her how it was going and named a particular situation that she had revealed on a previous 1-2-1 networking call. To his surprise, the lady was quite affronted and suspiciously asked, *"How do you know that?"* The defensive reaction imploded the conversation and wrecked any relationship building as trust had been damaged!

We do have to be mindful of what we are saying and be respectful so that we don't lose our credibility in future communications! Alongside this, is the raft of information about us online. Nothing said or written online is private – it's all in the public domain, so get organised and note things down to aid your memory and protect your reputation.

Online Visual Impact

Lesley Burton,
Franchise Owner: <u>House of Colour</u>

Networking online has created a fantastic opportunity for us all, however it does put us firmly in the spotlight. Our face, neck and shoulders are our *'cameo'* or communication area and it is on permanent display on the screen, which make it doubly important that we use this profile to its best advantage. As visual creatures, we often make up our minds (not necessarily fairly) if we like someone based on their looks. Welcome to my world! I help people enhance their 'First visual impressions' by the use of colour. Colour is something we can use and 'control' in our appearance.

Colour is a very powerful tool. It not only affects the way you feel, but the colours you wear make an enormous difference to the way you are viewed. The correct ones will brighten and harmonise with your face ensuring you look healthy and awake, whereas the wrong ones make you look pale, drawn and tired.

It is good for your business and online presence to look radiant so knowing what works with your palette and wearing those colours next to your face makes a huge difference. You also need to understand how to mix and match your colours and the way to wear your colours. It is best to have colour blocks for appearing online (because of pixelation).

At any other time, in offline settings, patterns are a great way to wear your colours.

Colours are part of your 'picture' adding both impact and authority to your profile. The choice is crucial; the right colour helps to build your online networking profile particularly from the shoulders up! Ladies can use both neck and sleeve detailing and statement accessories such as necklaces, scarves, earrings and hair adornments. These promote your personal brand. Makeup, particularly lipstick, in a shade that suits your natural colouring, will add wonderful contrast and elevate your profile.

For men, wearing a tie expresses your style and, with impact colour, helps you to stand out. When not wearing a tie, your shirt needs to add the impact. The choice is crucial: it needs to be of good quality and the correct type of collar for you.

Your online video is your best impression to others, who are often watching you on their screens for half an hour to up to two hours. The right colours and style will help you to project your own personal brand and be memorable.

Better Clues, Fewer Disability Issues

I prefer online to offline networking. I've realised that I find it easier to communicate on a video call when I can see the person.

I am a business woman living with autism and ADHD, which means I need facial expressions to give me better clues, and I've also realised I partially lip-read so it's much easier to absorb information via video call than by phone or in-person.

"Long live the video call!"

By Leah Leaves, Founder: Leah Leaves Hypnotherapy

Shout out for Online Networking Organisers

Where would we be without those who are willing to step up to the plate and organise networking events? They've had to learn a new way of networking, battling with technology they never thought they would have to learn, just to serve business people. They've been a cornerstone during lockdown in keeping business people connected with one another, expanding geographical reach and being supportive with networking endeavours.

The new business world of online networking owes organisers a huge debt of gratitude, as forerunners and pioneers, guiding us onto and into the realm of online networking. They're part of the evolving history of business networking, as we know it.

Additional Tips for Organisers

As an organiser, your role is to ensure your participants have the best opportunity to connect with one another. One of the best ways to achieve this is to put a post on LinkedIn after the meeting with @tags which link to everyone on the call – this is the equivalent to an attendees list (obviously, checking with each participant on the call for permission to do this first). It means participants can easily increase their networks by clicking on the @ and adding their fellow participants to their connections. An added benefit is, it also attracts new people to the next event.

Mark Jarvis `Author`   4d ...
Better business leads by unlocking the real power of your network re...

Wonderful way to start the week, bringing positivity to the world.
Great to hear from Eddie Palmer Jon Davies Andrew Wood Chris Rose Richard Holtom Sheila Stamp Judith Hamilton Rob Purle Ladey Adey Dawn Fear Adam Davey

Be brave, and encourage your members to measure their networking activity and how to know if it's good use of their time.

Ask your members to feedback on the event and if there's anything they'd like more or less of.

Your Online Networking Opportunities

As an avid networker who uses networking as part of their marketing or sales strategy *(why else would you have reached this chapter in the book?)* it's time to ask yourself some questions. It's worth periodically examining if you're making the very best of your online networking and using the opportunities wisely. Ask yourself:

- How are you effectively using your online networking calls?
- Are you engaging with the speakers, by comments or questions?
- If uninspired by the speakers (some are very dull #sorrynotsorry!), how are you maximising your time while on the call?
- Are you engaging with other participants on the call? Remember you can message the group or individuals in the chat box (providing this option has not been disabled by the organiser - grrrrr!). If it has been disabled, look participants up on another platform and request a connection.
- How often do you multi-task while on a call?

The only real way of ascertaining if networking online or in-person is working for you is to measure your outcomes and results.

Measure Your Networking Productivity

Now, you have your ducks in order. You have:

- Your bio at the ready.
- Practiced your elevator pitch.
- Booked in for a meeting.

Measuring Networking Effort

I measure networking through the number of leads I receive each week and then I keep a record of how many sales I make as a result of following up on those leads. These sales currently stand at hundreds of thousands of pounds - so I'm measuring my networking activity as pretty successful!

Mark Saxby, Founder: <u>Status Social</u>

- 🖥 Decided which networking group is for you.
- 🖥 Committed to attending for a while.
- 🖥 Followed-up with people and had great conversations.
- 🖥 Spoken with potential clients and perhaps gained a couple of new clients.

Now what? You need to *'rinse and repeat'* especially if you have a winning formula, but how do you know what works best? You need to measure. Have a system which gives you data, (remember *'Data is King!'*) so you can know with certainty whether this networking game is worth playing or not. Some look at their reach, impression, engagement, contacts and leads. *Note: others have alternative definitions but generally speaking:*

Reach is the number of posts which are read by others and the number of people you engage with; as geographic barriers are removed from online networking, this gives many more opportunities to reach people and for them to know about your business.

Impressions are the number of different people who engage with you for the first time to find out more about your business and to share about their business.

Engagement is a common metric for evaluating online activity. It measures the additional public shares, likes and comments. Occasionally, I will promise a small group of fellow networkers that I will give them a recommendation on social media. This is the type of engagement that can be measured (and asked for - *Call to Action* - as part of a one-minute pitch).

Contacts are the people you have added to your list, email address or app.

Leads are people who may have an interest in what you're offering and have been brought to your attention by someone in your network. They're people who don't yet know about your business, and you need to follow-up to introduce yourself to them and thank the person who has provided this lead. You may have heard of the sales terms: cold leads, warm leads and qualified leads. This gives an additional term referred leads.

Initiative

Time to Get Out There and Do It

Attend a Networking Event	10 points
Arrange and Diarise a 1-2-1 meeting	20 points
Follow-up with people and add them to your list	20 points
Gain a new customer from networking	50 points

Introduction

Referrals and Social Media Responses

Your affiliate link is used or you ask someone for their affiliate link	10 points
Your name is tagged or mentioned on Social Media	10 points
Someone contacts you after seeing you in a networking meeting	10 points
You refer someone or are referred by someone to a new contact	20 points

Networking Balanced Scorecard

Interactive

Low level Contact

Interact with an individual in a chat box	10 points
Leave a comment on a group page	10 points
Respond to another person's post	10 points
Add a constructive comment or question in chat box	20 points

Interfacing

Higher Level Branding

Ask a Speaker a question	10 points
Create and post an article, blog, video or webinar	20 points
Speak at a networking event	30 points
Contact an 'unknown' business person and start a conversation	40 points

The Networking Balanced Scorecard

The purpose of measuring your business networking activity is to give yourself feedback about your networking habits and practices. From this feedback, you can make business decisions on the future of your networking action.

My daughter, Abbirose, and I have devised the *Networking Balanced Scorecard* as an easy and effective way to measure your networking activity. It makes managing your networking purpose *'a piece of cake!'*

Inspired by the strategic performance management tool, *The Balanced Scorecard (1992)*, brought to us by *Robert Kaplan* and *David Norton*, the focus of our Networking Balanced Scorecard is on business networking (see Extras). We give you permission to copy the charts and use them. Our only *ask* is that you feedback to us on how you used it and how it's informed you about your networking activity.

The *Networking Balanced Scorecard* has four categories and you collect points for your activity within four divisions: *Initiative, Introduction, Interfacing, and Interactive.*

"What do points make? Prizes!" as *Bruce Forsyth* would say. Well, using the *Networking Balanced Scorecard* the prize is data! You can award yourself points for each time you take action in each sub-group.

INITATIVE: *Time to get out there and do it.*

Attend a networking event = 10 points
Arrange and diarise a 1-2-1 meeting = 20 points
Follow-up with people and add them to your list = 20 points
Gain a new customer from networking = 50 points

INTRODUCTION: *Referrals and Social Media Responses*

Your affiliate link is used or you ask someone for their affiliate link = 10 points
Your name is tagged or mentioned on social media = 10 points
Someone contacts you after seeing you in a networking meeting = 10 points
You refer someone or are referred by someone to a new contact = 20 points

INTERFACING: *Higher Level Branding*

Ask a speaker a question = 10 points

Create and post an article, blog, video or webinar = 20 points

Speak at a networking event = 30 points

Contact an 'unknown' business person and start a conversation = 40 points

INTERACTION: *Low Level Contact*

Interact with an individual in a chat box = 10 points

Leave a comment on a group page = 10 points

Respond to another person's post = 10 points

Add a constructive comment or question in chat box = 20 points

Count up your points at the end of each week. Remember, that you can have points for each engagement. For example, **Initiative:** if you attended four networking events in one week then you score 10 points x 4 = 40 points.

Once you have a month's data, you'll begin to notice your own patterns, see your own averages and notice which areas produce the most rewards for you such as, an ideal customer. Questions which you need to ask yourself once you have some data:

- 💻 Which activities positively affect the growth of your list or contacts?
- 💻 How is networking affecting your business growth?
- 💻 Which networking strategy could you develop and improve?
- 💻 How do the activities improve your personal networking and friendship groups?

Identify and add your own networking activity, with points to the scorecard. There are likely to be other networking activities that you employ that are not on this list. Identify these and add them to your own *Networking Balanced Scorecard* with the points you feel should be awarded.

The *Networking Balanced Scorecard* is a tool to use for you, and you only; there are no competitive elements and nor is there any point in comparing your results with those of another business. Your points will depend on your business. Your personal style of communication will affect which areas you perform best in. It then takes some analysis to work out which areas need improving and which benefit your business most. You can do this!

Overall, it's a tool to build a rapport, referral and relationship strategy and attract more customers. Do use the tables (see Extras) to print out tables to fill in your data easily. If you would like the Excel sheet to populate this information drop me an email: *ladey@ladeyadey.com*.

Number of Networking Groups Attended

This number will affect your scorecard as you can give yourself points in each section for each time you attend a group.

Networking Groups who Measure their Activity

BNI is a networking group which takes measuring its activities very seriously. It measures the participation of its members in seven categories, including number of referrals passed and the amount of business they've been thanked for by others.

ActionCOACH Garry Crosby runs the BNI Synergy Chapter in Peterborough, UK. The group is currently 4th in the country, based on measured performance and Garry has ambitions to be No.1. In the 12 months leading up to September 2020, his group has passed 2,610 referrals between the members, leading to over £2m worth of business being generated.

Business Networking Online is My Favourite

The beauty of business networking online is, people are more polite and give focused attention as screen time is usually on a 1-2-1 basis or in a small group. Have you ever been at an in-person event where you start a conversation with someone whose attention is obviously elsewhere? As the conversation progresses, they look over their shoulder, obviously on the lookout for someone else they'd rather talk to. What about the meetings where the background music is too loud, or the hubbub of the networking voices are so loud you can't hear the person talking to you? The worst networking groups for the latter are those with a speed-dating networking style! This can't happen in online meetings!

For me, these are just a few of the benefits of successful business networking online. I leave you to ponder this quote by fellow author, *Dr Daren Martin, 'Today you can be inactive, reactive, or proactive! Choose your 'active' wisely.'* I actively choose Networking ONLINE.

John McHale - ActionCOACH

Ladey Adey (LA): John, I know you have a lot of experience in networking. Can you tell me more about your networking history, please?

John McHale (JMcH): I've run a Business Coaching business for several years and for me, networking has been one of the marketing strategies I use for generating leads and growing my full time business as an ActionCOACH. This has accumulated to a huge amount of networking over the years, but it's changing!

Networking has changed remarkably since March 2020. Just as everything we had previous to that date, the whole world has changed. There were very limited options for where to go once the world was placed in lockdown and business turned online to survive. Online was already a very crowded space and it became even more crowded with networkers moving their meetings to this virtual platform. It became really interesting to see which networking groups were able to adapt and make a good transition.

LA: How long have you made networking a part of your business?

JMcH: I've used networking for ActionCOACH for the past six years, attending two or three networks regularly. BNI (*Business Network International*) was a staple of this networking, and I was part of a BNI group for five of these years.

LA: What are the key changes that you've seen since lockdown?

JMcH: Interestingly, there are some new networking groups that have set up because of lockdown. Previously, there were very few online-only groups already in existence. New ones have started up and the face-to-face networks have had to move online - the latter forced to take this action to survive. To quote *Charles Darwin*, *'It's not the strongest of the species that survives, nor the most intelligent, but rather, that which is most adaptable to change'*. Applying this to today, real-life networking had to move to the virtual platform and adapt to what was going on in people's lives. Some networking groups made this change simpler than others.

LA: What do you think the secret is to making change simple?

JMcH: I've been part of this change and watched how other networks have adapted. I've noticed the networking groups who recognised a need to change the structure or the format and had the flexibility to do it have been successful. Certain networks asked their membership to feedback on what they could do differently to improve their online networking, and then implemented those changes. These networks have not only maintained their numbers, but even increased them. I think the point of consulting members is a very important one.

Other new groups that I've seen were created just to offer help to business people during this particular period of our lives. Their message was simply, *"Do you need help? If you've got any issues with your business, jump on our webinars; we'll do whatever we can. This is completely free of charge; let's see what we can do to help you during this period - however long it lasts. We're here to help"*.

Effectively, they became a drop-in networking group to help all business people. These have proved really popular. In the long-run, I'd expect them to disappear as quickly as they were introduced.

My wife attends various networking groups in her role as Marketing Director for our business. As we share our offices, I hear what's going on in the networking groups she attends. The meetings are buoyant, lively, energetic, and fun. What else do you need to network well?

The networks that haven't worked well, to my mind, are the ones already in existence, who haven't changed their format in any way, shape or form as they moved from the offline to the online format.

LA: Was there an assumption that what works in face-to-face networking would work equally as well when put online?

JMcH: The assumption, possibly arrogantly, was, *"We've got a very successful networking group here, it's been in existence for many, many years. Therefore, we'll just transfer it online and it will be just as successful."*

This just doesn't work. Maybe the slowness, inability, or inflexibility to adapt is because some of the larger networking groups are part of a franchise. I guess it's a lot harder for them to change things very quickly. It's very inflexible when you're part of a franchise to be able to change things yourself; you need clearance at a higher level for that to happen. Do you remember the video renting company, *Blockbusters* - A video/DVD rental business? They thought they were impenetrable and didn't change when online film streaming came along – the company no longer exists! It's the same business principle here; if networks don't adapt, they're not going to survive.

LA: Can you explain more about what it is that doesn't work?

JMcH: The best way of answering is to consider the behavioural patterns which occur during a face-to-face networking meeting. By understanding body language and how people like to communicate, you can adapt your approach and presentation style to suit individuals and their different styles.

A lot of information is passed between people during the informal times of networking - those 'chitchat' moments when conversations are happening simultaneously in the same room. It means that the decibel level gets quite high, as there might be 10 or 12 conversations happening at once, and you can move between each of those separate chats at will. When you're on a virtual platform, that doesn't exist. When you've got a screen full of people, only one person can talk at a time, and the only way you can have any conversations is via the chat function or breakout rooms. It's hard to get banter going over the chat box or passing on informal business knowledge inside a virtual room with everyone else listening.

LA: Is there any way around this, or is it a case of accepting that there are some limitations with online networking?

JMcH: To my mind, this will be a limiting factor unless the organisers of these networking groups put some thought into this aspect. One networking group I'm a member of *Catena Network*. This works very well because of what they do before, during and after the meeting: prior to the meeting, they send out a delegate list and ask if people want to meet a specific person. Or, if there are no requests, they use their knowledge of people attending to suggest a meeting between delegates.

On arrival, the organiser introduces participants and what they do (no direct one-minute pitches). Participants then move into breakout rooms. People can stay in the breakout room for as long as they wish. When they wish to leave, they can go into another breakout group. This format has been explained beforehand so nobody takes umbrage when someone leaves. I've been known to stay talking to people who were relevant to my business for over an hour! The organisers are looking for chemistry or a good fit in advance of the meeting to aid in building networking relationships. It works because of the time and effort put in, in advance of the meeting.

LA: Each network is different, but overall, what do you think network organisers need to do as online networking becomes part of the networking mix?

JMcH: Good question. That is probably a two-pronged answer: firstly, the network organisers need to recognise they need to ask for regular feedback from their members to avoid assumptions. *Is it working? Are you getting everything out of it that you need? Is this format relevant to your needs?* Ultimately, every business owner will decide whether this networking group gives a return on their investment (in both time and money). Participants aren't there for a cosy chat with people, nice though that is. Networking is a marketing strategy and needs to produce contacts and ultimately clients. It's a marketing strategy and, as such, the only true indicator of success is the return on the investment.

Secondly, online networking needs to become more 'professional'. During the period of the Covid-19 outage, turning up 'casual' to a network meeting with views of your stairs, bedroom or your kitchen behind you is acceptable as not everybody has the space to have a home office. Going forward, that's not okay. You can't go to network meetings and have that behind you all the time. So, you either need to have a home office space where you can work from where it looks professional or invest in a green screen which can display your logo and business information in the background.

LA: How has the ActionCOACH Community coped online?

JMcH: The ActionCOACH Community is about 200-strong across the UK, from the top of Scotland to the southern-most part of Cornwall. Almost immediately, as lockdown period started, we started communicating dynamically on WhatsApp, updating each other on what we were doing and what was happening in our individual regions across the UK. We recognised we had to make ourselves available to any networking group or any business community - simply to be there for people and be willing to give a helping hand. The majority of the ActionCOACHES put on at least two or three webinars each week for anybody, literally anybody, to jump on. These ranged from: '10 things you need to do to get you through the recession' to 'How to do effective lead remote management'. For many business owners, these complimentary sessions were of a huge benefit in them understanding what they needed to be doing to survive.

LA: The majority of networking online during lockdown was free meetings or a significantly reduced membership fee. Going forward, what do you think will be an acceptable price point?

JMcH: I think the price point will ultimately come down to the perceived value their members see. Ultimately, as business owners, it always comes back to what is the return on the investment. Networking groups need to look for lifetime value - working with people in the long-term, rather than making a quick pound now. There's no point in today's sale if it means you might not have that customer tomorrow - we know relationships matter!

Networking groups, especially online networking groups, need to recognise that this is not a 'short-term' novelty because of lockdown – many business owners have seen a new kind of networking group and some will want this to be the norm when normality returns.

Business people like to feel part of a network and while fostering relationships, they may well invest for a little bit longer. We recognise that online means cutting down on venue hire and meals, as there's no need to leave your own home or office. So, from this, the price point has to be lower than face-to-face - maybe a difference of 50-66% less than what has been seen as 'normal' for in-person networking groups.

LA: Do you think online networking will threaten offline in-person networking?

JMcH: This period has forced a lot of people to think differently. My firm belief moving forward is yes, there will be a choice of online and offline networks to join. From a behaviour profiling perspective, people who are, by default, task-oriented people will welcome the new, more efficient way of networking. It saves on travel time – both ways – and it can still do everything you want it to do. Those people who are, by default, people-oriented people, hanker for the time when they can actually meet people properly again. They need it because it's the environment where they work best. For these people, online networking is something that they just have to put up with temporarily.

Consequently, the face-to-face networks will have another competitor in the marketplace. For some people, online networking meetings may well become the network of choice. So, there's a brand new competitor in the field that didn't exist only a few weeks ago. Going back to *Darwin*, adaptability will ensure longevity.

Online Overload

The currency of real Networking is not greed but generosity.
Keith Ferrazzi

The year 2020 brought with it a major shift to the world's landscape: environmental, political, legal, economic, technological, and social. Change was needed due to the pandemic Covid-19, the ability to adapt was essential for everyone and everything, especially business.

Business people need to be able to react, adapt and anticipate economic change. We see successful business people do this, it is as if they have an ear to the ground and are ahead of the game when they quickly and effectively implement changes in their companies. SMEs have the flexibility to do this quicker than large corporate companies.

On the day businesses were forcibly *'closed'* by governments world-wide, offices and retail outlets shut and face-to-face operations were no longer allowed, business people had to find a solution or cease trading. For those who use networking to generate business, lockdown took on a new meaning. The solution was found in the digital sphere, putting products and services online for their customers. Never before had technology been used so intensely by schools, universities, employers, older people, churches, and of course, for networkers.

This intensity has brought a darker side; heralding digital fatigue. This button has been pressed with the plethora of online groups and a feeling of FOMO (Fear of Missing Out) creeping in. Curiously, the networking world has been here before. During the 2008 recession, there was networking group panic and networking groups reached saturation point.

Blended Networking

I find the problem with online networking is I don't know anybody's emails, I don't get anyone's business cards or numbers and I don't get to do the soft networking afterwards. I think online puts guest speakers under pressure; they need to be much more dynamic to come over well. A good speaker needs to engage people by having a good vocabulary, excellent power linguistics, and a good message; they need to be more focused than in a face-to-face meeting. They can take advantage of strategically placing a banner behind them but if the speaker can't engage, people will tune out and go and check their emails etc..

If you ask me what the future looks like, I think now we've dragged people into the online world, people are gaining confidence. As they become competent, they will want to use it to reach out and connect. In the learning world, I use the term '*blended learning*', to describe teaching which combines online interaction with traditional, place-based classroom methods. In the future, when face-to-face and online networking are both offered would give us '*blended networking*'.

Cath Babbington, <u>*Coach Cath UK*</u>

Keep in Touch

My networking consists of staying in touch on the phone or a quick video conference call. I believe it's all about how you look after your customer during these challenging times, which will determine success when we return to '*normal*'.

Melanie Jackson, Director: <u>ARC Broker Services Ltd</u>

The Recession of 2008-2009

Let's go back to 2008 to the last recession - at that time I had bought into the franchise of the Athena Network® and built a network for business women in Lincolnshire. The network was membership based with a yearly fee and commitment to monthly meetings. On the network scale, it is at the high-end of networking. It fitted in well with other networks, town business clubs, BNI, Rotary Club, smaller women's business clubs and the golfing fraternity.

When the recession came in, overnight business people left their networking organisations and started their own groups. Within a month networking groups had mushroomed. It seemed that every other business person was setting up a networking group.

This led to the question why would business people pay into a membership base network (high-end expense) when they could meet the same people, down the road, for £5 a meeting? For me, it brought an end to my franchise. Within two years, a lot of these quick fix networking groups had gone and the balance had been restored with the original groups and networking channels remaining.

It was due to the commitment of the network organisers, which groups survived the 2008-9 recession storm. It takes hard work to sustain and maintain a networking group. It may look easy, but there is extensive activity behind the scenes to keep members motivated.

I see the same frantic networking activity happening online now. At the start of lockdown only a few networking groups had an online option. Some large groups (4N and MIBA) reacted quickly and provided their members an online networking outlet within days of lockdown. This quick reaction saved their businesses.

Meanwhile, within a few weeks into lockdown others have jumped on the networking bandwagon! Each day more networking groups are being set up online. In fact, not a day goes by when I don't get an invite to a new online network (*I'll try to attend them all!*).

Once the epidemic is over, when lockdown becomes a distant memory and we return to life post Covid-19, it will be interesting to see how many of these online networks continue.

I've even had a clash of two Zoom networking calls on same day at the same time. For the fun of it (and in the name of research), I attended both simultaneously! It was an interesting experience. I used two separate devices and different accounts so that Zoom would work on both without the technology getting in a muddle! I had to make sure that my video was stopped, and my photo showing on one device, whilst engaging on the other. I flip-flopped on this so the participants could see the real me from time to time! I had to discover the sound button so I could easily just take sound off one when talking on the other. It was made slightly easier by one video call beginning with a talk and the speaker used PowerPoint slides. I could watch these whilst listening to the other group giving their elevator pitches, and occasionally put comments to the speaker.

The challenging part came when I was waiting my turn to do my elevator pitch, and the other call suddenly went into break out rooms. It was, *'Oh, my goodness, what do I do?'* I realised to enter the *'Breakout Room'* it required a click of the mouse to accept the invitation to join and is was not automatic. Phew! I waited five minutes before entering and got my one-minute pitch in the other Zoom meeting before stopping the video so my photo appeared. Then, I went into the *'Breakout Room'* and joined the conversation.

At the end of it, neither group was the wiser but boy was I exhausted! My brain felt scrambled, which only a walk around the garden cleared and I didn't want to go on another video call for the rest of the day!

Would I recommend doing two video calls at once? Not really. Would I do it again? Unlikely. I'd choose one and commit to it 100%!

The question to ask yourself now: Are you experiencing Online Overload? Do you need to seriously consider how you are going to control your online activity and notice its effect on your health?

Digital Deluge

We have embraced the technical world and submerged ourselves in digital and online activities. Does this make online overload or online fatigue a new phenomenon? Probably not, since digital devices have become part of our modern word, digital fatigue has occurred.

We see digital usage everywhere; a mother with a child in a pushchair with a phone to her ear or texting away; a family sitting at a restaurant table each on a phone or tablets; at home, it's TV dinners and 'Alexa' at the ready. Everywhere we are, it seems impossible to be without smartphones, tablets or digital devices. Statistics say people are spending over eight hours a day involved in online communications.

We use it in our work and then become over stimulated. We've got

too much going on our heads - add to this the stress of perfectionism or competitiveness, trying to do too much, fighting a learning curve and setting high expectations. *Why are we surprised our bodies feel abused?*

As our bodies are affected, there will be side affects; eyesight is strained, body posture fall into poor habits, the chairs used are old and not fit for purpose and sitting in front of the screen for hour upon hour is bound to affect us. We've developed the mindset of responding very quickly to others through the technology. It is as though we are in competition with the computer itself. Speed of responding to messages can be demanding, if a message is left for more than an hour, we are left with guilt and a feeling that we have failed?

Where did these '*rules*' come from in the first place?

Online Fatigue

Hannah Long,
Founder: _Potential Occupational Therapy_

When Covid-19 hit, I questioned how my business would cope. What would happen to the connections I had made? Would I be able to continue to networking? So, when the opportunity arose to take my networking online - I grasped it with open arms.

Of course it didn't take long to become acquainted with my new friends _'online fatigue'_ and _'Zoom fatigue'_.

I refer to Zoom as a collective term for all video conferencing platforms and fatigue as _"a feeling of being extremely tired, usually because of hard work or exercise"_. I already supported clients to overcome fatigue following brain injury on a daily basis but Zoom fatigue was not something I was expecting. So, as any Occupational Therapist would, I decided to approach it by going back to the theory.

The person-environment-occupation model explains how

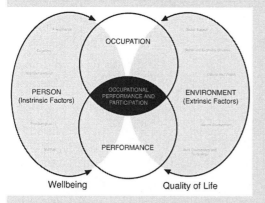

Wellbeing   Quality of Life

performance results from the dynamic relationship between people, their occupations, and the environments, in which they live, work and play. So, when I apply lockdown and the world of video conferencing to this model, it is clear to me why our performance can falter during a Zoom call.

The Person

F continued

- Are you "techy"?
- Do you become stressed at the first sign of computer malfunction?
- Are you sitting at your desk in pain?
- Is networking a choice or are you required to do it?
- What is your mood like?
- Are you a confident speaker?
- Do you think online networking can work?
- Do you miss face-to-face contact?
- Are your extended family video calling daily?

All these things are personal to each and every one of us and they all affect how you experience zoom fatigue.

The Environment

We are all at home. We cannot meet colleagues for coffee or get in our car to visit a client. Our social environment does not change and we are constantly in close proximity to our family. Ultimately, there is no variation in our environment. During an online video call, the dog starts barking, the kids are crying downstairs or your partner appears in their underwear… *yes, we've all seen the funny videos on social media.* Then, there's the issue of getting the lighting right for your call, setting a background or tidying your office. We spend the whole call staring at a computer screen whilst our environment throws distractions and obstacles our way.

The Occupation

I find there is an added social pressure during a Zoom call, you feel like everyone is watching you. It takes greater effort to read the body language or facial expressions of others. We use so much energy focusing on what others are saying, participating in the chat, and processing the array of visually distracting backgrounds whilst dealing with the constant distraction of seeing ourselves.

At the moment, our diaries are back-to-back with video calls; networking, meetings, client appointments and at the end of the day the family quiz night! The person, environment and occupation are simply not working harmoniously together, and as such, we are not performing to the best of our ability, we are becoming worn out and fatigued.

So, what can you do to restore harmony and reduce Zoom fatigue?

Before a video call:

1) Review your workstation set up. Sitting for long periods will increase pain.

2) Put a sign on your office door so your family knows you cannot be disturbed.

3) Check your webcam. Review the lighting and make adjustments to ensure you can be seen easily. This will help others to read your body language when you are speaking.

4) Make sure you have plenty of drinks and a snack (which you should eat with the camera off for online etiquette).

During a video call:

1) Turn off your video. This may seem controversial but it is ok to turn off when you are not speaking. Agree with the other participants that this is ok.

2) Hide your own video from your view. This will reduce the natural urge to look at yourself.

3) Look away from the screen regularly, close your eyes from time to time. You can still listen to the speaker.

4) Adjust your position, stand up periodically, particularly when you have your video off.

5) Do not multi-task during a video call. You may think it is the perfect opportunity to catch up on emails but this will increase your fatigue. Close down all background tabs or programmes for the duration of the meeting.

6) Reduce visual cues. Participants should use the background facility on video conferencing software to apply a plain or simple background.

7) Limit video calls to 2 hours maximum. Do not schedule more than two "long" video calls per day.

After a Video Call:

F
continued

8) Plan your week and schedule when you will network and when you will have downtime. Don't make video calling the new default option. Outside of business networking you can still speak on the phone and email as you normally would both personally and professionally.

9) Schedule breaks. I would recommend at least 10 minutes between video calls.

10) Get a good night's sleep (7-8 hours) and maintain a good routine.

BREAK up the Video Calls:

Here is an acronym to remind you to make your break affective:

Breathe – Take some deep breaths and close your eyes. Lay on the floor, if it helps, and stretch at the same time.

Rehydrate – Drink plenty of water and refill your drink before the start of a meeting.

Exercise – Move around the room and do some stretching exercises.

Adjust – Change your position. If the environment is not right it's beneficial to move, or adjust your computer's position.

Know Your Limits. Don't overstretch yourself; plan your week, with breaks and have breaks between Zoom calls.

As a final thought: as we all adjust to this new way of working, ensure you give people the best version of you, not the version crippled by Zoom fatigue. Plan your week and manage video calls to a sensible level (not back-to-back) and remember to include time for your own health and well-being.

Step Up Your Self-Care

Most of us tend to underestimate how important it is to put self-care above everything else. The temptation is to put our own needs way down the list, after our work and taking care of the family, but I've seen that go wrong time and time again. The chances are that if you became too sick to continue working, or take care of your family, the knock-on effects could be potentially devastating.

Over the years, I've seen countless people who have lost homes and families because they didn't take proper care of themselves and get help when they needed it. Stepping up your self-care can mean anything from: going to bed an hour earlier each night, to having a monthly massage (self-massage during lockdown), to going for an annual check up with someone like me.

Even small changes can make a big difference; whatever your situation there will always be something else you can do to move yourself in the right direction.

I was lucky (or unlucky!) to have learnt about this the hard way at a very early age. When I was just 14, I burnt out. Within minutes I went from a perfectly healthy schoolgirl to starting a two-year journey with Chronic Fatigue Syndrome.

Ever since I recovered, I've been on a mission to educate people that when we take 100% responsibility for our own health, there's really no limit to what we can achieve. I specialise in working with busy people who don't have much spare time; my YouTube channel has plenty of quick tips and bite-sized videos to help you on your way, a real boon to self-care online.

Hannah Charman: *Physic Health Consulting*

Are You in Control of the Apps?

With the onset of remote working or working from home, customers, staff, suppliers are using many apps to make contact but responding to many apps and remembering which one to return calls on creates additional pressure. Alongside this is the concept of 9-5 is being eroded and these messages can arrive outside traditional *'office'* hours and at weekends, too. This means we are *'on call'* for longer and feel we need to respond to customers at all hours, even at 10pm!

It should be you in control of the messages and the timing of answering them, not the other way around. We are constantly interrupted; our attention diverted by emails, apps and other social media activity during main work. This puts a stress on our brain and bodies, sapping our energy.

The speed in which technology works, muddles up our brains. We are not computers and therefore we should not be competing and hurrying to react at the speed of a computer. Do you know when you've had too much computer or app time? I think deep down we know. We feel overwhelmed. There's just too much choice, or conflict, such as attending a networking group, but the feeling that other activities are really the priority and you should be doing something else. The temptation then is to do two things at once, networking and dealing with emails!

It is us who make Zoom relentless, by scheduling calls back-to-back. It is time to put in time spaces between the online meetings. Alongside all this networking activity you still need to respond to existing customers and do the work of your business!

Perhaps, it is time to become comfortable and satisfied with what you're doing to help your business at this moment in time (especially when dealing with home working, home schooling and running a business!). If you're feeling irritable and anxious – then it's time to take a break, even just a short one (a walk round the block, garden or to the other side of the house). You need a break from the computer.

If you're feeling overwhelmed, over-eating and not sleeping, these are signs that something is not right with your mind, body and spirit.

A Regime for Your Voice

Helen J Millington, Vocal Expert and Founder: *Lincoln School of Speech and Drama*

One of the first things people notice about us is our voice and we all want to make a good first impression. We spend almost a third of our working lives in active conversation with others, speaking around 16,000 words a day, therefore looking after and protecting your voice from damage must be taken seriously.

As we adapt to spending more time online, and increasingly conduct our business via talking on video calls, we need to consider how this online medium can affect the way we use our voices. We need to know how to best protect our voices as we use this vital organ to deliver great meetings without compromising our vocal health. Here are some hints and tips to help you develop and maintain safe, clear and effective use of your voice whilst in online meetings.

Breathe correctly.

Unlike office-based meetings where we are often encouraged to stand, we are almost always seated when taking online meetings. This is not conducive to good breathing practice and leads to shallow breathing, or 'clavicular breathing', which can make us feel short of breath and fatigued, and in the worst instances can lead to anxiety and even panic attacks.

Try using a hard-backed chair to maintain a straight back, keep the shoulders relaxed and breathe deep down into the belly. Remember, the upper chest should only move slightly when breathing in, it is the lower abdomen that should appear to inflate which is harder to achieve when sitting, therefore make a conscious effort to sit up, breathe deeply and calmly, and relax.

Stay hydrated.

F continued

Have a warm drink to hand when online and sip regularly. Try to avoid coffee (sorry folks!) as it causes systemic diuresis and will dry out your vocal cords, (or vocal folds) making you sound hoarse. Also avoid alcohol for the same reason, it dehydrates.

Warm water with a little honey is great, as is green tea, but a glass of room temperature water is also fine. Avoid drinks made with large amounts of milk or cream such as smoothies or milkshakes as dairy products cause the mucus in the sinuses to thicken, which cause a whole set of other vocal issues.

Vocal warm–ups.

Most of us think vocal warm-ups are just for singers but this is not true. Warming up your voice will help you maintain safe and effective vocal production and doing a couple of vocal exercises before a meeting or presentation will significantly improve your vocal impact.

First, take three deep, smooth breaths into the tummy (this will also help calm any nerves or feelings of anxiety). Next, breathe in and as you breathe out, create a steady hum. Breathe in again, this time starting with a hum and turn this into *'Ahhhhhhhhh'*. Breathe in again, and as you breathe out create vowel sounds such as *'OO, OH, AW, AH, AY and EE'*. Then add a consonant to the start of the words, e.g. *'TOO, TOH, TAW'* or *'BOO, BOH, BAW'*. This will help to warm up your speech organs, too.

Don't strain.

Many people don't know how to use their voice effectively without straining, raising or even shouting. Good vocal production comes from effective breathing and support from the diaphragm, not from the throat. Breathe in deeply and engage (or 'tighten') your tummy muscles slightly so you can feel their presence in the process. Only then should you begin to speak. This provides the support necessary to create safe, sustainable and impactful speech.

F continued Ensure the microphone on your laptop or computer is sufficiently sensitive to pick up your voice effectively, or alternatively, consider investing in a headset with microphone incorporated. This will reduce the desire to raise your voice or strain your vocal cords, which can lead to significant damage.

Remember, voice comes from the entire body, only speech comes from the mouth.

Take regular breaks.

In between online meetings take as many breaks as you can where you stop talking altogether. Make a sign saying, 'I can't talk right now,' to display to family members who may be around and avoid answering calls during this time. Use this time to move around and practice the breathing techniques and vocal exercises mentioned previously (this time standing up).

Maintenance.

Looking after your voice following online meetings is also

important. Try steaming your vocal cords by putting two or three drops of Tea Tree or Eucalyptus oil in a bowl of hot water, place your head over the bowl with a towel over and breathe in the vapour. Sucking fruit flavoured pastilles (or sweets containing glycerine) will help to soothe a dry, irritated throat. However, avoid anything labelled as a 'cough' or 'throat' sweet as these often contain menthol which simply numbs the pain temporarily, giving you the impression that the underlying problem has been cured and therefore you are more likely to cause further damage to your voice.

By using these tips and techniques, you will begin to develop a better regime for your vocal health. Incorporate some useful habits into your daily routine and (after your tenth online meeting of the day!) your voice will thank you.

Online Overload and Fatigue

Online fatigue is a stress indicator. In these times of Covid-19 and fears of Covid-19 we are all suffering to some degree with additional stress. For some, Covid-19 has triggered mental health issues such as Depression, Post Traumatic Stress Disorder and Anxiety, and too much time spent online will probably not help.

The feature articles from Hannah Long and Helen Millington give some great tips and suggestions on how to take care of yourself and combatting online fatigue. Be gentle with yourself, it's not the end of the world if you miss a networking meeting - *note to self!* Check for balance in your life, simplified this is the balance between brain and body. For me when I've done a lot of 'head' working; writing, podcast/ blogging and networking then I need to do something to counteract this such as craftwork, bricklaying or gardening. Choose the physical part of your life, which counteracts your intellectual part; it could be sport, exercise or beauty treatments. This will help keep the balance, if you feel out of kilter (exhausted, overwhelmed or ill) it means that too much concentration has been put into one area.

Can You Step Away from the Computer?

Give yourself a break and cull the number of video calls you make in a day, Zoom burn out and technology burnout are a real thing! Our business and social life are both conducted in the virtual world so we need to be in control and not allow the technology to control us. Have a look at the *'To Do Planner'* from *The Passionate PA*, use it or be inspired to make your own planner which includes networking activity and online time-keeping (see Extras).

Overloading the mind has an official name; infobesity or infoxication and it encompasses information explosion and over-stimulation. When suffering from these conditions the ability to make good decisions or to understand the issues is compromised. Isn't this interesting? Physiologically it can; increase blood pressure, lower mood or energy, make concentrating difficult, cause vision problems and increase tiredness. It's not surprising our brains are complaining as they struggle to prioritise so much information.

Don't Isolate Your Business

We all realise that it will be some time before we can resume conventional networking – which involves lots of handshaking, lots of standing close together and even the odd hug. So, what do we do now – just allow all our business relationships to wither away? Of course not!

Online networking has been forced upon business folk because of the need to minimise physical contact. It has proved to be an effective way of staying in touch without spending money and without travelling time. Smart businesses carry on marketing during a crisis and online networking is an important part of that marketing effort. Once the crisis has subsided, and businesses are back on the physical networking scene, it is likely that online networking will continue - alongside the physical events.

Here are a few suggested ways of maintaining your contacts, and even finding a few new ones:

- Participate in as many online 'virtual' networking events as you can – nearly all of them are free, they take up little time (and of course there are no fuel or parking costs).
- Continue with newsletters, blogs, podcasts and social media activity to ensure folks don't forget about you. Share hints and tips with your fellow business people.
- The mail system or postal service, that thing we used to use years ago, still works well – so surprise your customers.
- Make sure you call your customers regularly.
- Make sure you call your suppliers regularly – boy, you may need them now!
- Finally, call people who are neither customers nor suppliers – just to be thoughtful and supportive.

Of course, in these times we need to isolate ourselves – but there's no need to isolate our businesses, too.

Mike Stokes, Founder: Positive Networking and *Exportential*

Online Networking Happiness

Online networking helps combat social isolation, as it's a talking machine with the opportunities to meet and communicate with other people.

Every piece of information that comes through the text message or WhatsApp, from emails to social media, triggers the brain to release dopamine to help us out. Dopamine is known as a happy hormone, the brain releases it into the body as a chemical reaction and as a major neurotransmitter. It sends messages to our nerves and other cells in the body. It is possible to become addicted to this reaction, and therefore go into the circle of more online interaction and then online overload!

Online networking is different in many ways than in-person communications so be observant of how these online practices are affecting you. Check your online activity is in balance; forming an integral part of your business strategy and in the main is a healthy and enjoyable experience.

Working from Home or Remote Working

For most of us home working has changed due to lockdown, especially when we have to share the workspace with our spouse, partner, children and even pets! The majority of people feel this is a better work/life/ environmental balance and appreciate the flexibility of working from home. It is expected that the landscape of home working will change in the future.

One day as I was immersed in the online zone, I suddenly thought, *"I'm hearing voices - I'm going mad!"* I look around my desk to find the source of the sound but nothing from any of my devices. I wonder, *Is it the residue of a video call overload and though I have shed the headset, I'm remembering it. No, I find my husband, had gone from the office leaving the radio on and it's those tiny voices coming from his headset that I can hear. Phew! I'm not going mad, well not today anyway!* The radio is now switched off when he leaves his desk.

Many business people, experiencing the advantages of working from home, and using technology to remain in contact with their team have decided to cut the overhead of the physical office. They've cancelled the renting of their offices, hot-desking has been put on hold, and office space businesses are under threat as remote working from home becomes more acceptable and popular.

Technology for Remote and Home Working eature

Clive Catton, Chief Information Officer:
Octagon Technology Ltd

At Octagon Technology Ltd, all our staff work from home. As a company, we gave up our office in 2007, mainly because we were never there, and clients turning up on spec would be greeted with a notice on the door asking them to call a mobile number. We decided it was rather unprofessional and knew that we either had to employ somebody to stay in the office all the time, or move out and go completely virtual.

In the end, it was a no-brainer so we moved out. Since then, we have become so adept at working remotely whilst still working together, giving us expert knowledge of all the traps and pitfalls (as well as all the benefits) of working from many venues; home, front seat of the car, train, hotel, campsite, mountainside and so on.

We get together regularly for video conference meetings, so the lockdown change was something we were used too. It is one of the tools we use to keep everybody happy and motivated, along with a very robust shared diary. However, the video conferencing tool we use has been rather forgotten in the excitement around Zoom and we were curious to know why that particular app had become so popular. It's very easy to use and I suppose the name says it all.

Zoom was originally developed for business use some years ago, but the recent take-up of the platform has exposed issues around security, which Zoom are racing to improve upon. The platform we use, however, has none of those issues. It is secure; people can work on confidential documents together using it. Best of all, it is cheaper than Zoom. The full version comes as part of Microsoft 365 including: Word, Excel, Outlook,

F continued PowerPoint, OneDrive and SharePoint for less than the cost of just the video conferencing with Zoom. It surprises me when people chose to pay for Zoom when they probably had a facility on their machines already. Maybe it's because the Microsoft video conferencing platform is called Teams – hardly an obvious name!

Microsoft themselves have been rather slow to the party in advertising Teams, although they have developed a TV advertisement recently. IT support companies may have promoted it, but again it would have been after the event. Lockdown came so suddenly and Zoom managed to get into the party very quickly. As a business networker, I found myself having to talk about Teams whilst in a Zoom meeting. As people had already made the investment into Zoom the advice regarding to security and versatility was largely ignored.

So, for the avoidance of doubt, here is a table with the pros and cons of Teams versus Zoom (only chosen for this because of its popularity, other platforms are available!).

Teams	*Zoom*
Great for business to business.	Good for business networking.
Simple meeting controls for confidentiality.	Easy to use.
Meetings can be recorded securely and automatically transcribed.	Meetings can be recorded.
No need for a Microsoft account to attend.	No need for a Zoom account to attend.
Cross platform stand-alone Teams app is available for people to join meetings without a Microsoft 365 subscription.	Standalone cross platform Zoom app is available for people to join a meeting without a Zoom account.
Integrated with Microsoft 365 for collaboration and scheduling - sharing of confidential documents	

Shoulda, Woulda, Coulda

Our Networking Group, Business Focus Burton only missed one week when lockdown began and everyone bought into the online networking really well. Some are saying they should have used video meetings years ago!

I've been using Google Hangouts and Zoom for quite a while but most people still liked meeting in-person, until now. I think lockdown has certainly made a difference to how we network and how we will carry out business in the future. However, some principles stay the same; you still need to be active and engaged.

Tony Walton, Founder: _Pollen 8 Social_ *and*
Business Focus Burton Networking Group

A 'New Norm' has resulted from Covid-19!

The unprecedented situation of Covid-19, lockdown and our response means there will be changes in the way we work. This creates new challenges for employers, and new policies have to be written. There is a concern over Health and Safety and use of equipment as few checks can be made, so what can a business do in terms of duty of care for their home-working employees?

It is helpful to carve out a dedicated work zone, which may be a challenge if living in a small house. Set yourself work and family life boundaries to set up a healthy balance. A friend of mine has set up an office in her sitting room and is using her ironing board as her desk! She says it works for her!

Home working must not mean isolation, but regular connection with colleagues, team and networking via online video is a must. Training needs to be on-going to keep you informed and keep your *'grey matter'* engaged. Find a person to be your accountability partner as you look after yourself; with meals, hydration, etc. to have a balanced working-at-home environment.

Alongside remote working comes choosing the way you divide the hours worked in a day. The 9-5 office hours or usual working day hours are eroded as work is conducted around family and personal priorities.

Economists will be watching the remote working space with interest, does it improve productivity, and are employees happier and more motivated when having the freedom to choose their personal office space? How is the technology developing so team working can still be activated, how does it affect the managerial role? All are very interesting challenges or dilemmas. Certainly, business and employment has changed and it cannot go back to how it was before the pandemic.

In our worldwide situation, the government approach to defeating Covid-19 and dealing with pandemics has provided a new way of working. Only time will tell how this improves the lives of society, in their business, work life and social interaction with one another.

Mandy Allen - Founder of CRM Insights

Ladey Adey (LA): Mandy, has anything surprised you about online networking?

Mandy Allen (MA): The biggest surprise has been how much money and travel time I am saving. Working from home was forced upon us due to lockdown, but I think I could easily make this a permanent arrangement. I'm saving a minimum of 10 hours travelling a week, that's 40 hours a month, which I can now invest elsewhere.

Pre lockdown I would often attend face-to-face meetings at numerous London networking groups. However, this took a full day out of my diary.

An average day looked like this:

1) Drive to the station and park my car (car parking fees are obviously an extra cost).

2) Take the train to Peterborough, change trains at Peterborough for Kings Cross.

3) Take the tube to my London location followed by a short to walk (approx. 10 minutes).

4) A 2-hour meeting followed by post meeting 1-2-1s (often adding another hour) before I start the journey home.

The cost to the company is over £100 plus a day out of the office.

With the new style of remote networking, I've been able to make new connections online with people who were not previously on my radar. The main reason for this is people have decided to network out of their area due to the accessibility of online networking.

Suddenly the conversations I'm having are not just ten-minute conversations (scheduled in a face-to-face meeting) but they are followed up with longer conversations, which have real depth.

These deeper conversations are also possible because in the one-minute pitch I can articulate exactly what I want and direct it to exactly the right people. This direct approach attracts the right people I need to connect with and then we arrange to have a follow up conversation.

LA: I know what you mean, I have known some people on the networking circuit for over 10 years and we've never got past, *"Hi, how you doing?"* or *"How is business for you?"* and *"Isn't the weather nice?"* then we'd move on to the next person. We never really understood what each other's business was really about. Since, networking has gone online this has changed and I'm now connecting with the same people and talking to them on a deeper and more personal level.

MA: It matters to me who I connect with, as I am keen to build genuine relationships, engage in compelling conversations even though it doesn't always follow that they will necessarily become a client.

I like to be around interesting people. This is one of the key things about developing positive relationships with people who you want to be around rather than the fake type of relationships which happen simply because people want business from you.

I value people's friendship, camaraderie, and their business knowledge. I look for people who have contrasting skill sets that are complementary to us as a business.

I'm regularly *'Wowed'* by people and these are the people I like to have in my network. When someone asks, *"Do you know anybody who..."* I want to have the confidence to refer a business connection, which I know most suits, plus someone who I can trust to deliver it. It's always humbling when they reciprocate because we recognise each other's worth alongside business acumen.

LA: Has this changed since going online?

MA: I still like to explore relationships and I am curious about people. Being online provides new opportunities to follow up and to know more people. There are a couple of recent conversations that stand out for me which I'll always remember.

You know when you begin a conversation and realise *'you get'* one another. You both speak the same language and your instinct; is there will be opportunities for great referrals between each other.

One guy said, *"You are really challenging me and making me think deeper, I don't usually talk about this side of the business with people."* It was a conversation where we both realised *'we got'* one another. We spoke the same language and instinct tells you there will be opportunities for great referrals between one another.

Of course, this doesn't happen with everyone. By comparison, I recognise in a face-to-face environment people are often conscious of time and also conscious of making a sale. They are not always conscious of getting to know somebody and building a relationship.

At the end of an event, I'll follow up; to keep in touch with people I've spoken to. If the connections do not respond I just think they are not the right kind of connections for us as a business. It's important for the friendship and relationship to be validated both ways for it to be beneficial.

LA: Do you run a networking group?

MA: Several years ago I used to run a 'traditional' networking group. Now at CRM Insights, I facilitate our own referral group, which operates in a different way to networking groups.

Our referral networking events are by invitation only. It includes people who we've known for a while. The members share the same values and also have a great reputation in their field. The difference is we do not charge a membership fee.

By aligning ourselves with the right people who we know, like and trust, we appreciate they will be able to support us on specific projects when required. I'll leave you with this example: recently, we worked with a large local construction company. The project was to undertake a transformation of their business processes providing each department with a structure. This resulted in an improved workflow for their internal processes as well as an enhanced customer journey for their clients and prospects. As part of the overall process, we were able to recommend two further suppliers from our referral network to support their other business requirements.

E pilogue

The Future of Business Networking Online

Networking that matters is helping people achieve their goals.
Seth Godin

The 'Jury may be out' on the future of business networking online, but the initial feedback is positive - with the view that it is attracting new customers and reaching potential clients. In conversations with organisers and owners of business networks I believe there's an appetite and 'market' for business networking to be conducted online.

Talking with business people, it became clear that online networking doesn't diminish the principles of face-to-face networking, it gives a new dimension. In fact, the online transformation brings networking up to date. A consensus between business people is that networking must centre on deepening relationships and using online networking is a fabulous tool in this pursuit.

More For Sure!

I have connected with more people and engaged with many online meetings during lockdown. I think it's because I have time to do it. However, going forward I will ensure I make time to continue engaging online as I have found it supportive and I've learnt loads, which means I continue to grow as a professional coach and trainer.

Debra Pitchford, Founder: <u>Debra Pitchford Development</u>

The New Networking Norm

Diana Catton, Managing Director:
Octagon Technology Ltd

Networking online boomed during the Covid-19 Crisis but has it become the 'new normal'? On the whole I would say that I am in favour of networking online. There are various reasons for this, some of them personal, some of them not so personal.

To begin with, networking online saves time and money. There is no travel time or petrol costs – and we can meet more people from further afield; no time spent eating and drinking (although I miss the variety of networking meals!). At a time of uncertainty, when every business is trying to cut costs to the bone, this is a real bonus. Pressure of the arrival and leaving times are better as online meetings open and close spot-on agreed times.

In a wider context, we are not using precious fossil fuels to travel to our meetings, thus reducing pollution and our carbon footprint. Have you noticed how much bluer the sky is, how much sharper the contrasts in colours in nature, how beautifully the birds sing? This is no coincidence. Apparently the Himalayas can be seen from the *Taj Mahal* for the first time in thirty years. Another way some of us are saving the planet is not washing our clothes so often – we don't have to worry about that so much now, and also only our top halves can be seen online, so we can wear old gardening joggers and slippers if we want! I don't wear the gardening joggers, but not having to wear smart and often slightly uncomfortable shoes is a bonus. Normally, I wash my business jacket every weekend, but now that I only put it on for my meetings, I don't need to wash it so often. I can wear all my tops until they get properly dirty and even I can smell them - too much information?

F continued

Of course, there are some disadvantages, and having a one-to-one online meeting is not the same as meeting people face-to-face, and giving a presentation to a screen sea of faces with no sound, or no face at all (if they turn the video off) is probably unnerving. For this reason I smile and laugh, give thumbs-up signs and so on, so that the speaker has some feedback.

Letting people into our working-from-home spaces means being presentable and moving the clutter outside the range of the camera, putting up banners or a nice bouquet of flowers behind us, or blurring the background. I personally am not in favour of the generic backgrounds that come with online networking platforms as they do not keep up with people's movements and attendees can look as if they are calling from outer space with a very dodgy connection!

We also have to ensure nobody else comes into our space whilst we are in the meeting; and keep our microphones on mute, unless we are actually speaking. I have seen meeting attendees getting video-bombed by pets, children and partners, some of whom are either dressed inappropriately (or not at all). I have also heard arguments and other unsuitable comments. As a tip, if you get interrupted (or need to do something like blow your nose), make sure your microphone is on mute and turn your video off temporarily!

As business people are attending online meetings from further afield, it can result in multiple people representing the same industry. They have to think on their feet to make sure they are not all saying exactly the same thing and need to have several sixty-second introductions to hand so that they can switch at a moment's notice.

As for the future? I hope online networking becomes the new normal, alongside the option of face-to-face. For the wider business community, I believe this lockdown has brought in a new way of working which will benefit many who previously could not attend networking meetings (as well as those who are seasoned networkers) because of the savings in time, money and carbon footprint. It's all good!

A World of Opportunity

I've found online networking to be an amazing way to keep connected. With no travelling to be done there are huge time savings and no location constraints. In the past, I would have probably said that I was more of a face-to-face networker, yet with no choice but to join in virtually, I've found that it has opened up a whole world of opportunity.

It's really a game changer on the future of all networking. It's also convenient - from the comfort of your own home!

Lisa Davies, Chief Inspiration Officer:
Get the Edge UK Training and Consultancy Ltd

Addicted to Online Networking

I run a network for 80 Indian entrepreneurs to meet online. It's a smaller network than a global networking organisation, specific to its community, speaks in their mother tongue and based on building relationships.

We appreciate online networking because of the time saved by not travelling. In a city like Mumbai, people spend two hours in heavy traffic for 30 minutes of networking. Now, it's on their doorstep, they can Zoom at home with their own choice of refreshments. I see this continuing, especially as venues are restricting the number of people allowed in. People will be so addicted to online that they will say, *"Okay, let's stay online right now. Let's not go offline?"* I don't think there will be much interest for in-person networking, except a few instances.

Bharat Jethani, CEO Asentiv Central India

I believe Business Networking Online will Stay

The depth of people's responses regarding the use of online technology to communicate with other business people has overwhelmed me (in a good way). There has always seemed to be someone else with another perspective, or experience of online networking whom I wanted to invite for comment.

I had to extend my target of publishing this book to within six months (instead of three) as I didn't want to draw a line and stop inviting people to contribute. Consequently, contributors have grown from 25 to over 100 business people giving a viewpoint. As online networking becomes the norm, we're all gaining knowledge about the best way to communicate and use this forum to increase business. If you want to comment or know of someone who ought to have been in this book – there's always Edition 2 - contact me via ladey@ladeyadey.com.

Businesses Abroad

I was curious as to how business networking had been affected in other countries, and if these business communities reacted in the same way as the UK, in terms of going online. I approached my networks and asked if they knew any business which networks in other countries; *Lisa Davies* and *Phillip Burton* referred me to some of their contacts.

Amal Loring Founder of MBD reported, *"Business people in the UAE have gone online the same as the rest of the world. I'm focusing my time in the UK, although I live in Dubai."*

The viewpoints of *Amal, Bharat, Niraj* and *Rizwana* in this chapter, and *Mike Kim, Robert Middleton, Lauren Davis* and others from USA show the pandemic has given us a world-wide shared experience. The approach to networking means moving their networking activity online.

We know the next generation of business people will have been born in this digital age. They'll have no memory of life before the mobile phone and will automatically use the online medium as a matter of course. Despite this, there's an innate need in us all to have a physical human connection and collaborate with others face-to-face.

The future may be more of a *'blended'* nature and we may even see *'blended networking'* (a phrase coined by *Coach Cath Babbington*) where there'll be a mixture of online and offline networking offered by networking organisations and groups.

Increased Productivity

When lockdown initially started in India, there was panic: everyone buying emergency supplies. Then

people relaxed into almost a holiday mode, but businesses realised this was unsustainable in the long term: they started to explore digital marketing to promote themselves.

In my networking group, most discussions are now conducted online. We don't have to worry about social distancing and people are developing new skills and improving their skill set.

More attention is focused on home working and people have converted a corner of their homes to office space. I think working from home is going to be popular. In terms of productivity levels, I believe they have increased.

Niraj Agarwal, Founder: *Digital Assist*

Increased Networks Abroad

Inside Kuwait, various organizations have taken to online collaboration tools used to conduct official business. Personally, I have increased my network globally, in Europe, North America, Far East and Australia. It has been an excellent platform to collaborate and obtain cross-cultural knowledge.

Along with a not-for-profit organization in KSA, I initiated a working group of Business Management Consultants with the aim to network, share knowledge and support one another. This has been well received and is an excellent opportunity to network online, support one another, obtain exposure to the market, and also to give back to society.

Rizwana Narvel, Founder: *HiPPO Associates*

In Conversation With

Steff Wright - Chairman of Gusto Group Ltd

Ladey Adey (LA): Steff, you were telling me about a new kind of network, which involves the community as well as business people. Can you tell me a little bit more please?

Steff Wright (SW): It's a network called the Community Conversation, and it's a post Covid-19 inspired idea. I'd like to give a little bit of context, thinking about how communities have evolved over the centuries; our communities were excellent ways to communicate with each other. People would walk around and say, *"Hello!"* meet in local pubs, walk their dogs and take their kids to the local parks or meet and play sport on green spaces. Everybody dealt with each other within the community. Once we had the local butcher, baker, candlestick maker, business professionals, vicar, doctor, postmaster, headmistress, teacher, and even the local policeman - everybody knew who everybody was because they all lived within the same community.

Communities, as I remember them growing up in a small village, included the butcher's vans and other mobile businesses driving round and having its own fire station. Over time, people had more opportunities to move away. Car ownership grew, people started working away from village life - in towns and cities rather than necessarily working in the communities where they lived. This was seen as progress with new technologies such as mobile phones and the Internet enabling us to build virtual business communities and social communities away from our physical communities. Local community life became less important as our wider network provided everything we needed.

Then, suddenly, we're shoved into this lockdown situation where people are actually locked within those physical communities for an extended period of time. Gradually over time, people are getting to know their neighbours again, and actually taking notice of the community in which they live - a lot more than they ever did. This is where the idea of the Community Conversation network came in.

LA: How has the idea developed?

SW: I organised a large networking event lasting over five hours with the Lincolnshire Chamber of Commerce. The agenda covered different sections of life - education, travel and areas covered by government departments. We had speakers from all over the country.

LA: Following this inspiration, how was the first Community Conversation group in Collingham, Nottinghamshire, established?

SW: I wanted to know if we used a video meeting platform to link up leaders and motivators who all shared an interest in improving their local community, we could improve life for those living there. I spoke to local business people, Parish Councillors, the District Council, the leader of the Women's Institute - everyone I could think of - from the local football club and tennis club to shop-keepers. Would there be an appetite to bring together different people from the local community?

I believe Collingham has vitality and a forward-thinking energy. We have a medical centre, churches, sports clubs, a school, a fantastic community pub, and there are over 100 organisations within the village covering everything from toddlers groups to the University of the Third Age - a wide variety of people across all generations. We formed a video conference call and Facebook Live broadcast and trialled it for three weeks at Wednesday lunchtime for an hour and a half. Since then, we've moved it to a Thursday evening for an hour, and it's been very well received. Resident, *Kerry Lummus* said, *"I attended the lunchtime ones and spoke from a business perspective on the second one. We were in 'deepest darkest' lockdown at the time, and it was an absolutely brilliant way of bringing the community back together and hearing how everyone was getting on – just when we needed it most."*

LA: What has come out of the Community Conversation that surprised you?

SW: People who would not normally speak to each other are now finding out about each other and understanding one another. The feedback I'm getting from people is; *"This is brilliant. I didn't know about... Now I've spoken to that person or heard their view on things I can see things differently."* We're developing the conversations as we learn more, using the group to talk together on a variety of topics, for instance, the feasibility of creating a local market.

LA: What type of people do you need to form a Community Conversation network?

SW: I'd say if anyone is interested in founding this type of network, they must have a positive entrepreneurial mind-set and be a good host. We want Community Conversation to be about people interested in developing ideas and having constructive conversations about their community, and in using video conferencing to communicate these. This is opposite to what can happen on local Facebook groups, which can result in opinionated, critical and judgemental people who get bogged down with reasons why things can't work.

Our Collingham Community Conversation is in its infancy, but I can see projects coming from it. It's a great platform to move ideas forward by having lots of different people who are all *'on the same page'*, bringing different expertise, and who are eager to take action.

LA: Has Community Conversation only been made possible by online technology?

SW: Yes. This technology is giving us a larger reach and making it easier for people to contribute. We use video conference technology like Zoom, then stream it live on Facebook. This often gets re-streamed and shared across other local Facebook groups. Typically, we'll have 30 people on the call. Then, as it's posted out, a few hundred people listen and consume it in the same way as they do a local news programme. It gets people talking together within their community on pertinent points, in ways that are modern and make sense to them. We are looking at open source software to replace Zoom and Facebook as this fits better with the community ethos.

LA: How do you keep people on-topic and being constructive without personal agendas coming out?

SW: I think it's the power of people actually sitting and talking together, and finding ways to solve issues constructively. It's self-censored because they are viewed via the video screen. Being an anonymous faceless keyboard warrior on Facebook is not encouraged. Within the conversational group, people tend to react positively. If needed, we've got the power to switch the microphone off if someone chooses to disrupt a meeting. So far, we've found it very constructive.

LA: Do you plan to have Community Conversation networks in other villages and towns?

SW: This would be great. The Collingham group is the first, but we're looking to develop the model. We've created a brand, logo and website, and had a small film produced by *Matthew Hamilton*, a neighbour who's an Emmy award-winning cameraman - all without charge! The concept is, the network ownership sits within the community, as it's the community who create the conversation. I'm not looking at this as a commercial enterprise or to monetise it. It would have great benefit to every village or district if they were to roll it out within their community.

LA: How would a vision of Community Conversation throughout the UK and internationally work?

SW: I think it's a model that's repeatable and scalable anywhere around the world. There are lots of really strong communities with different cultures in the world. I feel that UK communities have lost a crucial element of community life because people have lost local focus. It's time to embed that important extra layer back into the physical community.

LA: I think the Community Conversation is inspired, and it could bring new life into the reducing participants within organisations like the local Church, Women's Institute and Parish Councils! If somebody was interested in setting up a Community Conversation network for their community, how would they go about doing this?

SW: Go to the website *http://www.communityconversation.org*.uk. We're putting resources there to give people the tools to get their local Community Conversation started.

LA: Is there a type of person that you think will take the initiative and 'run with it'?

SW: I think it needs to be someone confident, motivated, a good communicator and a good listener, who can help ideas develop without taking over. It needs to be a collaborative community project. I'd suggest someone with business acumen (so they are solution finders rather than problem dwellers) someone who can take ideas forward and has a burning interest in their local community.

LA: When you say, *"a community"*, is there a minimum number of people? Are we talking a single village, collection of villages, a town or district?

SW: I think the smaller, the better. There may be overlaps into other streets, or it may evolve into a larger area. In general, we're looking at a small community. For instance, there's no point in doing the Community Conversation network for the whole of a town the size of Newark, UK. It's just too big - people aren't going to connect with it in the same way as they would do if it were their street or their immediate community.

I think we need to get the Parish and District Councils on board with it so that they can give contributions each week. My motivation and drive were spurred by watching TV and listening to broadcasts from No.10, Downing Street with *Professor Stephen Powis* (the *National Medical Director of NHS England*), who's trying to come up with a solution that satisfies everybody in the country. For Covid-19, it's impossible. He can't come up with one answer that fits everybody. The answers need to come from the communities themselves; this is what will drive Community Conversation to thrive.

A culture of criticism has been created about the Prime Minister, *Boris Johnson* and the government every time they come up with a new set of rules, mainly because the rules are not always relevant to our community. If you live in a small rural village or town with lots of space, then the rules put in place for social distancing aimed at the centre of London aren't as relevant and will be interpreted in a very different way to make them so.

In my view, the best way for us to be a functional and healthy society is to decide how we reorganise ourselves. To achieve a good quality of life for ourselves and our children going forward, off the back of the

Covid-19 situation, respecting social distancing and other factors that we're going to have to sort out over the coming months and years, the decisions need to be implemented by and thought through by, the local community.

LA: This book has been looking at business networking online but obviously learns from general networking etiquettes and so forth. How do you see Community Conversation fitting in with the new online way of communicating?

SW: It absolutely fits perfectly with it. If you've got people engaging on a local community platform with each other, then the next thing they're going to do is start to trade with each other as well. So the business aspect continues. In the Collingham Community Conversation group, we've created business shout-outs in the meeting. Effectively, we're advertising local business like the ones who're featured in the village magazines and newsletters. They are people known, liked and trusted by their community. Our agenda isn't fixed but changes as we evolve. In a one hour meeting, we have 20 minutes of community notices where we ask organisations from our community to give a short talk about what they do, and we keep the all-important factor of having a conversation around a theme or topic.

LA: At the beginning of this book, I compiled a plausible history of business networking. It makes sense to me to finish the timeline with the development of Community Conversation in the belief that they will mushroom and be part of our business networks in the future.

SW: I think that's a natural progression. As you've said, at one time we'd have gathered round the fire to discuss the best way for our community to develop their lives in work and play. Today, we're gathered around our home computer, able to use this as a platform to engage with members of the community who want to make a difference and improve their lives. We have started with Community Conversation as a model, and it's really scalable. I mean, massively scalable.

Final Comment from Ladey

A brave new world of business networking is evolving. As we live the experience, it's time to invest in this change. Successful networkers will be the business people who embrace this and utilise the time to forge ahead to the betterment of their business.

This book was written and published over a span of six months, (April - September 2020) and already networks groups have come and gone, businesses folded and new ones started as we all come to grips with a prolonged lockdown and its affect on business.

You may have noticed some repetition such as *'Stop video'* when eating and *'Data is King'* - there are some points which can't be emphasised enough!

It has been a delight talking with contributors to this book (over 100 networkers) via the *'In Conversation With'*, *'Features'* and *'Viewpoints'*. Some common themes have emerged from people who have never met delivering strong messages about the principles of networking such as: networking is about relationships and building positive interaction between people, the difference virtual meetings have made but this process needs to be part of a strategic plan, and how business people have embracing the evolving change in the world of business networking.

I look forward to seeing online networking mature and be an accepted and crucial part of business. I expect it to be used to further companies' sales and marketing, build strong relationships and for significant achievement through Successful Business Networking Online.

Additional Tools and Information

*Networking is a mindset - it is a strategy for life,
a way to create connections that could last
a lifetime and in all areas of your life.
That is why I say Networking is 24/7.*

Andrea R Nierenberg

trust you'll find the following Extras useful. If you have any questions feel free to contact me on ladey@ladeyadey.com.

Extra 1:   50 Billion Users *(from Introduction)*.

Extra 2:   Chatham House Rule *(from Chapter 2)*.

Extra 3:   The Athena Network® Monthly Minute Template *(from Chapter 3)*.

Extra 4:   Balanced Networking Scorecard and Your Networking Scores Tables *(from Chapter 6)*.

Extra 5:   The Passionate PA - To Do List *(from Chapter 7)*.

Extra 6:   Services from *Federation of Small Business* (FSB).

Extra 1

NUMBER OF YEARS IT TOOK FOR EACH PRODUCT TO GAIN 50 MILLION USERS

Airlines	68yrs
Cars	62yrs
Telephones	50yrs
Electricity	46yrs
Credit Cards	28yrs
TV	22yrs
ATM	18yrs
Computers	14yrs
Mobile	12yrs
Internet	7yrs
LinkedIn	6yrs
Ipod	4yrs
Zoom	3yrs
Facebook	3yrs
Twitter	2yrs
Pokemon Go	19days

Compiled by Abbirose Adey, Pink Parties Press

The Chatham House Rule

The Chatham House Rule reads as follows:

"When a meeting, or part thereof, is held under the Chatham House Rule, participants are free to use the information received, but neither the identity nor the affiliation of the speaker(s), nor that of any other participant, may be revealed."

The world-famous Chatham House Rule may be invoked at meetings to encourage openness and the sharing of information.

Explanation of the Rule

The Chatham House Rule began at the UK Royal Institute of International Affairs based at Chatham House, St. James Square, London. The rule originated in June 1927 with the aim to provide anonymity to speakers and to encourage openness and the sharing of information. It is now used throughout the world as an aid to free discussion. Meetings do not have to take place at Chatham House, or be organized by Chatham House, to be held under the Rule.

Meetings, events and discussions held at Chatham House are normally conducted *'on the record'* with the Rule occasionally invoked at the speaker's request. In cases where the Rule is not considered sufficiently strict, an event may be held *'off the record'*.

Monthly Minute Template

No more than 120 words will ensure that you keep to the minute in the meeting.

Opening – 10 Seconds

Your Name
Your Business Name (if you have one)
Where you are based or where you are looking for business

```


```

Middle – 30 Seconds (maximum)

A BRIEF overview of products/services you offer, what you require

```



```

Call To Action – 10 Seconds (maximum)

```


```

Conclusion – 10 Seconds (maximum)

Your Name:
Your Business Name (if you have one) or Profession:
Strapline:

```


```

V3.0 24.7.18 AC

Initiative

Time to Get Out There and Do It	
Attend a Networking Event	10 points
Arrange and frame a 1-2-1 meeting	20 points
Follow-up with people and add them to your list	20 points
Gain a new customer from networking	50 points

Interactive

Low level Contact	
Interact with an individual in a chat box	10 points
Leave a comment on a group page	10 points
Respond to another person's post	10 points
Add a constructive comment or question in chat box	20 points

Networking Balanced Scorecard

Introduction

Referrals and Social Media Responses	
Your affiliate link is used or you ask someone for their affiliate link	10 points
Your name is tagged or mentioned on Social Media	10 points
Someone connects you after seeing you at a networking meeting	10 points
You refer someone or are referred by someone to a new contact	20 points

Interfacing

Higher Level Branding	
Ask a Speaker a question	15 points
Create and post an article, blog, video or webinar	20 points
Speak at a networking event	30 points
Connect an 'unknown' business person and start a conversation	90 points

Your Networking Scores

Print off this page and use this table to add up your score on a weekly basis. Give yourself points for EVERY time you do an activity.

The only competition here is within your business. It provides vital data to your networking activity; to help decide whether you are receiving a good return on your investment.

Your Networking Scores		
Week Commencing: _____		
Activity	**Points**	**Your Score**
Initiative (Get Out There & Do It)		
Attending a Networking Event	10	
Arrange and Diarise a 1-2-1 Meeting	20	
Follow up and Add Contact to List	20	
Gain a New Customer from Networking	50	
Total		
Introduction (Referrals and Social Media)		
Your affiliate link is used or you ask someone for their affiliate link	10	
Your name is tagged or mentioned on Social Media	10	
Someone contacts you after seeing you in a networking meeting	10	
You refer someone or are referred by someone to a new contact	20	
Total		
Interfacing (Higher Level Branding)		
Ask a Speaker a question	10	
Create and post an article, blog, video or webinar	20	
Speak at a networking event	30	
Contact an 'unknown' business person and start a conversation	40	
Total		
Interaction (Low Level Contact)		
Interact with an individual in a chat box	10	
Leave a comment on a group page	10	
Respond to another person's post	10	
Add a constructive comment or question in chat	20	
Total		

For each month do a summary sheet using your weekly score results.

Your Networking SUMMARY Scores	
Month: _____	
Activity	**FINAL Scores**
Initiative (Get Out There & Do It)	
Attending a Networking Event	
Arrange and Diarise a 1-2-1 Meeting	
Follow up and Add Contact to List	
Gain a New Customer from Networking	
Total	
Introduction (Referrals and Social Media)	
Your affiliate link is used or you ask someone for their affiliate link	
Your name is tagged or mentioned on Social Media	
Someone contacts you after seeing you in a networking meeting	
You refer someone or are referred by someone to a new contact	
Total	
Interfacing (Higher Level Branding)	
Ask a Speaker a question	
Create and post an article, blog, video or webinar	
Speak at a networking event	
Contact an 'unknown' business person and start a conversation	
Total	
Interaction (Low Level Contact)	
Interact with an individual in a chat box	
Leave a comment on a group page	
Respond to another person's post	
Add a constructive comment or question in chat	
Total	

If you would like a copy of these tables (in excel) email me: ladey@ladeyadey.com and I will send them to you.

Extra**5**

THE PASSIONATE PA
REAL PEOPLE. REAL BUSINESS. REAL VALUE

Date

Today's TOP Priority	My Health & Well-being

Business Development To Dos	Business Admin & Planning To Dos

Money Making To Dos	My Personal To Dos

www.thepassionatepa.co.uk   T: 0330 002 0200

Thanks to Kate Chastey & Laurey Buckland both Passionate PAs

Federation of Small Businesses (FSB)

Katrina Pierce, Development Manager for Lincolnshire,

As an organisation that is built on the power of people joining together, the FSB has a strong heritage in hosting networking. Since 1974, we've helped small business owners and self-employed people to forge connections and influence change. When nationwide lockdown kicked in we moved our entire event and networking programme online, and we learnt a very quickly what our members needed.

I found that giving people good notice that their *'60-seconds'* are coming up worked well – people seem more relaxed and their one-minute pitches were more succinct and memorable.

In the early days, people were flocking to online events, not only to get updated but also to connect with each other. It was clear just how much our members relied on FSB. The desire to reach out, to seek help, to stay in touch was really strong and it's been an honour to provide people with these opportunities. As time has gone on, it has become a positive habit for people – long may it continue.

Member Benefits

- FSB Payments
- FSB Business Banking
- FSB Funding Platform
- FSB Debt Recovery
- FSB Workplace Pensions
- FSB Cyber Protection
- FSB Legal Hub
- FSB Tax Investigation Protection
- FSB Legal Protection Scheme
- FSB Employment Protection
- FSB Health & Safety Advice
- FSB Care
- FSB Insurance Service
- FSB PR/Crisis Management

Thank You

*Networking is not about just connecting people.
It's about connecting people with people, people with ideas,
and people with opportunities.*

Michele Jennae

I'd like to acknowledge and publicly thank the people who made such a difference to how this book evolved. They include some of my business networking heroes and heroines. I was so made up and honoured when they responded to my invite, and agreed, to be part of the book.

Have you've realised this book is also a networking tool where I have introduced you to a number of businessmen and women who are experts in their field and have a high respect for networking? Do use their links to contact them and introduce yourself – say I referred you. Keep enjoying networking whether on or offline.

Following is a list of my guests with more detail about them. Meanwhile, I look forward to meeting everyone again - Networking online.

*The main thing I wanted to say, and thankfully
it's what most people say they get out of the book,
is simply an acknowledgement that we do affect
each other in ways we can't predict.*

Jay Asher

Photo by Caleb Chen on Unsplash

Foreword

Nigel Botterill is famous for building nine separate million pound businesses of his own in the last 12 years. As a Sunday Times best-selling author, serial entrepreneur plus founder and CEO of Entrepreneurs Circle - the UK's largest private organisation dedicated to helping entrepreneurs to get & keep customers, he has shared the stage with luminaries like Sir Richard Branson, Lord Sugar and President Bill Clinton and he excels in front of large audiences. Nigel is known as UK's most sought after business growth expert.

Author of: *Botty's Rules, It's all Changed and Co-author with Martin Gladdish: Build Your Business in 90 Minutes a Day.*

https://entrepreneurscircle.org/

In Conversation With

Anthony Thomson, Co-founder and Chairman of 86 400 and Goldman Visiting Professor of Innovation and Enterprise, Newcastle Business School.

Anthony is not your typical banking executive. A marketer by background, *Anthony* has founded two banks in the UK, *Metro Bank*, the UK's first new bank in 150 years, and *Atom Bank*, the UK's first bank for mobiles. *Anthony* has raised in excess of $1billion in capital over the course of his career. He is a highly respected financial services expert worldwide and is a member of the Advisory Board of *Bank ABC, Bahrain*.

As Chairman of Australia's first Smartbank *86 400*, *Anthony* brings his extensive experience in the financial services industry and hunger to shake up the banking landscape in the Australian market. *Anthony* collects wine and guitars and loves to race cars (not all at the same time).

Co-author with Lucian Camp of: *No Small Change, Why Financial Services needs Better Marketing.*

Alisoun MacKenzie is a TEDx & Keynote Speaker, Coach, Author, Mentor and Retreat Leader. Alisoun is often described as one of the most authentic and inspiring souls you can meet.

Alisoun is on a mission to improve the lives of 100,000+ people - by making it easy for women to feel good, enjoy meaningful success and have more impact in the world (personally or through their business) and also through her support of causes that tackle poverty, education and social justice. *Alisoun's* keynote talks, training, mentoring and best-selling books have favourably changed the fortune of thousands of people worldwide. She loves doing humanitarian work, travelling, fundraising and living by the beach in Scotland.

Author of: *Give to Profit, How to Grow Your Business by Supporting Charities and Social Causes*, and *Heartatude – the 9 Principles of Heart-Centered Success.*   *https://www.alisoun.com*

Brad Burton, the UK's No.1 motivational speaker, was born in Salford in 1973, and was regularly told he would amount to nothing: except, perhaps, a bank-robber. Proving all his detractors wrong, he entered the computer games industry, becoming a commentator of the Channel 4 show, Gamesmaster.

In 2004, *Brad* started a marketing business in London, financing the company by delivering pizzas. In 2006, *Brad* shut down his marketing business and set up *4Networking*, a business networking company. *Brad* has given many interviews about business and entrepreneurship appearing on *Working Lunch, BBC Newsnight* and the *Jeremy Vine Show*, to name a few.

Having combatted many struggles with life and love, he now describes himself as *"no longer skint, no longer depressed and actually quite balanced and happy"*. He lives in Somerset with his wife and three children.

Author of: *Life. Business. Just Got Easier, Now What?*, *Get Off Your Arse* and *Get Off Your Arse Too*. *https://www.bradburton.biz*

Jacqueline Rogers launched The Athena Network® in December 2005. It's the leading International Networking, Training and Development Business Club for Female Executives and Entrepreneurs.

Jacqueline heads up the operation and says, "It's a network business that's just grown and grown." She rather wryly admits. "It wasn't so much a question of choosing networking but networking choosing me – it just made such good sense!"

The Athena Network® now encompasses over 130 groups countrywide and to keep her *'hand-in'*, *Jacqueline,* personally runs East Chiltern region and blesses the fact daily that she has an outstanding support team to enable her to do that.

https://theathenanetwork.com

Mike Kim is a speaker and marketing strategist who specializes in brand strategy and copywriting. He's been hired by some of today's most influential thought-leader brands including: John Maxwell, Donald Miller, Suzanne Evans, and Catalyst.

For years he was the Chief Marketing Officer of a successful multi-million dollar company near New York City. Nowadays, you'll find him speaking at conferences, looking for the next great place to scuba dive, and sipping a glass of *Macallan 15* — all while teaching everything he knows about branding, entrepreneurship and life through his hit podcast, *Brand You*.

http://www.mikekim.com

Mike Luxford has over 30 years experience in computer networking work with many of the major IT companies. His philosophy is to prepare clients for the future so that adoption of new technology is more straight-forward.

Mike has been amazed that lockdown has shaved 10 years of the prediction that most Mike Luxford 3 people will work from home, or work from venues of their choice with any device to hand and the majority of households would use video conferencing as their main platform of choice for communication. The tipping point for this was anticipated to be 20030, but this is now the reality for many – 10 years early!   *http://www.mlcs.co.uk*

John McHale is a dynamic, motivated and a result orientated professional with a proven business and corporate track record of success in helping business owners achieve high profitable growth year

on year (including the Best Client Results for the Lincolnshire/Yorkshire region for 2018 and 2019 and the Best Client Results for Europe, Middle East and Africa for 2019).

John is a down-to-earth communicator who dislikes jargon and really understands what drives people. He cares enough not to tell clients what they want to hear, but instead will function as a critical friend and hold them to account to bring about changes needed to create the business they want, and the life they deserve.

https://actioncoach.co.uk/coaches/john-mchale/

Mandy Allen has been involved with networking for the over 15 years and has seen a noticeable change in formats over that time. In 2008, Mandy started *'The Newbiz Network'* supporting start-up businesses and it ran for two years.

Mandy is the Business Relationship Manager of CRM Insights, holding responsibility for generating leads through both online and face-to-face networking.

She established *The Referral Network* in 2018 to support the business at *CRM Insights Ltd* by aligning with relevant business partners. Mandy says: *"The power of building relationships online should never be underestimated. As human beings we naturally thrive on relationships, online networking has continued to help us achieve and manage that."*

A true people-person, she has an innate ability to engage in conversation with just about anyone. A key aspect of her approach; the ability to listen, and to know instantly who she can refer people to - whether that's internal or external to CRM Insights.

www.crminsights.co.uk

Steff Wright started his first company as a mobile DJ at the age of 17. He says, ***"I have always had an enthusiasm for developing businesses and innovating in different sectors."*** I bought my first  fully electric car 20 years ago and our Gusto Homes business has led the way in developing sustainable communities and low energy housing for over 20 years. Our *Rototek* rotational moulding company is now the world's largest manufacturer of sailing dinghies employing over 120 staff and innovating across a wide range of products.

Alongside building innovative companies within *Gusto Group*, I have a passion re-investing profits back into start-up companies and social enterprises, especially those focused on innovative ways of tackling the climate crisis.

I spent 10 years as a Director and Chairman of *Lincoln City FC*, we put in place a sustainable business model whilst trying to gain a promotion.

My passion for travel and lifelong learning is channelled into the growth of *GlobalGrad.com* where we are creating a new learning ecosystem to inspire the next generation through combining online education with global and purposeful volunteering.

When not at my laptop, I enjoy kite surfing and snowboarding and am slowly getting into cycling!" *http://www.gustogroup.co.uk/*
http://www.communityconversation.org.uk/

Guest Features (in order of appearance)

Margot Grantham, Meryl Shirley, Felicity Francis, Robert Middleton, Nathan Eaves, Graham Todd, Dr David Cliff, Lauren V Davis, Tony Smith, Louise Third, Simon Goodchild, Mark Jarvis, Lesley Burton, Hannah Long, Helen Millington, Clive Catton, Diana Catton.

Viewpoints (in order of appearance)

Sandra Garlick, Deborah Firmstone, Julie Taylor, Chan Abraham, Rob Purle, Nicola Gaughan, Melanie Smith-Rawlings, Kieran Willis, Rachel Haith, Ellie Hiam, Mark Jarvis, Stephen Goddard, Neil Jones, Andrew Kotek, Bill Partington, Hannah Thompson, Robert Drury, Kim Penney, Sarah Coleman, Marie Elizabeth Edwards, Belinda Roughton, Jon Davies, Kathryn Colas, Chris Moody, Claire Bicknell, Leona Burton, Stav Melides, Jackie Forbes, Nicola Ellwood, Lorraine Lewis, Chris Rose, Jo Keen, Tim Ladd, Bryan Cohen, Charlie Whyman, Bev Thorogood, Leah Leaves, David O'Brien, Mark Saxby, Joe Glover, Cath Babbington, Melanie Jackson, Mike Stokes, Hannah Charman, Tony Walton, Debra Pitchford, Lisa Davies, Bharat Jethani, Niraj Agarwal, Rizwana Narvel.

Screenshot Models

Abbirose Adey, Denis P Adey, Keith Girling, Kayleigh Nicolaou.

Stories

Kris Cavanaugh Castro, Ron Clark, Kathryn Colas, Adam Davey, Pete Davis, Mike Garner, Tom Huberty, Ian Johnson, Neil Jones, Lorraine Lewis, Amal Loring, Ken Marshall, John McHale, Chris Messina, Glenn Salter, Sheila Stamp, Nicola Watson, Joanna Weave, Ben Wright.

Additions

Taseer Ahmad (Taz), Laurey Buckland, Kate Chastey, Catherine Rannus, Angela Scott, Harmeet Singh.

Kiss-off Line

Niraj Agarwal, Nicky Armstrong, Ernie Boxall, Katya Bozukova, Nicola Ellwood, Paula Finch, Dewi Hughes, Mark Jarvis, Kim Penney, Bruce Roberts, Emma Rose, Lyndon Sanders, Tony Smith, Jason Spering, Faye Stenson, Bev Thorogood, Paul Tompsett, Cristina Vannini-Goodchild, Neil Wainman.

Support from

Peter Jones, Alert PR *https://www.linkedin.com/in/redalertmedia*

Katrina Pierce and **Andrew Masters,** Federation of Small Business

fsb.org.uk

Karen Wilbourn is owner of Leicestershire based Design and Media company Quack Media. With a long career in design and manufacturing *Karen* now designs and writes content for client social media accounts and in her capacity as a Shopify Partner, designs and manages Shopify websites. Karen also works with individuals and businesses on re-branding projects.   *https://quackmedia.co.uk*

Kerry Lummus is an experienced virtual assistant or PA, but she is so much more. She is an ambassador for her clients' businesses. Kerry helps to bring in new business by introducing her clients to useful connections and by identifying opportunities for them. She likes to think of herself as her client's *'wing woman'*. As a qualified proofreader, she was delighted to *'cut her teeth'* on Ladey's ground-breaking book.   *http://klss.co.uk*

Alan Long took the Cover Picture in 2018 at a wedding using a green screen – who know that it'll be used for this book? *Alan* is a Freelance Event Photographer & Videographer. He photographs in Commercial Promotions & Education, Corporate & Entertainment and Digital Conversions & Non linear editing.

http://www.the-event-photographer.com

Last but not least –

Joanne Whitlock is a Storyteller, Writer & Cartoonist. She has been working as a speaking skills coach for the last fifteen years, committed to helping people who feel they are held back by poor speaking skills.

With a quirky, and often self-deprecating, sense of humour she combines her teaching with cartoons and conversations about the Hero's Journey, with a goal of helping others feel good about themselves, their abilities and wherever they are at on their journey.

Author of: GROW, The Ups and Downs of Transforming Your Life

http://www.joannewhitlock.com/

I don't think I've missed anyone but just in case I have

THANK YOU

Check These Out

Networking is an enrichment program,
not an entitlement program.

Susan RoAne

Books

Auel, Jean M, *The Clan of the Cave Bear,* (Bantam Books), 1991

Barnum, PT, *The Art of Money Getting, or Golden Rules for Making Money,* (Createspace) 2016

Booher, Dianna, *Communicate with Confidence: How to Say it Right the First Time and Every Time,* (McGraw-Hill), 2011

Botterill, Nigel, Gladdish, Martin, *Build Your Business in 90 Minutes a Day,* (Capstone), 2015

Botterill, Nigel, *The Botty Rules: Success Secrets for Business in the 21st Century,* (Glazer Kennedy Pub), 2011

Bounds, Andy, *The Jelly Effect - How to Make Your Communication Stick,* (Capstone), 2007

Burg, Bob, *Endless Referrals, Network Your Everyday Contacts into Sales,* (McGraw-Hill), 2005

Burton, Brad, *Now What? Moving you and your business onto the next level, that's what,* (4Publishing), 2016

Burton, Brad, *Life. Business. Just Got Easier,* (Capstone), 2013

Burton, Brad, *Get Off Your Arse Too* (4Publishing), 2011

Carnegie, Dale, *How to Win Friends and Influence People,* (Vermillion), 2006

Chaney, J.N, Hopper, Christopher, *Ruins of the Galaxy* (Variant Publications), 2019

Colas, Kathryn, *How to Survive Menopause Without Losing Your Mind,* (Pink Parties Press), 2020

Goodchild, Simon, *Make People Buy Your Stuff,* (Traffic For Sales), 2020

Heppell, Michael, *17 - The Little Way to Get a Lot Done* (Gloop Books), 2020.

Kaplan, Robert S, **Norton, David P,** *The Balanced Scorecard: Translating Strategy into Action,* (Harvard Business Review Press), 1996

Lerner, Gerda, *Early Community Work of Black Club Women,* (University of Chicago Press), 1974

Marshall, Ken, *Beyond Traditional Training,* (Kogan Page), 1999

Misner, Ivan and Hilliard, Brian *Networking Like a Pro: Turning Contacts into Connections,* (Entrepreneur Press) 2017

Moore, Michelle, *Selling Simplified,* (Forty Four Publishing), 2013

New International Version, *NIV Holy Bible,* (Hodder Classics), 2015

Nierenberg, Andrea R, *Savvy Networking - 118 Fast & Effective Tips for Business Success,* (Capital Books), 2007

Schreiter, Keith, Tom 'Big Al', *The One Minute Presentation,* (Fortune Network Publishing), 2017

Shakespeare, William, *As You Like It,* (The Arden Shakespeare) 3 Rev Ed, 2004

Sinek, Simon, *Start with Why: How great Leaders Inspire Everyone to Take Action,* (Penguin), 2011

Whitlock, Joanne, *GROW: the Ups and Downs of Transforming Your Life,* (Cantomax Limited), 2019

Music

Youssou N'Dour featuring Cherry Neneh, McVey Cameron and Sharp Jonathan, *7 Seconds,* (Columbia), 1994

Pictures

Bruno Emmanuelle, *The New Normal,* (Unsplash), https://unsplash.com/photos/azsk_6IMT3I, 15/08/20

Caleb Chen, *Thank YOU,* (Unsplash), https://unsplash.com/photos/l9Vrl5RT-jw 15/08/20

Celpax, *How Was Your Day?,* (Unsplash) https://unsplash.com/photos/OtV1OXDX94I 15/08/20

Clker-Free-Vector-Images 29580, *Female Avatar,* (Pixabay) https://pixabay.com/vectors/user-female-avatar-woman-307993/ 01/08/20

Open Clipart-Vectors 27406, *Avatar Picture,* (Pixabay), https://pixabay.com/vectors/avatar-face-glasses-male-man-1294776/ 08/08/20

Open Clipart-Vectors 27407, *Business Woman Avatar,* (Pixabay), https://pixabay.com/vectors/avatar-cartoon-comic-female-girl-2027367/ 15/06/20

Unattributed, P T Barnum - *Picture,* (Harvard Library, Public Domain), https://en.wikipedia.org/wiki/P._T._Barnum 08/04/20

Wikipedia contributors, *The Syndics of the Drapers' Guild by Rembrant 1662,* (Wikipedia, The Free Encyclopedia), https-//commons.wikimedia.org/w/index.php?curid=13411875 08/04/20

Websites

Aaron Garner, *The Truth about the Communication Formula – 55/38/7,*(EIA Group), https://www.eiagroup.com/communication-formula/ 24/08/20

Alex York, *How to Create a Hashtag for Your Brand,* (Sproutsocial), https://sproutsocial.com/insights/create-a-hashtag/ 23/06/20

Alfred Lua, *21 Top Social Media Sites to Consider for Your Brand,* (Buffer Marketing Library), https://buffer.com/library/social-media-sites/ 06/08/20

Alison E Berman, *Why Grappling With Digital Overload is Now part of the Human Condition,* (Singularity Hub), https://singularityhub.com/2016/01/15/why-grappling-with-digital-overload-is-now-part-of-the-human-condition/ 07/05/20

Ben Sailer, *How To Use Hashtags Effectively Without Being Annoying,* (Coschedule Blog), https://coschedule.com/blog/how-to-use-hashtags/ 03/05/20

Brian DeChesare, *Investment Banking Networking: The Definitive Guide,* https://www.mergersandinquisitions.com/investment-banking-networking/ 10/04/20

Caroline Forsey, *18 Quotes About Networking that'll help you connect with People,* (Hubspot), https://blog.hubspot.com/marketing/networking-quotes 09/05/20

Conrad Hackett and **David McClendon,** *Christians remain World's Largest Religious Group but they are Declining in Europe,* (Pew Research Center), https://www.pewresearch.org/fact-tank/2017/04/05/christians-remain-worlds-largest-religious-group-but-they-are-declining-in-europe/ 14/04/20

Doreen Dodgen-Magee Psy. D, *Why Video Chats are Wearing Us Out,* (Psychology Today), https://www.psychologytoday.com/us/blog/deviced/202004/why-video-chats-are-wearing-us-out 01/05/20

Dr Matthew Green, *The Surprising History of London's Fascinating (but forgotten) Coffee Houses,* (The Telegraph), https://www.telegraph.co.uk/travel/destinations/europe/united-kingdom/england/london/articles/London-cafes-the-surprising-history-of-Londons-lost-coffeehouses/ 31/05/20

Editorial team, *7 Second Rule of Websites,* (Gumas), https://gumas.com/the-7-second-rule-of-websites/ 21/05/20

Editorial team, *10 Symptoms of Information Overload and How it Affects your Brain & Body,* (Learning Mind), https://www.learning-mind.com/information-overload-symptoms/ 07/05/20

Editorial team, *11 Reasons you need a Social Media Management Tool,* (e-clincher), https://eclincher.com/blog/11-reasons-you-need-a-social-media-management-tool/ 03/05/20

Editorial team, *18 Easy Ways to Network,* https://www.scienceofpeople.com/networking/ 07/04/20

Editorial Team, 25 Most Important Days In Computing, (Galaxy Visions) http://www.galaxyvisions.com/the-25-most-important-days-in-computing/ 1/9/20

Editorial team, *27 Eye-Opening Website Statistics: Is Your Website Costing You Clients?*, (Sweor), https://www.sweor.com/firstimpressions/ 11/04/20
Editorial team, *77 Best Network Marketing Books Out There,* (Direct Selling Star), https://directsellingstar.com/network-marketing-books/ 14/04/20

Editorial team, *Business Networks and Networking Groups in the UK*, (Entrepreneur Handbook), https://entrepreneurhandbook.co.uk/business-networks/ 14/04/20

Editorial team, *Chatham House Rule,* (Chatham House), https://www. chathamhouse.org/chatham-house-rule 15/04/20

Editorial team, *Conference Software,* (Source Forge), https://sourceforge. net/software/conference/ 03/05/20

Editorial team, *Ergonomic Computer Workstation Set-up Advice,* (Posturite), https://www.posturite.co.uk/help-advice/useful-resources/learning-guides/ ergonomic-workstation-setup 03/05/20

Editorial team, *History of the Chamber Movement,* (International Chamber of Commerce), https://iccwbo.org/chamber-services/world-chambers-federation/history-chamber-movement/ 14/04/20

Editorial team, *How to Behave - Tips!,* https://www.businessballs.com/ building-relationships/networking/ 21/5/20

Editorial team, *IoD - Our History*, (Institute of Directors), https://www.iod. com/about/our-history 14/04/20

Editorial team, *Interview with Brad Burton, Founder of 4Networking.biz*, (Easyspace), https://www.easyspace.com/blog/2013/11/28/interview-with-brad-burton-founder-of-4networking-biz/ 09/04/20

Editorial team, *Tenth Annual Report of the Tuskegee Woman's Club (1905)*, (Harlan and Smock 0 University of Illinois Press), http://www.nzdl.org/ gsdlmod?e=extlink-00000-00---off-0whist--00-0----0-10-0---0---0direct-10---4-------0-1l--11-en-50---20-help---00-0-1-00-0--4----0-0-11-10-0utfZz-8-00&a=d&d=HASH97165bf98d513706050103/ 14/04/20

Editorial team, *The Difference Between Cold, Warm and Qualified Leads,* (Success Agency), https://www.successagency.com/growth/2014/06/26/ the-difference-between-cold-warm-and-qualified-leads/ 27/06/20

Editorial team, *The History of Network Marketing,* (Betterhealthworkx.com), https://www.betterhealthworx.com/network-marketing-history.html/ 14/04/20

Editorial team, *What is a Social Media Bot?* (Cloudflare), https://www. cloudflare.com/learning/bots/what-is-a-social-media-bot/ 03/05/20

Editorial team, *What is Pestle Analysis?* (Pestle Analysis), https://pestleanalysis.com/what-is-pestle-analysis/ 06/05/20

Editorial team, *Why networking is important for Christian Business Owners,* (Christian Biz Connect), https://www.christianbizconnect.com/networking-important-christian-business-owners/ 14/04/20

Emily Bary, *Zoom, Microsoft, Cloud Usage are Rocketing During Coronavirus Pandemic,* (MarketWatch Inc), https://www.marketwatch.com/story/zoom-microsoft-cloud-usage-are-rocketing-during-coronavirus-pandemic-new-data-show-2020-03-30/ 08/04/20

Erica Julson, *10 Best Ways to Increase Dopamine Levels Naturally,* (Healthline), https://www.healthline.com/nutrition/how-to-increase-dopamine/ 07/05/20

Graham Todd, *Why Your Networking Follow-Ups Suck* (Spaghetti Agency), https://www.spaghettiagency.co.uk/blog/why-your-networking-follow-ups-suck-and-what-you-simply-must-do-about-them/ 16/05/20

Hannah Charman, *Quick Eye Refresher Trick,* https://youtu.be/QfN4LAlFxEE/ 03/05/20

Herminia Ibarra and Mark Lee Hunter, *How Leaders Create and Use Networks,* (Harvard Business Review), https://hbr.org/2007/01/how-leaders-create-and-use-networks/ 07/04/20

Jackie Mansky, *Eight Secret Societies You Might Not Know,* (Smithsonian Magazine), https://www.smithsonianmag.com/history/secret-societies-you-might-not-know-180958294/ 09/04/20

Janelle Raney, *3 ways to Use Polls in Meetings,* (Zoom blog), https://blog.zoom.us/wordpress/2016/09/20/3-ways-to-use-polls-in-meetings/ 03/05/20

Jo Ciriani, *Online Networking Events – The 'New Normal'?,* (Spaghetti Agency), https://www.spaghettiagency.co.uk/blog/online-networking-events-the-new-normal/ 16/06/20

Joel Schwartzberg, *How to Elevate your Presence in a Virtual Meeting,* (Harvard Business Review), https://hbr.org/2020/04/how-to-elevate-your-presence-in-a-virtual-meeting?/ 17/04/20

John Harrington, *The client is not the enemy: 14 quotes on PR measurement you need to read,* (PR Week), https://www.prweek.com/article/1455538/the-client-not-enemy-14-quotes-pr-measurement-need-read#ptzPg7VBzEK4sYgc.99/ 11/06/20

John Lee, *Learning from Paul to Leverage Networking for Missions,* (Christianity Today), https://www.christianitytoday.com/ct/2017/august-web-only/learning-from-paul-networking-evangelism.html/ 14/04/20

Josh, *Best Ring Lights,* (Vloggergear), https://vloggergear.com/best-ring-lights/ 11/07/20

Julia Sklar, *Zoom Fatigue is Taxing the Brain,* (National Geographic), https://www.nationalgeographic.co.uk/science-and-technology/2020/04/zoom-fatigue-is-taxing-the-brain-heres-why-that-happens/ 07/05/20

kjw2, *Baths & Bathing as an Ancient Roman,* (depts.washington.edu), https://depts.washington.edu/hrome/Authors/kjw2/ BathsBathinginAncientRome/pub_zbarticle_view_printable.html/ 31/05/20

kjw3, *Jamaica Wine House,* (depts.washington.edu), https://en.wikipedia.org/ wiki/Jamaica_Wine_House/ 12/07/20

Kris Hart, *Networking - Why Golf is a Top Networking Tool,* (Nextgengolf.org, https://blog.nextgengolf.org/golf-industry/networking-why-golf-is-a-top-networking-tool/ 14/04/20

Lieutenant Joseph A Hendry Jr., CLEE, *The Origin of Lockdown,* (Alice Training Institute), http://hartlake.org/wp-content/uploads/2015/12/ Origin-Of-Lockdown.pdf 12/04/20

Mandy Barrow, *Roman Baths (Thermae),* (Primary Homework Help), http://www.primaryhomeworkhelp.co.uk/romans/baths.html/ 31/05/20

Melonie Dodaro, *Is your LinkedIn Content Strategy Making you Look Desperate?,* (Social Media Today), https://www.socialmediatoday. com/news/is-your-linkedin-content-strategy-making-you-look-desperate/569900/ 03/05/20

Minal, (Marketing by Minal), https://www.marketingbyminal.com/what-is-social-media-tagging/ 03/05/20

Nancy Taylor, https://www.naylor.com/associationadviser/why-are-hashtags-important/ 03/05/20

Patrick Whatman, *Social Mythbusters: Does Using Instagram Hashtags Mean More Engagement?,* (Mention.com), https://mention.com/en/blog/ instagram-hashtags-engagement/ 03/05/20

Pete Davies, *What's in your LinkedIn Feed?* (LinkedIn), https://www.linkedin. com/pulse/whats-your-linkedin-feed-people-you-know-talking-things-pete-davies/ 03/05/20

Peter Aspden, *Art and Commerce: A Difficult Meeting,* (Financial Times), https://www.ft.com/content/064cb214-5fe9-11e2-8d8d-00144feab49a 08/05/20

Peter Geaumont, *How UK coronavirus lockdown compares with other countries,* (Guardian News & Media Ltd), https://www.theguardian.com/ politics/2020/mar/23/how-uk-coronavirus-lockdown-compares-with-other-countries/ 12/04/20

Shalini Umachandran, *Blame it on the virus, it's the largest lockdown in history,* (Livemint), https://www.livemint.com/news/india/blame-it-on-the-virus-it-s-the-largest-lockdown-in-history-11585159348758.html 12/04/20

Simon Parkin, *Has Dopamine got us Hooked on Tech?,* (The Guardian), https://www.theguardian.com/technology/2018/mar/04/has-dopamine-got-us-hooked-on-tech-facebook-apps-addiction/ 07/05/20

Stephanie Thurrott, *Quarantine Fatigue and Stress is Real,* (Today), https://www.today.com/health/quarantine-stress-fatigue-can-online-therapy-help-t180688/ 07/05/20

Thomas DeMichele, *The History of Modern Banking and its Origin: From Early Merchant Banking to the Modern International Banking System,* (Factmyth.com), http://factmyth.com/the-birth-of-modern-banking/ 18/09/16

Tim Brookes, *The 9 Best Social Media Management Apps in 2019,* (Zapier), https://zapier.com/blog/best-social-media-management-tools/ 03/05/20

Trevor Haynes, *Dopamine, Smartphones & You: A battle for your Time,* (Harvard University), http://sitn.hms.harvard.edu/flash/2018/dopamine-smartphones-battle-time/ 07/05/20

uz-idn, *Oldest Coffee House in London,* (Reddit), https://www.reddit.com/r/pics/comments/d0uear/oldest_coffee_house_in_london/ 31/05/20

Wikipedia contributors, *Ancient Roman Bathing,* (Wikipedia, The Free Encyclopedia), https://en.wikipedia.org/wiki/Ancient_Roman_bathing/ 08/08020

Wikipedia contributors, *Dale Carnegie,* (Wikipedia, The Free Encyclopedia), https://en.wikipedia.org/wiki/Dale_Carnegie/ 09/04/20

Wikipedia contributors, *Fight-or-flight Response,* (Wikipedia, The Free Encyclopedia), http://en.wikipedia.org/wiki/Fight-or-flight_response/ 08 August 2015

Wikipedia contributors, *Guild,* (Wikipedia, The Free Encyclopedia), https://en.wikipedia.org/wiki/Guild/ 08/04/20

Wikipedia contributors, *History of Banking,* (Wikipedia, The Free Encyclopedia), https://en.wikipedia.org/wiki/History_of_banking/ 10/04/20

Wikipedia contributors, *History of Golf,* (Wikipedia, The Free Encyclopedia), https://en.wikipedia.org/wiki/History_of_golf/ 14/04/20

Wikipedia contributors, *Margaret Murray Washington,* (Wikipedia, The Free Encyclopedia), https://en.wikipedia.org/wiki/Margaret_Murray_Washington/ 14/04/20

Wikipedia contributors, *Rotary International,* (Wikipedia, The Free Encyclopedia), https://en.wikipedia.org/wiki/Rotary_International 10/04/20

Wikipedia contributors, *Round Table (Club),* (Wikipedia, The Free Encyclopedia), https://en.wikipedia.org/wiki/Round_Table_(club) 10/04/20

Ladey Adey

Everything you want in life is a relationship away.
Idowu Koyenikan

Ladey has written nine books, including three books in the Little Unicorn children's series co-authored with her daughter, Abbirose, and has published numerous books for other authors. She has been featured on the ALLi blog, and is the host of the Ladey Adey Show, a podcast all about books.

She started her professional publishing career in the 1990s as a typesetter, layout artist, editor and designer for a technical publications department. She was the editor of the Company's newsletter and co-editor of *Northern Newfoundland Club* newsletter with one of her best friend, *Chris Tedder*. She is continually amazed at how far technology has come and has genuinely fallen in love with *InDesign* and subtitling apps. (Yep, every video needs sub-titles; a great marketing tool.)

Ladey heads up the family-run publishing business called Ladey Adey Publications, helping ambitious business people, poets, children's authors and other writers to write and publish their books. She invariably has her own book in production. When not writing, or publishing, you can usually find her in the garden, talking to God and doing activities including brick laying, dry stone walling, or creating mosaics. She loves to listen to and watch musicals. Her favourites are, *The Greatest Showman* and *Disney's Frozen I & II* .

Ladey says, *"I design and build features in my garden, it's always open for visitors - especially if you arrive with cuttings or seeds from your own garden! (Consider this a genuine invite). This is me. I would love to speak with you about your author journey."*

Networking View

You are never too old to ride a Carousel
Ladey Adey

Ladey has always loved meeting people and learning about their businesses. Now, an avid networking online fan who has doubled her client list since lockdown. She says, *"My business life is so rich due to networking. Communicating online has opened more doors including opportunities to give talks to networking groups. I am looking forward to travelling around the world - online - talking about: Your Online Presence - from Study to Back Bedroom - How to get the Professional Edge."* Contact Ladey to be a Speaker at your next event.

Founder: World Online Networking Day - 29th October.

Networking CV

4Networking (Newark) - 2019 - Group Coordinator.

The Selling Network - 2015 - Co-Founder with Abbirose Adey.

Women's Golf Network (Lincolnshire) - 2012 - Director/Founder.

Pink & Blue Networking Group - for men and women - 2011 - Founder.

Spotlight Networking (Business raising money for charity) - 2011 - Founder.

Athena Women's Network® - 2008 - Regional Director for Lincoln, Grantham, Sleaford and Boston.

Networks Membership: Lincoln Business Club, Kingdom Business, Catena, MIBA, Bizznet, Talk Networking, Women of Impact, The Marketing Meet-up, Mark Jarvis' - PURE, 4Networking, Woman Who Achieves Academy, the list goes on... Invite me to your network (online) and I'll be there.

Previous Books:

Start Writing Your Book Today, - e-book (2019) Pink Parties Press (PPP).

Colouring 101: The Ultimate Guide for the Colouring Addict, (2016), Co-Author with Abbirose Adey, Pink Parties Press (PPP).

Colours of Unfrozen: Reflecting, Relaxing and Rejoicing: A Believer's Colouring Book for Adults, (2016), Co-Author with Abbirose Adey, Author Academy Elite (AAE), UK Edition.

Unfrozen: How to Melt your Heart from Life's Disappointment, Disillusionment and Discouragement by Opening the Door and Stepping into God's Warming Light, (2015), Author Academy Elite (AAE), Version 2 (2017). Audio version on Amazon Audible.

God's Gifts: What are the Gifts and Fruits of the Holy Spirit and Where to find them in the Bible, (2013), Pink Parties Press (PPP).

Contribution to other Books

17: **The Little Way to Get a Lot Done,** *Michael Heppell,* (Gloop Books) 2020

PR on a Beermat. The Entrepreneur's Guide to using Public Relations, *Louise Third MBE,* (Beermat) 2020

Children's Books

Little Unicorn Discovers the Dinosaurs,
Co-Author with Abbirose Adey,
Ladey Adey Publications, 2020.

Little Unicorn and the Nativity,
Co-Author with Abbirose Adey,
Pink Parties Press (PPP), 2019.

Little Unicorn - What's Your Name?,
Co-Author with Abbirose Adey,
Pink Parties Press (PPP), 2018.

Contact via Social Media

Email:	ladey@ladeyadey.com
Facebook:	https://www.facebook.com/ladey.adey.3/
Instagram:	https://www.instagram.com/ladey_adey/
Linked In:	https://www.linkedin.com/in/ladey/
Pinterest:	https://www.pinterest.co.uk/LadeyAdey/
Podcast:	https://shows.acast.com/ladeyadeyshow/
Twitter:	https://twitter.com/ladey_adey/
Website:	http://www.ladeyadey.com/
You Tube:	https://www.youtube.com/user/LADEY2/videos/

Affiliated Links

ALLi (Alliance of Independent Authors) https://allianceindependentauthors.org/?affid=4559

T4S (Traffic for Sales) https://t4s.site/introducing-t4s-to-create-online-course/your-killer-idea/

Is there a Book In YOU?

*L*adey Adey Publications runs an Author Mentoring Programme to guide authors and ensure they receive 100% copyright, 100% control and 100% royalty for their books.

We help ambitious business people write their book which will put them head and shoulders above their competitors, raise their company's brand and be seen as an expert to their customers.

If you could write a book about any part of your business or your life - what would you choose?

Author, *Kathryn Colas* used her book, *How to Surviving Menopause Without Losing Your Mind* to respectfully challenge the medical profession's viewpoint on Menopause. Kathryn said, *"It's a real pleasure to work with Ladey and Abbirose. Through our monthly calls, I realise how much there is to know about publishing but Ladey guided me, with sensitivity. The Author Mentoring Programme has taken me from being overwhelmed to making my book happen."*

*A*bbirose heads up our Children's Books division. She is a Primary School teacher and an incredible artist so makes sure the digital images *'pop'* in the book.

Author, *Katie Goodacre*, used her experience of mental health issues: anxiety and being bullied, to help children, troubled in the same way, through a character called *Miley* (a dog) in her book. She said, *"I'm so impressed with my book now Abbirose and Ladey have done their magic – it's more professional than I ever envisaged."*

We're Changing Lives
- One Book at a Time.

Index

Networking, whether off or online, should always be purposeful, and *Successful Business Networking Online* is an essential read for those who really want to maximise their online networking results. As founder of one of the UK's fastest growing referral networking organisations, I am excited about the potential of online networking and this book will be a proactive companion for experienced and inexperienced participants alike.

Nicky Thomas, Founder: The Growth Community

Ladey's book sets out some of the fundamental principles of good business networking in the modern world. I particularly like the reminders that networking is not just a means for direct selling, and that, for networking to work, you need a long-term commitment. It's not about making a fast buck!

John Espirian, Technical Copywriter and Author: Content DNA

Networking often receives a bad press, yet it's the lifeblood of any business. Who you know, or more importantly, who knows about you and what you can do, or offer, makes the difference between having a successful business or not. Ladey Adey has written a very timely book here. A new type of virtual networking has sprung up in response to recent events. Be assured, this won't go away, and we can expect a mix of online and offline networking events in the future.

This well researched, thoroughly engaging book combines insightful interviews with networking experts, practical exercises and excellent advice. It's a treasure trove, containing just about anything you will need to help you gain confidence in the online networking world and make your presence felt. If you're just dipping your toe in the water, or you're a more seasoned networker looking to make the move into the virtual world, then this book is well worth a read!

Susan Ritchie, Author: Strategies for Being Visible

As an experienced business networker, for over 12 years, I was very interested to read Ladey's book. I figured it would be preaching to the converted… how wrong was I! It turns out you can teach an old dog new tricks!

A fascinating read, and lots of new ideas that I plan on implementing in my networking straight away. I highly recommend all business owners read this book, especially the networking novices, as well as the seasoned professionals.

Andrew Martin, Founder: Success Networking Grantham

In an ever changing landscape, this is a jam packed guide to the new world of networking.

Michael Heppell, Speaker, Coach and Author: How to be Brilliant

A very insightful book, and, in today's world, very important. It's called 'net-WORK' not 'net-SIT-AND-HOPE'. And Ladey shows the best way to do it virtually, so you get the best, quickest return for your work. A revelation'

Andy Bounds, Award-winning sales consultant and Best-selling author: The Jelly Effect and The Snowball Effect

As Chairman of a Business Parks Association and the owner of a PR Business which is approaching 35 years old, I have always known how important networking is to success. Ladey Adey's book takes this a step further, offering a deep and thoughtful insight into the history of business networking as well as looking to the future as more of us go digital. We can all learn something from her principles, whether we are starting out or have been successfully trading for years.

I highly recommend this book, and I'm sure the wisdom imparted in its pages will be at the forefront of my mind as I meet business people online and when we re-start networking in person.

Susan Fleet, Founder and MD of Lea Graham Associates, PA to the late Dame Vera Lynn.

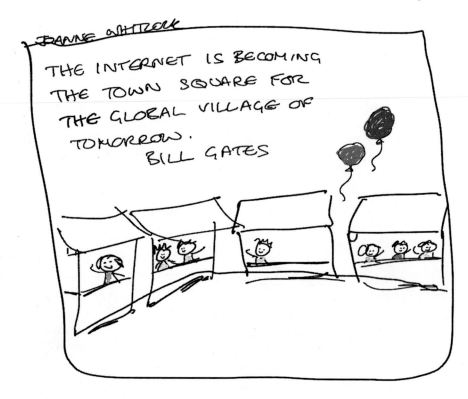